THE VIEW AND PRACTICE OF QUINTESSENCE DZOGCHEN

THREE RARE TEXTS ON NYINGTHIG DZOGCHEN FROM DZA PATRUL'S COLLECTED WORKS

BY TONY DUFF
PADMA KARPO TRANSLATION COMMITTEE

The texts in this book are secret and should not be shown to those who have not had the necessary introduction to and instructions for the Thorough Cut system of Great Completion (Dzogchen) meditation. If you have not had the necessary instructions, reading this text can be harmful to your spiritual health! Seal. Seal. Seal.

First edition, November 2018
ISBN paper book: 978-9937-572-64-4
ISBN e-book: 978-9937-572-65-1

Janson typeface with diacritical marks and
Tibetan Classic typeface
Designed and created by Tony Duff

Produced, Printed, and Published by
Padma Karpo Translation Committee
Kathmandu
Nepal

Committee members for this book: composition and translation, Lama Tony Duff; cover design, George Romvari.

Web-site and e-mail contact through:
http://www.pktc.org/pktc
https://www.pktcshop.com
or search Padma Karpo Translation Committee on the web.

Contents

Introduction v

From the Supreme Vehicle Ati: Foremost Instructions Clearly Showing Actuality by Dza Patrul 1

"Lamp for a Dim Room" The Meanings of the Key Points of The Secret, Quintessential Great Completion's Tantras, Protected wth the use of Thorough Distinctions by Dza Patrul 31

"Luminosity's Appearance Aspect", The Ultimate Key Points in the Practice of Great Completion: Root Text and Commentary by Dza Patrul 65

Glossary of Terms 85

Supports for Study 123

Introduction

This book presents three texts concerned with the "Dzogchen", or in English "Great Completion", system of teaching that explains reality and how beings can return to it from their current, confused state. The Dzogchen system has several levels of teaching, the most profound being called the "Nyingthig" or in English "Quintessence" level of the teaching. The texts presented in this book are concerned with that most profound level of teaching.

In Tibet, there were several lines of transmission of this Quintessence Great Completion level of teaching. One came through a master named Longchen Rabjam, so it was called the "Longchen Nyingthig" transmission meaning "Longchen Rabjam's transmission of the Quintessence Great Completion teaching".

This Longchen Nyingthig came down to a Tibetan man who grew up in the Dzachuka town of Eastern Tibet and came to be a great master of this particular teaching not to mention the Buddha's teachings as a whole. He was therefore known as "Dza Pal Trul" meaning "the glorious (pal) manifestation of enlightenment (trul) from the town of Dza". Strictly speaking, his name should be transliterated into English as "Dza Paltrul", but nowadays it has become so common for non-Tibetans to call him "Dza Patrul" that we have followed that way of referring to him in this book.

In his early adult years, Dza Patrul received the Longchen Quintessence teachings from great masters at Dzogchen Monastery, which is not far from his home-town of Dzachuka. Having done so, he spent the rest of his life in retreat with his disciples in the mountains behind the monastery. A number of his oral teachings on Longchen Nyingthig were recorded in writing by his disciples and he wrote a number of texts on the subject himself. These and other writings were gathered and preserved in his *Collected Works*.

Three of his texts on Longchen Nyingthig that so far have not been translated into another language are presented in this book. These texts show these very high level teachings in a way that is rarely, if ever, seen. I am sure that anyone who is interested in the Quintessence Great Completion teachings, whether he or she follows the Longchen Nyingthig or some other line of transmission of the teachings, will find the teachings contained in these texts to be fascinating at very least. And for those who do follow the Longchen Nyingthig, there is a revelation from early in the lineage that has not been seen in English before, and which is just amazing in its content.

Great Completion

The Great Completion system of dharma came from a land called Uddiyana, which early writings say was "north-west of the vajra seat", the vajra seat being the place where the Buddha attained enlightenment, now in Bodhgaya, India. The name of Great Completion in the language of Uddiyana is "mahāsaṅdhi" literally meaning "great juncture". The Tibetans translated this name with Dzogpa Chenpo, commonly abbreviated simply to "Dzogchen", and literally meaning "great completion". The words "juncture" and "completion" have the same meaning in this case; they refer to that one all-encompassing space, that one juncture, in which all that there could be—whether enlightened or unenlightened, whether belonging to nirvana or samsara—is complete.

The name Great Completion refers both to an all-inclusive space that beings including humans could realize and to a system of instruction designed to bring beings to the realization of it. When a being does realize it, there is nothing more to be realized or done because all is complete within that being's space of realization and the work of spiritual practice is complete. In a Buddhist way of talking, Great Completion is the final realization that happens when a being manifests truly complete buddhahood.

Great Completion is often called "Great Perfection" in English, but that presents an incorrect understanding of the name. The final space of realization is not a state of perfection but one that contains both perfection and imperfection. The name is not intended to connect us with the idea of perfection but with the idea of the juncture of all things perfect and imperfect, to the idea of a state of realization in which all things are complete. There is also the problem that the incorrect translation "Great Perfection" feeds into the theistic habits of the West and can easily mislead people into thinking of a godly state of perfection. Last but by no means least is the unavoidable point that Longchen Rabjam's definitive explanations in his revered text *The Dharmadhatu Treasury*[1] make it clear beyond a doubt that the meaning of the name is Great Completion and not Great Perfection. He mentions in several places that the name is intended to convey the inclusion—just as the original name from Uddiyana states—of all dharmas within dharmadhatu wisdom. He makes it clear in many places that this is not a condition of perfection but of inclusion.

Completion in Great Completion means that all phenomena are included at once in a single space of realization. *Great* is used to distinguish something known by wisdom in direct perception from

[1] Tib. chos dbyings mdzod. Longchen Rabjam wrote a set of seven texts on Great Completion called *The Seven Treasuries*. This one concerns the practice of Thorough Cut. An exceptionally large commentary to it is currently being translated by Padma Karpo Translation Committee.

the same thing known by dualistic mind as a concept. Thus *Great Completion* is not the completion understood through the use of concept, but the greater version of that, the actual state of completion known through wisdom.

While that is the ultimate meaning of "great" in the name "Great Completion", great also gives the conceptual understanding of the greatest possible state of completion, one which is greater than any other. Because of this, the wording "greater completion" is also used in the Great Completion teachings. For example, this wording is found several times in the third text in this book, *Luminosity's Appearance Aspect*, when it explains how various facets of what is—appearance, emptiness, self-liberation, and so on—are, in the context of Great Completion, at a greater level of completion than in other system for attaining enlightenment. This again points at why the name is Great Completion rather than Great Perfection.

Levels of Great Completion Teaching

The Great Completion teaching is divided into three main sections, arranged in a sequence of increasing profundity. The three main sections are Mind, Space, and Foremost Instruction sections, with the Foremost Instruction Section containing the most profound teaching of Great Completion. The Foremost Instruction section can be further divided into outer, inner, and secret sections. Going further again, there is a fourth section literally called "more secret again" or "extra-secret" which contains the most profound teaching of Great Completion. This term has regularly been translated as "innermost" but that is mistaken; this term indicates that there is the secret section which is the third of the outer, inner, and secret sections of the Foremost Instruction section and then there is this section which is one step beyond that secret level again, so is the "extra-secret" section. This extra-secret section is not surpassed by any other level of Great Completion teaching, therefore it is also called "unsurpassed". The two names are usually put together with the result that this most profound level of Great Completion teaching is usually referred to as "extra-secret, unsurpassed Great Completion".

There is a second, equally common name for the extra-secret, unsurpassed level of the Great Completion teaching. The original Sanskrit name for it is "hṛidaya tilaka" which was literally and exactly translated into Tibetan with "nyingthig (snying thig)". The literal translation of the Sanskrit and Tibetan terms into English is "heart drop" but it would be misleading to use that given that in actual use in the Sanskrit language, it does not mean "heart drop" but "the very essence of all", which corresponds exactly to the English "quintessence". It is a mistake then to think of and to translate the name as "heart drop" or "heart essence" as has commonly been done; the name means "quintessence" or "quintessential" level.

Thus, "extra-secret, unsurpassed" and "quintessence" are alternative names for the most profound level of teaching of Great Completion that has appeared in our era of human society.

The Early Lineage of the Teaching

The Quintessence Great Completion teaching was first taught in the current era of this human world by Garab Dorje who was born, roughly speaking, in Northern India. It was passed on through other Indian masters until it arrived in the hands of the masters Padmasambhava and Vimalamitra. They brought it to Tibet where two main lines of transmission arose from their teachings. The main line of transmission from Padmasambhava came down through his consort, Yeshe Tshogyal, and was known as the Khadro Nyingthig or Dakini Quintessence because of it. The main line of transmission from Vimalamitra was known as the Vimala Quintessence because of it.

Longchen Rabjam's Tradition of Nyingthig or Quintessence Great Completion

Longchen Rabjam [1308–1363][2] had a special connection with the transmission coming from Padmasambhava and also had the transmission coming from Vimalamitra. He passed on these teachings in a number of ways. For example, he passed the teaching to Jigmey Lingpa [1730–1798] in a transmission which became known as the Longchen Nyingthig or Longchenpa's Quintessence. It was very powerful and spread through Tibet, though it flourished strongly in Eastern Tibet, where it caused a major resurgence of the quintessence teaching. Following on from that, Longchen Nyingthig or Longchenpa's Quintessence has become the most commonly practised transmission of Quintessence Great Completion at this time.

Longchen Rabjam transmitted the teaching to Jigmey Lingpa [1730–1798] in a series of visions. A brief story of the transmission follows. At one point in his life, Jigmey Lingpa went into strict retreat near Samye Chimpu, and practised the guru yoga of Longchen Rabjam for a long time. In 1759, at the age of 31, he stayed in two different caves which had been named the Nyang Caves after Nyang Tingdzin Zangpo who had practised in them long before. It was in those two caves that Jigmey Lingpa met Longchenpa's wisdom body in a series of three visions. The first vision occurred in the Upper Cave of

[2] The Tibetan term "longchen" literally means "an vast space that one experiences as being in the midst of that space". This sometimes results in the idea that "Longchen Nyingthig" means "the Quintessence Great Completion that is like a vast space". However, the Longchen Nyingthig tradition itself clearly explains that the "longchen" in Longchen Nyingthig is the first part of Longchen Rabjam's name so that Longchen Nyingthig means "Longchen Rabjam's transmission of the Quintessence Great Completion teaching".

Nyang and the two later visions in the Lower Cave of Nyang. Jigmey Lingpa later named the lower cave Flower Cave of the Great Secret.

The following description of Jigmey Lingpa's three visions was given by the late Tulku Urgyen and translated by Andreas Kretschmar. It is a condensation of Jigmey Lingpa's own record of his visionary experiences called *The Water Moon Dancer, The Story of the Realizations that Appeared as Very Secret Experiences.*[3]

> On the sixteenth day of the eighth month, after I had composed a praise to this great and holy practice place, while sleeping in a state of unchanging luminosity, ordinary fixations on the five sense objects were purified and coarse object fixations dissolved into the ocean-like consciousness. In this non-conceptual state of the alaya, the interdependent origination of phenomena subsided and the appearing luminosity of luminosity, rigpa wisdom, arose.
>
> In this mirror-like state, I saw the glorious master from Samye, the All-Knowing Lord of Speech, like a magical apparition. His noble body was beautified with the threefold monk's robes and he was a little advanced in age. As with the Buddha, one could see no imperfection in him.
>
> I heard him say in a clear voice, "May the mind transmission of the meaning be transferred to you! May it be transferred! May you perfect the transmission of words! May you perfect it!"
>
> At that moment an unbearable faith and devotion, similar to falling unconscious, was born in me and without wasting time to prostrate, I immediately grabbed both hands of the All-Knowing Lord and placed him on top of my head at the Great Bliss Chakra. Almost fainting with

---

[3] This autobiography is found in the *Collected Works of Jigmey Lingpa.*

devotion, I prayed to him, "All-Knowing Dharma King, think of me! All-Knowing Dharma King, think of me! All-Knowing Dharma King, think of me!"

He replied, "I knew that in later times someone saying this would come". When I came back to my senses, I understood this to be an unhappy statement because when he was still dwelling in his physical body, beings of lesser merit had no faith and devotion toward him, and through the power of their bad practice they had brought sadness to his mind.

I said to him, "Thinking of your great kindness and how you benefited the dharma and beings with your *Seven Treasuries* and the mind treasure of the Quintessence alone, I have a constant devotion, seeing your outstanding qualities to be equal to those of buddha in person."

He looked straight at me and said, "Son of noble family! Now I have transferred the realization of the transmission of meaning to you by means of aspiration and entrustment. Erect the life-fortress of practice and teach extensively to the destined ones! And, your songs are excellent." As he said that, I thought of asking him for teachings but the vision of the three kayas dissolved like a magical apparition into the dhatu.

After that, I thought unceasingly of the All-Knowing Lord. "I would have thought that, for a poor beggar yogin like me, who practises in caves and is young in age, such realization would be impossible. However, just by seeing your face, all my latencies, negativity, and obscurations are gone. Just by hearing your voice, the great expanse of realization has burst forth and, without having studied the words of the teaching but merely by seeing the writings, I understand all the key points of instruction. In one day, your kindness has transformed me from a sentient being into an enlightened one."

Thus I was blessed with the transmission of meaning through various symbolic methods: outwardly through the tamer of beings, the Great Humkara; internally through the master Manjushrimitra; and secretly through the dharmakaya of Longchenpa. This was the first vision, in which I was blessed with his body.

At that time, I stayed in Nyang Tingdzin Zangpo's practice cave, which in the old guide books to holy places is referred to as the Upper Cave of Nyang. It is an overhang type of cave and now, to the right side of the entrance there is a white bush growing out of a crack in the rock and on the side of the rock are the outlines of three stupas, and the grass on the floor of the rock is moved by a continuous breeze.

People of former generations have written about the southern cave, also known as the Lower Cave of Nyang, as the Nyang cave. Through a vision, I gained confidence in what was previously written about it and I remembered it to be the practice cave of the Dharma King Trisong Deutsen and of Nyang Tingdzin Zangpo. Therefore, I gave the Lower Cave of Nyang the name Flower Cave of the Great Secret.

While I stayed in this holy place in very strict retreat, I felt strong renunciation in my mind and had a vision in which all the solidification of grasping collapsed. I met the All-Knowing One, the second buddha, Longchenpa, again. This time, he gave me a book with one chapter and said, "In this, all the hidden points of the *Great Chariot*[4]

---

[4] Longchen Rabjam wrote a set of fifteen texts gathered into three parts that are considered to be a "stages of the path" presentation of Great Completion. The collection is named *The Great Completion Resting-Up Trilogy* and *The Great Chariot* is part of that trilogy. An exceptionally large commentary to it is currently being translated by Padma Karpo

(continued ...)

are clarified". At that time, he taught the cycle of *Unravelling the Symbols of the Great Secret Treasury*.

Again he said, "This is a record of your former lives and predictions for the future", and handed me a scroll. When I opened it, I found that it contained two lines, one above and one below. The upper one read, "In your previous life, you were the All-Knowing Dharma Lord[5]". As I began to read the lower one, the vision faded out like a cloud within space. At the time of this vision, I had no gross grasping that would think, "His body shape is like this or that". Thus he blessed me with his speech and I received the authorization to compose writings. This was the second vision.

After a few months, I met the All-Knowing Lord again. He was magnificent, wearing the robe of a pandita. He had the body of a very youthful man aged twenty. On his head, he was wearing the pandita hat with long flaps. With the mandala of his body and through the symbolic union of the five spontaneously-existing male and female buddhas, he conferred the empowerment of infinite luminous purity upon me. Without saying anything at all and with a kind and joyous smile, the wisdom vision of great purity dissolved into the dhatu. Thus he blessed me with his mind and I received authorization as a master who has realized the transmission of actual meaning. This was the third vision.

At that time, my perception of objects became liberated, freed of all reference points, and my realization during meditation was without any restrictions. Internally, I was freed from the grasping mind stream and therefore everything was purified into limitless natural liberation.

---

[4] (... continued)
Translation Committee.

[5] Longchenpa.

> In my post-meditative wisdom perception, I spent the time in a happy yet saddened state of mind. With devotion and powerful longing, I composed the praise to Longchenpa called the Longing Song of the Spring Queen.
>
> The meaning of Longchenpa's *Three Chariots* and *Seven Treasuries* arose in my heart and I wrote many instructions concerning key points, and quintessential teachings on view and meditation, and on the essentials of practice. All were written in an easy-to-understand way with an economy of words, for example, *Words of the Omniscient One*, *White Lotus*, *Annihilating Deviations*,[6] and so forth.

Jigmey Lingpa transmitted this to many disciples and the teaching of the Longchen Quintessence flourished, especially in Eastern Tibet. His two closest disciples were Jigmey Thrinley Ozer and Jigmey Gyalway Nyugu, both of whom became very highly realized. The former was an incarnation of the great treasure revealer Sangyay Lingpa and became the first of the very famous Dodrupchen incarnations; much has been written about him and his works are well known. The latter was also very famous in Tibet but is less well known. The teachings of both of these masters went to a number of disciples, primarily in Eastern Tibet, and the teachings of Longchen Quintessence became firmly established.

One of the several very important homes of the Longchen Quintessence transmission was the major Nyingma monastery in Eastern Tibet called Dzogchen Monastery. Dzogchen Monastery had been founded some time earlier and was one of the six great homes of Nyingma teaching in Eastern Tibet. It was established by Padma Rigdzin who became known as the first Dzogchen Rinpoche and was tended by his incarnations following that. The fourth Dzogchen Rinpoche, called Mingyur Namkha'i Dorje, was a student of both Jigmey Thrinley Ozer and Jigmey Gyalway Nyugu and became one

---

[6] These three are all found in the *Root Volumes of Longchen Nyingthig*.

of the two figures of his generation in the Dzogchen Monastery lineage of Longchen Nyingthig.

A second person from that generation was included in the Dzogchen Monastery lineage of Longchen Quintessence. His dharma name was Orgyan Jigmey Chokyi Wangpo, though he became commonly known as Dza Paltrul "the glorious manifestation of enlightenment from Dzachuka". As mentioned earlier, nowadays his name is usually written in English as "Dza Patrul". He was born in 1808 in a neighbouring county to Dzogchen Monastery, called Dzachuka. Dzachuka has been a hub of dharma activity for many centuries and still is today; it is home to many monasteries, lamas, and yogins of Nyingma and Kagyu traditions. Dza Patrul passed away in 1887.

Dza Patrul learned much Kagyu and Nyingma dharma in his home town of Dzachuka. Later, he went to study with his main teacher for Longchen Quintessence, Jigmey Gyalway Nyugu. Dza Patrul was a contemporary of the fourth Dzogchen Rinpoche of Dzogchen Monastery, and took teachings together with him at Jigmey Gyalway Nyugu's feet. After that, Dza Patrul went to Dzogchen Monastery and stayed there for many years, making it his home. Through him the system of Longchen Quintessence coming through Jigmey Gyalway Nyugu was firmly established at Dzogchen Monastery and has flourished there until now because of him.

Dza Patrul lived for many years at Dzogchen monastery, mostly staying in retreat in the high mountains at the far end of the valley which, in those times, had not been built up at all and was purely a place where yogins lived and practised. His fame spread and many people came to visit. Some stayed and a few, such as Padma Vajra of Dzogchen Monastery and Lungtog Nyoshul from Lungtog district, became his principle disciples who then carried on the lineage in their respective places. Dza Patrul became such an important figure in the transmission of the Longchen Quintessence teaching at Dzogchen Monastery that he was, together with the fourth Dzogchen Tulku, officially set down as the lineage holder of that system at the monastery. He was so much a part of the monastery, that he became known to Tibetans in general as Dzogchen Patrul and is still more often that not called by that name. Most non-Tibetans on hearing the name Dzogchen Patrul assume that it means "Patrul who was a great Dzogchen master" when it actually means "Patrul of Dzogchen Monastery".[7]

That is the story of how Longchen Quintessence or Longchen Nyingthig came about and how it came to Dzogchen Monastery. Because the texts in this book focus on Jigmey Gyalway Nyugu and his disciple Dza Patrul, and also because of the special teaching in one of them given by Jigmey Gyalway Nyugu to Mingyur Namkha'i Dorje, it would be appropriate to give more of their amazing life stories in order to make this explanation of the transmission of Quintessence Great Completion as it happened at Dzogchen Monastery complete. However, to do so would make this introduction go on for too long. Therefore, the reader is directed to the excellent book *A Marvellous Garland of Rare Gems*[8] which gives excellent summaries of their respective lives and shows clearly how they each fitted into the overall Longchen Nyingthig transmission that happened in Eastern Tibet.

---

[7] With this book, we have translated all of the texts on Quintessence Great Completion that are available in Dza Patrul's *Collected Works*. After that, we will publish Lungtog Nyoshul's teachings on the same, which come in two very famous and lengthy texts, one on Thorough Cut and one on Direct Crossing. In this way, we are making the Quintessence Great Completion teachings that came through Dzogchen Monastery available.

[8] By Nyoshul Khenpo and translated by Richard Barron, published by Padma Publishing, 2005, ISBN: 1-881847-41-1.

The Writings of Dza Patrul

Dza Patrul was not only highly accomplished but very learned as well. He knew the Buddhist teaching thoroughly and taught and wrote on all aspects of it. Modern-day Nyingma practitioners often assume that, because he is such an important figure in the transmission of Great Completion, he was purely Nyingma. In fact, he had great knowledge of the Kagyu system of teaching as well. This should not be surprising given that his birthplace in Dzachuka has many Kagyu monasteries, lamas, tulkus, and well-practised yogins. The extent of his knowledge of the Kagyu system can be seen in the text in here *From the Supreme Vehicle Ati: Foremost Instructions Clearly Showing Actuality*. From that text it is clear that he has an extensive and practical knowledge of the Kagyu Mahamudra teachings sufficient that he could incorporate them into a complete presentation of the steps of Great Completion meditation.

Dza Patrul's *Collected Works* appeared originally in a set of six volumes carved on woodblocks and printed at the famous Derge Printery in Eastern Tibet. His writings are not as extensive as those of some Tibetan figures, occupying a total of six volumes only. This does not mean that he did not teach very much; to the contrary, he was famous for his continuous teachings given to disciples in the mountains of Dzogchen Monastery and many of those teachings have been passed on in an oral tradition which I know from personal experience is still passed on today at the centres in Eastern Tibet of the Longchen Quintessence teaching.

The first text of the first volume in that edition of Dza Patrul's *Collected Works* is an explanation of the content of the six volumes. It is like a table of contents, but also has explanations of the organization of the texts and a short description of each text. From it, we learn that the collection of texts is arranged primarily according to the four turnings of the wheel of dharma: the first three volumes deal progressively with matters related to the three sutra turnings of the wheel; the fourth and fifth volumes deal with the fourth turning or Secret Mantra teachings; and the sixth volume is filled with items such as short praises and liturgical procedures which do not fit into the scheme of the first five volumes.

The fourth volume contains texts specific to the Longchen Quintessence. There are not many of them, with the main ones being:

- The Key Issues of Visualization: Four Nails Pinning The Life-Forces, "A Melody of Brahma Playing Throughout The Three Realms";
- From the Supreme Vehicle Ati: Foremost Instructions Clearly Showing Actuality;
- "Lamp for a Dim Room" The Meanings of the Key Points of The Secret, Quintessence Great Completion's Tantras, Protected with the use of Thorough Distinctions;
- "Luminosity's Appearance Aspect", The Ultimate Key Points in the Practice of Great Completion: Root Text and Commentary;
- Feature of the Expert Glorious King, root and commentary texts
- Profound Foremost Instructions for The Chod Practice Sound of Dakini Laughter.

I am pleased to say that with the publication of this book, all of these indispensable texts have now been translated into English and made available for the use of practitioners. (In fact, there is a group of texts in this fourth volume that we have not translated—they are empowerment manuals for the *rig pa'i tsal wang*, which I do not think need to be translated at this point.)

The fifth volume also contains a text specific to Longchen Quintessence. The entire volume is taken up by one text on the preliminary practices of Longchen Nyingthig Great Completion, known in

English as *The Words of my Most Excellent Guru*. This also is very important to Longchen Nyingthig practitioners and also has been translated into English.[9]

The Texts in this Book

The three texts selected for this book that have not been published before are all of short to medium length.

The First Text

From the Supreme Vehicle Ati: Foremost Instructions Clearly Showing Actuality is in two parts. It starts with a main teaching and ends with a section of "various pieces of instruction heard in person from gurus, which are important to understand".

The main teaching shows the way to practise Great Completion for all types of person, starting with the ones who are most capable and going down to those who are least capable. Dza Patrul tells us in a note at the end of the main teaching that "it is extracted from a Mind Section Great Completion text". However, one of the very interesting features of his teaching is the way that he combines Great Completion and Kagyu Mahamudra teachings into one. It is exactly the style which Shakya Shri of the Drukpa Kagyu made famous a few decades after Dza Patrul wrote this text and which is now taught in the West by Drukpa Kagyu lamas of Shakya Shri's tradition, for example by Tsoknyi Rinpoche. This shows how well Dza Patrul was acquainted with the Kagyu teachings, because of growing up in Dzachuka where the Kagyu tradition, and the Drukpa Kagyu in particular, was flourishing strongly. As a matter of interest, there is a text in Dza Patrul's *Collected Works* just prior to this first text called *The Foremost Instructions of Mahamudra, a Guidebook to the Instructions of the Highly Accomplished Marpa the Translator*. This is one of many

---

[9] This has been published by the Padmakara group, which should not be confused with Padma Karpo Translation Committee.

things that show how Dza Patrul was not only a mainstay of the Longchen Quintessence tradition but knew Kagyu theory and practice very well.

The second part consists of various pieces of instruction heard in person from gurus and has five shorter teachings. These short teachings are Foremost Instruction Section teachings which are full of interesting instruction for anyone who is practising Quintessence Great Completion.

The first shorter teaching starts with an explanation of how ground, path, and fruition should be at path time, which includes some instruction on how deity practice, guru yoga practice, and other such things that involve visualization should be done. It ends with a summary of the Three Lines teaching of Garab Dorje presented in the way it is taught in Longchen Quintessence. Dza Patrul is famous for his explanation of this teaching of Garab Dorje, which appears in a text called *The Feature of the Expert Glorious King*[10] that he wrote for his disciples practising in retreat in the mountains at Dzogchen Monastery. Today, this text with its particular style of explanation has become the basic text for Thorough Cut used by most Great Completion practitioners. The text does not cover all of Garab Dorje's teaching, which has caused some Westerners to question whether the explanation given in *The Feature of the Expert Glorious King* was already in the tradition or whether it was something Dza Patrul arrived at through his practice. This text in this book answers that question definitively, showing that it was not something that Patrul arrived at but something that was already in the tradition. Note also the very nice explanation of the meaning of "the four without the three" contained within the summary of the Three Lines teaching.

---

[10] Tib. khyad chos shri'i rgyal po. Translated into English by Tony Duff and published by Padma Karpo Translation Committee, second edition 2010, ISBN: 978-9937-8244-3-9.

The second shorter teaching explains the interesting topic of how the key points of Great Completion's Mind and Space Sections are incorporated in the Foremost Instruction Section.

The third shorter teaching is a teaching in general on how a Quintessence Great Completion yogin's practice should be. It makes several points, some of which are quite profound and some of which relate to Direct Crossing practice. All of these points have to be understood through personal instruction from a qualified teacher, so no further comment is made about them here.

The fourth shorter teaching continues with and expands on some of the themes raised in the third shorter teaching, again giving many pieces of advice on how a Quintessence Great Completion yogin's practice should be.

The fifth shorter teaching is a very short but beautifully-stated teaching that shows how the main practice of Thorough Cut leads to sudden enlightenment. This text, with its main teaching having a broad approach and initial occupation with Mind Section and Mahamudra teaching, is a little less profound than the remaining two texts, therefore it comes ahead of them. However, this does not mean that the reader should skip over this text or deem it less important—the main teaching is applicable to all levels of practitioner and the following teachings all are important advice for a practitioner of Quintessence Great Completion.

The Second Text

"Lamp for a Dim Room" The Meanings of the Key Points of The Secret, Quintessential Great Completion's Tantras, Protected with the use of Thorough Distinctions is a text about the view in particular. It shows clearly the view as taught in Foremost Instruction Section. The text is self-explanatory, though the points being covered are very profound.

Dza Patrul makes the point at the beginning of the text that the profound view of Foremost Instruction Section has become badly distorted because of having become mixed up with Bon teachings. This is thoroughly applicable to our current situation, where a number of Tibetan teachers have been spreading the idea that Bon teachings and Buddhist teachings on Dzogchen are the same. Anyone who has done the slightest comparison between the two systems will know that they are not. Unfortunately, this type of talk seems to fall right in line with the erroneous concept that many Westerners have fallen for, which is that all traditions are speaking to the same point and therefore that all of them can be combined.

I saw this problem personally during years of translating for Tibetan lamas in the West. Dza Patrul mentions only the problem of Buddhist Secret Mantra having become mixed up with and degraded by (that is the literal meaning of his words "laced with" which you will see in his text) Bon ideas about Great Completion. In the West, the problem has developed even further: Buddhist Secret Mantra has become very mixed up in the minds of people who, not really knowing the details involved, run around insisting that Advaita Vedanta and Bon teachings and Buddhist teachings all are the same, are compatible, and can be simultaneously relied on. I found again and again in my own experience that these people did not actually understand the details of the view. That is exactly the point that Dza Patrul makes here: he has to provide some protection for the Buddhist view of Great Completion in order to shed enough light on it that it will not be degraded by becoming mixed up with other views—Bonpo, Hindu Advaita, or anything else one cares to name.

Of course, it is not popular in the modern climate of lack of precision and cuddly embracing of all views to talk like this. Doing so could be verging on committing suicide.

However, Dza Patrul has said it plainly here, the vidyadhara Chogyam Trungpa said it straightforwardly in his writings, and many Tibetan masters publicly and privately express their deep concern at the ideas which have been fostered by a few individuals that Bon or for that matter Advaita Vedanta, can be successfully mixed with Buddhist systems. The bottom line is that their views are different from the Buddhist view, so they cannot be mixed.

The second interesting feature of this text is that it is based on the view section on Longchenpa's *Meaning of the Words Treasury*.[11] This is the most profound of Longchenpa's seven treasuries. The first of its eleven sections deals with the view at length. That exposition shows the view exactly according to Quintessence Great Completion and in full detail. It is exceptionally profound and very difficult to understand. For example, when receiving teachings on this text at Dzogchen Monastery, my guru Padma Kalzang Rinpoche gave masterful explanations of this first section, but the chief khenpo, who was also taking the teachings, told me straightforwardly that there were many points in this section which he had trouble penetrating. It really is a profound subject which is not easy to penetrate! Nevertheless, this text does a good job of explaining the ground, so it will be of help when a reliable translation of Longchenpa's *Meaning of the Words Treasury* finally appears.

This text also focusses on a key point of the Quintessence Great Completion presentation of the ground in which an important distinction is made between ground and ground appearances. A full treatment of this topic entails a full explanation of "the eight doors of the basis of shining forth of spontaneous existence's precious ground appearances" which is one of the most difficult topics of Quintessence Great Completion. Dza Patrul skirts this issue and rightly so, for a presentation of it would defeat his purpose of making a clear explanation of the ground that could be understood by most readers.

---

[11] Tib. tshig don rin po che'i mdzod. The title more fully stated is "the meaning pointed at by the words used to explain Quintessence Great Completion".

That said, the second part of this text gives a general explanation of the ground and ground appearances with the use of many quotations. These quotations come from Longchenpa's *Seven Treasuries*, giving the reader insight into Longchenpa's works. There are also some quotations from the tantras.

The Third Text

"Luminosity's Appearance Aspect", The Ultimate Key Points in the Practice of Great Completion: Root Text and Commentary is a text which first chronicles then explains an "after-passing" teaching that occurred in Dza Patrul's time. After-passing teachings are a special feature of the transmission of Quintessence Great Completion in which a great master appears to his main student after the master has passed away and then provides him with a potent, foremost-instruction-style teaching. This kind of teaching happened for a few generations at the very beginning of the current transmission of Great Completion in this human world—Garab Dorje, Manjushrimitra, and Shri Singha all gave this kind of teaching during that time.

It is generally accepted that this sort of teaching has not happened since. However, Jigmey Gyalway Nyugu gave this kind of teaching to his closest disciple, the fourth Dzogchen Rinpoche, Mingyur Namkha'i Dorje in a dream-like vision. Mingyur Namkha'i Dorje recorded the events of the vision and the advice-filled verses which his guru Jigmey Gyalway Nyugu spoke to him. Dza Patrul then put the record of the teaching at the beginning of a text, calling it the "root text", and added a simple yet very clear commentary. I must say that the words of the advice have the unusual quality of becoming clear in the mind very easily, rather like the words of Guru Rinpoche.

The after-passing teaching from Jigmey Gyalway Nyugu covers all of the ground, path, fruition, view, meditation, and conduct of Quintessence Great Completion, so it is a very nice text for Great Completion practitioners. It covers very profound material transmitted in a pure vision, so it is the final text of the series.

An Unusual Event with the Second and Third Texts!

When translating these two texts, I had the distinct impression of a sudden, major shift in the style and content of the material about half way through each text. After translating them, I saw that a major part of the explanation that should have been present was missing. I also noticed discrepancies; one of the texts referred to an earlier quotation which was not in that text but was in the other text and there were several other problems, too. A very careful examination of the Tibetan texts showed that the second half, approximately, of each text had been swapped with the second half of the other text!

It is not common to see such a major error within the contents of someone's Collected Works because Collected Works are, usually, put together carefully before committing them to print. However, these errors do happen. Having looked closely at this particular situation, I am convinced that the original handwritten leaves were dropped just before the woodblocks were cut and not correctly re-assembled. This is a known occurrence so it is not far-fetched and would not overly surprise a Tibetan person familiar with his own literature.

I looked at a modern edition of Dza Patrul's *Collected Works* recently re-published by Tibetans in China. This edition copies the faults of the original Derge edition to the letter, without even a note about this major problem. This lack of care in re-publication is all too common these days, I am sorry to say.

At any rate, this left me with a decision to make. Should I leave the translated texts as they appear before translation or should I correct the problem? To make a decision, I read through uncorrected and corrected versions of the translations carefully. Doing so, I saw that the uncorrected versions made reading both texts difficult to the point that much of their value was lost. Unless they were corrected, two thirds of the main content of the books bordered on being unreadable, therefore, the texts were corrected and I note with satisfaction that both of the book as a whole read very well after doing so.

An important factor in deciding whether to make the correction or not was that I was able to pinpoint where the mixup had occurred in each text. Because of that, swapping the pieces to their rightful places worked well. I think that there is the loss of perhaps a line or two in either text but this happened when the original mix-up occurred, not as a result of doing the correction. In particular, it seems as though there is a loss of one line in the first of the two texts resulting in the loss of the name of the source text for the quotation which follows. Other than that, several very careful inspections of both texts leads to me say that I think that the two texts have been almost perfectly returned to their original form. I have marked the changeover point in each text with a footnote so that those studying the Tibetan text can more easily follow what has been done.

This leads on to mentioning that, as usual with our books, I had electronic editions of all of three texts made and those texts are included at the back of the book. They have not had the text moved around as described above, that is, they represent what is found in the Tibetan of the Derge Edition.

I found, while preparing the Tibetan texts that there were many spelling mistakes in the woodblock prints and many places where the woodblocks themselves had been retouched. Derge editions are usually very reliable but the Derge edition of Dza Patrul's *Collected Works* has mistakes throughout and more frequently than usual. When preparing the Tibetan texts found at the back of this book, I corrected many of these errors. For some discrepancies between the root and commentary sections of the third text, there was no way to know which wording was correct, so I left them as is. Thus, those who use the Tibetan texts here should note that such discrepancies are in the original edition.

About the Transmission of Great Completion

Three Lines of Transmission

In our human world, there are three main ways that the extra-secret unsurpassed or Quintessence Great Completion teaching is transmitted: direct mind to mind transmission which only occurs between buddhas and tenth level bodhisatvas; transmission via symbolic means which occurs mainly between beings who are advanced on the path—the vidyadharas as they are known in this system; and aural transmission which is the main means for transmitting Great Completion to ordinary beings.

Nearly all teaching today is done via the aural transmission for ordinary beings, for example the content of the first and second texts here is given via that kind of transmission. However, the third text in this book chronicles a transmission of this quintessence dharma at either the mind or sign transmission level. This high level transmission occurred in relatively recent times, making it another interesting chapter in the events of the Longchen Quintessence lineage, one which I don't think has been known amongst Westerners until now. I found the story and the transmission particularly interesting because they shed some light on Jigmey Gyalway Nyugu, an essential part of the lineage but whose writings and life story have not been widely known amongst Westerners. Needless to say, the teaching itself becomes of great interest given the weight of blessing that accompanies this style of transmission.

The Requirements for Transmission

Having said that, we have to move on to the fact that it is a fundament of the tantras as a whole that no-one should hear the tantra teachings or be exposed to their profound methods for directly transmitting their ultimate meaning without first receiving what is called empowerment.[12] Great Completion is extremely particular about these two points of secrecy and correct procedure. The tantras of Great Completion clearly state that, before any formal teaching of the system can be given to a person, the person must have the introduction mentioned just above. In other words, the introduction must be received before a person can be given any explanations of Great Completion. This has to be done so that the disciple "gets it" based on what is real, what is fact. If it is not done that way, it says in the tantras and general instructions of the system, the disciple will not be able to avoid going down a mistaken path.

The Warnings

There are three points which are particularly noteworthy given the state of affairs of the transmission of Quintessence Great Completion in the West today. First, the tantras offer no alternatives or escape clauses on the point just made; it has to be done and done in the order stated. Second, the introduction has to happen in person, with the disciples actually present before the guru. Third, the tradition gives a very strong spiritual health warning: do not attempt to read the material in this or any other book on Great Completion unless you have already received the introduction to the nature of mind or have been given explicit permission to do so by someone in a position to give it. Study of the words without the introduction to the nature of mind will lead you astray and could, as the tradition warns, even prevent you from connecting to the actual fact of Great Completion in this life. In conjunction with this, there are many instructions

---

[12] A clear explanation of empowerment in general and how it connects with Quintessence Great Completion can be found in *Empowerment and Atiyoga* by Tony Duff, published by Padma Karpo Translation Committee, second edition, 2010, ISBN: 978-9937-8244-5-3. It also contains the root empowerment text for the Longchen Quintessence Great Completion and instructions by Dilgo Khyentse Rinpoche on the practise of Thorough Cut, making it a useful support for this book.

which explain that the introduction has to be, at this aural level of transmission, given in person.

The Terminology and Style of Expression used in the Aural Transmission for Ordinary Persons

Great Completion has its own vocabulary and style of expression. The former has not been part of the English language, leaving us with the task of understanding it and translating it into English. To assist the reader with this, I have over the last thirty years gradually developed a vocabulary in English which for the most part captures the vocabulary of the Great Completion tantras. Of that, the vocabulary needed for this book is explained in ample notes and an extensive glossary.

An important point of vocabulary is that I use it consistently. I do not take the simplistic approach in which several important terms, each with its own specific shade of meaning, are translated with one English term, and eschew the approach of inconsistent translation where an important term will be translated with varying English words throughout a text. Instead and just like in the original Tibetan, every single term is given its own unique equivalent in the English translation and the equivalents are used consistently throughout. This has two effects: firstly, it opens the door to the reader being able to follow the many and profound threads of meaning in a text in the same way that a Tibetan would be able to do; and secondly, merely by reading the translation the reader is educated in the use of the vocabulary of Great Completion in a manner which is completely consistent with its use in the original Tibetan texts.

Great Completion also has its own, unique style of expression which is an important part of the transmission of meaning, one that does not fit with standard Tibetan or English expression. This style of expression has to be learned and appreciated, otherwise part of the transmission will be lost. I make no apologies at all for maintaining that style of expression in English where it is part of the lineage's way of transmitting Great Completion. If it is hard to read at times, then know that that is part of the transmission.

Summary

This section has been a summary of explanations given in the tradition of the transmission, and the need for secrecy, and need for doing things the right way. A more complete explanation is given in the introduction of PKTC's *Flight of the Garuda*[13] publication.

Points of Translation

Notes

Copious notes have been provided to ensure the clearest possible understanding of the texts.

Use of the Second Person

I have often abandoned the use of the more formal English "one" in favour of the less formal but much more personal "you" simply because that is the tone of teaching in these texts; their style of composition is very personal and goes straight to the heart.

Sanskrit and diacriticals

Sanskrit terminology is properly transliterated into English with the use of diacritical marks. These marks often cause discomfort to less scholarly readers and can distance them from the work, therefore, they have been left out of this book.

---

[13] *Flight of the Garuda, a Complete Explanation of Thorough Cut by Zhabkar* by Tony Duff, published by Padma Karpo Translation Committee, 2011, ISBN: 978-9937-572-05-7.

Health Warning

The texts in this book are about a subject that is normally kept secret. Anyone who has had these teachings in person will be able to understand them or at least go to his teacher and ask for further explanation. As mentioned in the earlier section on the transmission of Great Completion, anyone who has had the introduction to the nature of mind upon which the teachings hinge, please use and enjoy the text as you will! However, if you have not heard these teachings and especially have not had the requisite introduction to the nature of mind, you would be best off not reading this book but seeking out someone who could teach it to you according to the ways of transmission laid out in the lineage itself. Today there are both non-Tibetans and Tibetans who can do that for you and who are available in many countries across our planet. In short, the content of this book could be dangerous to your spiritual health if you are not ready for it, so exercise care.

These days charlatans present the profound oral instructions
Without lineage and even tell their students that
This is a time of great consolidation where the teachings
From any and every source can be successfully combined.
Aaach! The students are cut off from lineage.

There is a pure lineage of the teaching here,
Unadulterated by the ideas of other traditions
Passed on by Patrul from Dza who spent a lifetime
Obtaining and purely practising the purest of instructions
From the purest of lineages.

I prostrate to him and the succession of brilliant beings
Who passed Quintessence Great Completion
Down through the ages and especially to those

Of the Dzogchen Monastery transmission—
Jigmey Lingpa, Jigmey Gyalway Nyugu,
Mingyur Namkha'i Dorje the fourth,
Patrul Jigmey Chokyi Wangpo, Padma Vajra the first,
Jigmey Yontan Gonpo, Padma Kalzang the second—
My glorious and unutterably kind guru—
Who poured their blessings and goodness
Into this Western vessel who likewise
Spent a lifetime obtaining and purely practising
The purest of instructions from the purest of lineages
In the hope that a few Westerners might have access
To pure teachings from a Westerner with pure lineage.

Thorough Cut!
What's left? That's it!
Direct Crossing—
Don't be deluded,
It's only for a very fortunate few!

Lama Tony Duff,
The Field of Lotuses
Dzogchen Monastery
Tibet, Summer, 2010

Thangka of Dza Patrul

From the Supreme Vehicle Ati: Foremost Instructions Clearly Showing Actuality

by Dza Patrul

I prostrate to the holy gurus.

People following the path of Nature Great Completion fall into three grades of faculty: best, middling, and least. The following presents the way that each of them preserves Nature Great Completion's actuality.

All of them initially set a basis for the actual preservation by honing in on the matter using the steps of seeking mind and being properly introduced to the inexpressible fact[14]. After that comes the actual way of preserving, as follows.

People of the best faculties are such that, for them, mind abiding is all right and mind moving is equally all right. These people arrive at a clear understanding that mind is empty then, having decided on that, it henceforth makes no difference to them whether mind is abiding or moving—for them, all discursive thought that shines forth

[14] The "inexpressible fact" is the fact that can be known only by wisdom, not by any mental or verbal expression of dualistic mind. For wisdom, see the glossary.

is the play of wisdom, all of it is the conquerors' mind process of profound emptiness.

So, set yourself in just that, not spoiling it by contriving it in the slightest. Sometimes discursive thought as discursive thought itself[15] might be present, but it will of itself, that is, automatically, be liberated in which case it is known to be part of the concentration itself[16]; it is dharmakaya, it is self-arising wisdom, it is Mahamudra, it is Prajnaparamita. It cannot, like a rope that has been burned down to an ashen thread, bind you because its entity is that it is empty. That, which is nothing more than a facsimile of discursive thought, is the output of the emptiness shining forth. Here, there is no difference between discursive thought and emptiness, so the great one from Uddiyana[17] said, "Discursive thought, because its entity is empty, is the dharmakaya!"

If you were to meditate, that would involve rational mind, so there is no meditating at all to be done. Leave discursive thought as itself, untouched! Doing this and that to discursive thought in order to fix it gives autonomy to the discursive thought, following which it turns into a chain of confusion, so do not do anything at all to fix it! If you become distracted during this, then, because you have set yourself right on yourself, you will have entered actual confusion; therefore, it is necessary not to become distracted—just that alone is sufficient.

---

[15] Tib. rnam rtog rang ga ma. Discursive thought as discursive thought itself means discursive thought functioning as such in a dualistic mind. The other possibility is discursive thought which, because it is self-liberating itself is only a facsimile of discursive thought, as mentioned further down.

[16] Discursive thought has become part of the concentration on actuality.

[17] Padmasambhava.

This is the one thing of simply never focussing on any reference[18] and not being distracted. The Great Completion guru Shanti said,

> Not knowing meditation and not knowing separation;
> Not separated from no meditation's meaning!

That means: "What shines forth is the meditation. That being so, there is no meditation which is a contrivance of rational mind to be done. Hence, it involves 'not knowing meditation'. It is not a lax primordial absence of meaning but a setting of yourself right on yourself without 'knowing separation' from it. Through that, you continuously stay 'not separated from no meditation's meaning!'"

In regard to this, those of outstanding faculties will not need to work at holding to it for seven days or fourteen days or one month in order not to be distracted from it, but will be able without conceived effort simply to place themselves in being over whatever shines forth. In Great Completion they are referred to as having "the mind of Great Completion, primordially liberated vast space" and in Mahamudra, they are referred to as having "the aware process of self-illumination".

With continuous preservation of that, you have what is called "common awareness". That common awareness has superficies that are not in the slightest bit different from the discursive thoughts as such of worldly people. However, it has the clearness and stillness[19] that comes with not grasping at its having an entity. Its equipoise has the excellence of objects, with post-attainment thereby voided[20]. It

---

[18] Focussing on a reference is what dualistic mind does; it uses dualistic reference points and focusses on them instead of direct knowledge.

[19] Tib. sa le hrig ge ba. A special term of Great Completion that does not simply mean being tranquil.

[20] Equipoise or the time practising meditation is without objects because it is focussed on emptiness. Post-attainment or the time of being off the cushion is the time when there are appearances. However, in Great

(continued ...)

is an awareness free of the blemishes of latencies, free of identification, yet within which a facsimile only of discursive thoughts can come. That is the actual dharmakaya. Those who think in Great Completion terms also refer to this as "while not possessing discursive thought, everything is known in clearness.[21] Mahasiddha Mitra Dzoki[22] said, "If you put yourself directly in whichever appearance occurs, there will be activity-free[23] spontaneous existence". If the discursive thought which is the subjective grasper is, like that, allowed to self-liberate by itself, the external objects grasped by it—visual forms, sounds, and so on—also will automatically proceed to self-liberate. It is a case of setting yourself, without manufacture or contrivance,[24] in the eye's objects of visual form whether good or bad, the ear's sounds nice or not, and likewise smells, tastes, and touches whether good or bad, and mind whether happy or sad, attached or averse, knowing enemy or friend, knowing earth, water, fire, air, and so on—in short in just exactly what shines forth and appears. Great Completion says,

> If for the consciousnesses of the five doors
> The thought involving mental clinging is not entered,
> Just that is the conqueror's mind.

---

[20] (... continued)
Completion, equipoise and post-attainment merge, with the result that the equipoise has appearances (this is the emptiness having the excellence of all superficies, explained in the glossary) and a post-attainment separate from the equipoise has been left behind.

[21] Tib. sa ler mkhyen bya.

[22] Mitra Dzoki was an ancient Indian adept of Mahamudra.

[23] "Activity-free" means that a yogin stays in spontaneous existence without needing to make any concept-driven endeavour to stay in the spontaneous existence.

[24] Tib. bzo bcos. "Manufacture" is the step of newly creating something that was not there before and "contrivance" is the process of changing what is already there so that there is now an artificial form of it.

and Pacifier[25] asserts,

> If you know the shortcomings of thought that
> intellectually knows the meaning,
> When discursive thought shines forth there is great
> meaning and
> When there are coarse afflictions wisdom is evident.

Thus, for the mind of Great Completion, it is stated that whatever shines forth is neither to be abandoned nor not abandoned and not to be followed after, and when you set yourself in just that without doing anything to fix it, that's it! Being that way, none of the things[26] made by rational mind are involved and, because of that, there is not something to be abandoned and no antidote for abandoning it, so there is no furtherance and suppression, no adoption and rejection, and so on. Therefore, it is also what is called "beyond-rational-mind dharmakaya suchness".

The above explanation was in relation to someone of best faculties, which should be understood to mean that it was instruction for those three types who are the best, middling, and least of the persons with best faculties.[27]

---

[25] Tib. zhi byed. Pacifier is the general name for the system of dharma practice that features the practice of Severance (Tib. chod).

[26] "Things" here and elsewhere in all of these texts usually means the things we perceive in our ordinary worldly way which are conceptualized, solidified inventions.

[27] In this text, he will explain nine types of people graded according to the ability of their mental and physical faculties: the best, middling, and least for each of best, middling, and least. What he has just explained are the best, middling, and least types of the best type. These are the ones who are able to approach Great Completion practice directly and be successful at it.

The three[28] of middling faculties are instructed in terms of the joining together shamatha and vipashyana. Gyalwang Yang Gonpa[29] said,

> Do primordial meditation through not meditating with
> rational mind!
> Leaving it alone, do not contrive it through
> manufacture!
> Not viewing rational-minded thoughts as faulty,
> Not meditating in order to not think,
> Leave mind to go its own way and stay there!
> Meditation will happen, coming in palm of shamatha!

Familiarizing yourself through meditation by doing it as he says will cause your time in the innate to be lengthened, the movement to be gradually lessened, and mind's abiding to be gradually stabilized. If thought process comes along, it is dealt with through the joining of shamatha and vipashyana. Meditating by preserving the continuity of that will cause all discursive thought, subtle and gross, to cease. In that way, a concentration that has no establishment of anything will come about, so it is empty, and at the same time, its luminosity has no thoughts, so there is no sensation of body and mind existing. With that, a blissful experience in which it is not possible to separate from that concentration will shine forth. By continuing with the meditation, the good qualities of the five eyes and the extra-sensory perceptions also will arise, which is referred to as absorption.[30] Culti-

[28] … the best, middling, and least …

[29] Gyalwang Yang Gonpa is one of the very famous early Drukpa Kagyu masters, well known for his great attainment of these practices. He wrote widely on Mahamudra practice.

[30] Skt. dhyāna. An absorption is a deep, highly stable, one-pointed, concentration.

vating that thick type of shamatha[31] will result in the four absorptions[32] and the one-pointed concentrations of the four sets of ayatanas[33], and finally, the levels of the nine equilibria[34] will be accomplished. The Tirthikas also have the nine[35], so this is a path common to both insiders and outsiders[36], nevertheless, it is necessary at first to find shamatha because there is no way to shut off the elaboration of many discursive thoughts without it. Still, the levels and paths will not be traversed unless there is vipashyana with that. Therefore, one first finds the mere factor of abiding mind and then, when the thought arises within it of being pleased with the non-elaboration of discursive thought, one simply recognizes the presence of that thought in the abiding then looks right at it, causing it to vanish. In that way, the looking and the abiding are joined into one, which is the activity of unifying or joining together shamatha and vipashyana[37].

---

[31] It is a thick because it does not have insight being developed with it.

[32] The four absorptions or dhyanas are the states of absorption corresponding to existence in the four form realms.

[33] The one-pointed concentrations of the four sets of ayatanas are eight levels of concentration that correspond to the eight formless levels.

[34] The nine equilibria are the nine steps of deepening one-pointedness that a person passes through while developing shamatha. A true shamatha is the final level of the nine levels.

[35] ... because they too have the practices that develop the absorptions and one-pointed concentrations, but they only have ones that are within samsara, they do not have ones that transcend samsara.

[36] Insiders are the Buddhists and outsiders are all the others following a spiritual path.

[37] This is explained by Padma Karpo in his Mahamudra text *An Explanation of the Four Yogas Points out Superfact* published by Padma Karpo Translation Committee in the book *Drukchen Padma Karpo's Collected Works on Mahamudra* by Tony Duff, 2011, ISBN 978-9973-

(continued ...)

The Dvagpo Kagyu refer to this as "the barrier between abiding and movement dropping away".[38] Essentially speaking, it is rational-mind-made meditation. In this, it is necessary to remain unseparated from the thought process with its factor of recognition, so the Kagyu refer to it as "thought process apprehending emptiness". Meditation done as a preservation of its continuity causes that apprehending thought process to turn into the thought process of self-illumination. If this remains of itself unnon-distracted, then that is on the side of a great kindness! Otherwise, after about one month of practice it can be mixed with daytime appearances[39]; as Gyalwa Gotsangpa[40] said,

> Appearances all together are not meditated on as empty nor are they meditated on as not empty; if whatever shines forth is apprehended by thought process, it will, of itself, be fine in about one month—abiding in the first level of Freedom from Elaboration will naturally happen.[41]

If the process described above is distilled down, what happens is that the initial phase of shamatha practice develops self-recognition which causes the joining of shamatha and vipashyana, which is referred to

---

[37] (... continued)
572-01-9.

[38] As do the Drukpa Kagyu, and again, this is clearly explained, *ibid.*

[39] ... meaning that process of merging with post-attainment can be started.

[40] Gyalwa Gotsangpa is another of the very famous early Drukpa Kagyu masters, well known for his great attainment of these practices. He wrote down many of his songs about Mahamudra practice. His name means "the conqueror who lived in a vulture's nest" given to him because he made his home for practice high in the rocky crags, near vulture nests.

[41] Freedom from Elaboration is the name of the second of the four yogas of Mahamudra. Its first level is the point in the overall practice at which one for the first time recognizes the nature of mind with vipashyana.

as "Mahamudra" and also "Maha Ati". Yang Gonpa summed it up when he said,

> The movement of rational mind's thoughts is the doorway to actuality. Self-recognition is the key point of developing experience in it.

In regard to this, if both the middling and least of the middling do not take the mental stance that discursive thought as discursive thought is the meditation, then, by looking at discursive thought that shines forth, all of it will dissolve into emptiness. On the heels of that thought and within the state of that dissolution, another thought will shine forth. If that also is looked at, it will dissolve as did the previous one, and exactly that is what is continuously to be preserved. A doha says,

> Mind without identification, an empty dhatu,
> Shining forth as the variety is the door to rigpa.
> While in the state of this rational-mind-free,
> Naked luminous-emptiness, look at the dhatu!
> Meditation will happen, coming in vipashyana's palm!

Do the meditation like that. In regard to this, Mitra Dzoki said,

> What shines forth is identified and in rigpa self-liberates in its own place.

That contains the meaning of being easy to do and of great effect.

The approach to meditation that is common to all three of both best and middling persons is as follows. A doha says,

> Do not lose the strength of undistracted mindfulness!
> Do not manufacture not meditating's actuality!
> Do not wish to speak about the thought-less rigpa!
> Preserve for a while that which is unspoiled with permanence and nihilism!
> Meditation will happen, in which shamatha and vipashyana are put into unification.

That is easy to understand in theory, but you must actually use undistracted mindfulness to ensure that you do not manufacture or contrive what shines forth! It will shine forth but do not view it as existent! It will dissolve but do not grasp it as non-existent! Allowing discursive thoughts to poke up their noses, let yourself function simply in recognition. From Great Completion's Mind Section:

> Within the state of the primally pure dhatu,
> Rigpa directly born in an instance of thought process,
> Comparable to gaining a jewel from deep in the ocean,
> Is the dharmakaya not contrived or made by anyone.

With that, there has been introduction.

——— ◆◆◆ ———

The three of least faculties are usually those who have no trust in vipashyana. They also are unable to give rise to real shamatha; they are either sinking or agitated with the result that meditation does not come on for them. Thus, for them, the preliminaries must be completed and then, on a comfortable seat, they must establish the seven dharmas: crossing the legs, putting the hands into equipoise pose, joining the tongue to the palate, setting the eyes down the tip of the nose, and so on.[42] Then they must do a set of nine expulsions of stale air, visualize the guru at the crown or heart, and supplicate.

Body and mind are allowed to relax and, in that state, you look right at any discursive thought that shines forth then relax right over that. And, if it shines forth again, then you relax as before right over that. Do not be pleased at its disappearance into absence! Do not be upset at its turning into a mass of discursive thoughts! Do not either hope for meditation to come on nor be concerned that it will not. Set yourself completely at ease on top of what shines forth and a great

---

[42] These are the Seven Dharmas of Vairochana; see the glossary for more.

relaxation might come on in which there is no movement of thought process at all, a discursive thought-less no-thought. Mindful of that, if you do not tighten and be aware of what is happening, there will be an undercurrent of thought which, not sensing itself, is like water moving underneath a stack of hay.[43] If you allow it free reign to do as it pleases, like you would with something that is not causing harm, that will not give rise to a complete meditation, so it is necessary to tighten. If you do not do so, then, as with water flowing under a stack of hay, you will not know of the thought. However, the movement of thought is the life of the identification of thought process, so relax over it and set yourself there. Then, discursive thought might not decrease but increase and you could become angry at yourself, thinking, "Meditation is not happening for me", but there is no fault—the first temporary experience to arise is like water crashing down a steep mountain face, which the Kagyu refer to as "being disturbed by the waves of thought of one-pointedness"; it is the lesser level of One Pointedness. You endure its production while continuing to meditate, which leads to thought sometimes staying still and sometimes proliferating, like a small bird in water by turns sits in the water and rises up from it, and to its sometimes sitting still for a while as though stationed on a rock. That is how the second temporary experience arises. If you to continue with the meditation, there will be times when it proliferates but mostly abides; the example is that of an old man—mostly sitting down. That is how the third temporary experience arises. Continuing still further, there will be times when, like water flowing inside a pipe, proliferation of thought will not be evident. Even at this time mindfulness has to be tightened

[43] This is an example used in the Mahamudra tradition to indicate how subconscious thought is damaging to meditation. A pile of hay (a meditation) which has moisture or a flow of water develop beneath it (an undercurrent of thought, subconscious gossip, etcetera) remains unknown to the farmer (the meditator). Additionally, although it will not seem to affect the pile of hay (it will seem that the meditation is going fine), it will cause it to rot away from below (the meditation will be going to ruin).

a little. That is how the fourth temporary experience arises. Continuing on, if thought continues to decrease, eventually there will be no proliferation at all in mind and it will be always abiding night and day; due to it craving for food and clothing will not arise and you will be able to abide, relieved of all movement of thought for days and months, so the example is that of a mountain. If this goes wrong, it will be that, by taking it too far, it will go onto being a shravaka's cessation. If it goes well, it will be that thorough processing[44] of body and with it perfected shamatha will be obtained. That is how the fifth temporary experience arises. Note that this progression accords with what happens for the majority of people, but, according to an individual's channels and elements and level of faculty, a different progression which does not fit the specified one is possible.

At that point, whereas the best of the least does continue on according to sequence, both the middling and least find it hard to produce the abiding so, for them, the key points of body are taken up as before, then a small piece of wood is set on the ground in front about one full arm-length from the point between the brows. Then, the three of mental mind, references, and wind are rolled into one. In this case, mind is treated as nothing more than a basis for developing non-proliferation; if overly tightened, it will become upset, and if overly relaxed, the meditation will be lost, so a balance should be found in short sessions done many times. From that, you can gradually move to longer sessions done fewer times. When mind has started to abide, meditate as before but on a white letter A visualized atop that small piece of wood. Then, by stages shift to a white sphere, a yellow one, and so on[45], and meditate on each reference for one, three, or more days as needed, yet not to the point of being irritated by it. Again, in place of the small piece of wood, put a pebble and meditate on that in using the same steps as before. Then meditate using whichever reference is suitable of syllables,

---

[44] Tib. shin sbyangs.

[45] … as described in the sutras …

small spheres, and the like, visualized externally on the three places of one's body and internally at the throat and heart centres, and so on, and through that the abiding will gradually be stabilized.

Moreover, it is very important not to be small-minded about this but to become fully involved with it and not allow yourself to be irritated by it. It has been said that you should not allow yourself to be overwhelmed when doing this shamatha practice but should engage the techniques for abiding described above with your fullest attention, like the swordsman in the midst of battle. The swordsman not losing his attention for a moment, raised his sword to an incoming spear and prevented it from hitting him, but then his eyes wandered momentarily to the sight of a beautiful woman, a spear hit him, and he arrived at his death. He said,

> This is not the fault of the spear; it is the fault of the
> distraction.
> Henceforth all you swordsmen
> Do not become distracted for even a moment!
> Within that distraction, your life will be lost!

It is important not to be distracted, exactly as shown in the example.

Now to expose vipashyana. Vipashyana is what is called "Prajnaparamita". Without Prajnaparamita you cannot traverse the levels and paths of the journey to buddhahood, which is why the other paramitas are said by themselves to be without eyes. Also, Lord Gampopa said, "I can maintain an equipoise for seven days", to which Milarepa replied, "That means that you have been introduced to the concentration of the gods of the four absorptions."[46]

---

[46] Gampopa, in his first meeting with Milarepa, presented his accomplishment of meditation achieved through the instructions of the Kadampa tradition. It is reported that Milarepa said, "That is your meditation, it is not mine!" He was saying that Gampopa's meditation was a mere shamatha style of meditation without vipashyana, a low grade

(continued ...)

There are three types of vipashyana. Of them, the one which utterly distinguishes dharmas is the vipashyana whose meaning is intended in all the sutras and tantras and is referred to as "an unmistaken awareness". The one which knows the actuality that is the natural purity of mind is the one being discussed here, the one introduced and meditated upon in the present. And, through familiarization with that one, there is the vipashyana of unmistaken actuality made manifest, which happens at the time of fruition, when buddhahood is obtained.

Now, as in the shamatha context, there is the explanation of discursive thought being part of the equipoise, but in this case it has to be defined as nothing more than identification. Discursive thought flashes out in a variety of ways, but that occurrence is treated in this case by setting oneself in the state of mere recognition of it. In short, it is exactly setting yourself in the state of merely recognizing that something has shone forth or arisen. In this, there is nothing at all to be meditated on through the use of meditation.

If you take the view that there is something to be abandoned and an antidote to be applied, the conceived effort and striving for accomplishment done on account of that will not take you past the causes and effects of samsara.

Moreover, discursive thought is that which is not conducive to concentration yet it does not have to be abandoned, instead, setting oneself right on it again and again, it proceeds to self-purify. As has been said,

> It does not involve turning away and abandoning
>   grasping at confused appearance.
> The non-conducive thing itself is a complete antidote.

---

[46] (... continued)
of accomplishment.

The least person of least faculties does it that way. However, if his mind is not serviceable, when discursive thought arises, he identifies it, then looks to see how it sits and then where it goes, with the result that it goes onto self-purification, and, by preserving a continuity of that, without needing to eliminate something out of consideration for future development, the discursive thought itself performs its own liberation which is called "self-arising wisdom". The meaning is as has been said: "If you hone in on movement, that alone will cause the thoughts and thought process to vanish into the dhatu".

Generally speaking there is what is called "common awareness": if you leave the entity of discursive thought that shines forth alone, not doing any manufacture or contrivance in relation to it, then remain undistracted from that, that alone will be sufficient. That does not happen for those of least faculties, so they preserve an equipoise that has conceived efforts connected with it. If they look at the discursive thoughts that shine forth but are unable to pacify them and the thoughts proliferate greatly, then they should relax by dropping the key points of the body altogether and allow the proliferator to proliferate, then, looking right at his ambassadors,[47] the proliferator will go back to being at peace in his own place. Both proliferation and abiding are mind, so they will become one in their own place and developing endurance with this practice will cause it to become deep.

Moreover, this example shows it:

> No matter how a crow flies off from its perch,
> After circling and circling it descends there again.

A crow about to be released from the edge of an ocean should have a thin metal chain attached to its leg! When it has arrived out over the ocean, if it flies up, there is empty sky in every direction; it is up in the emptiness of space. There is water below still; it has not escaped the water, so it flies here and there in all directions, but

---

[47] Thoughts are the ambassadors of the proliferator.

wherever it goes it does not find a way to return to ground. It needs to return to its perch! Similarly, discursive thought proliferates of itself but can be empty and equally, not proliferating, can be empty. It can abide, it can move, but it never goes beyond being empty. Thus, whichever way it shines forth, by coming down into just its own state, even the person with the least of faculties will be able to place himself in the freshness of the person of best faculties, and therefore, after examining this with great care, it would be excellent to train in this.

——— ◆◆◆ ———

People having the three faculties of best, middling, and least divided into a set of nine are used like that to show the way to practise; it is what is intended when the Great Completion Hearing Lineage[48] says,

> Those of best faculties are able to meditate right over the view; those of middling faculties are able to meditate right over meditation; those of least faculties are able to accomplish right over conduct."

Furthermore, it is necessary to generate strong determination towards meditation; the dharma is profound, but if it is not meditated on, the profound oral instructions become, as is said, lost to being just words off a page, which really is true. At this time we might have familiarized ourselves a little with meditation, but if we do not cultivate that continually, our minds, dharma, and practice will not actually meet with the dharma, then what we have done will not help at the time of death, so we must be careful. Gyalwa Gotsangpa said that it is necessary to have all six of these:

---

[48] This is the third of the three lineages through which Quintessence Great Completion is transmitted. It is also called the aural lineage for persons. It is the basic means by which these instructions are transmitted in these times.

Outwardly, put yourself in mountain tracts.
Inwardly, put yourself in a thatched wooden shack.
Secretly put yourself on your bed.[49]
Put yourself on the non-dual view.
Put yourself in un-distracted meditation.
Put yourself into detached conduct.

Generally speaking, in meditation outer and inner restrictions apply. When mind is unworkable, it is necessary to have outer restrictions so that you do not lose mindfulness. Then when discursive thought applies its own, inner restriction, whatever shines forth turns into meditation. Moreover, it goes on to being the state of the common awareness in which it has no grasping at itself.

A full-time meditator lets go of meditation, though it is known as the time when meditation does not let go of the meditator. When that happens, it is necessary to meditate without interruption. If you do not meditate like that, you might produce some slight experiences now, but they will dissipate and the meditation will be a case of "filling-it-in not functioning". "Hook not functioning" means that mindfulness, which could catch something, is not doing so and might as well not be there; if that is happening you need to tighten the watcher of non-distraction. "Split not functioning" means that, while having mindfulness, you do not allow yourself to become separated from compassion; for that, it is necessary at the beginning of a session to think, "I am going to meditate for the sake of all sentient beings", and at the end of the session to dedicate with, "May this merit cause all of them to attain buddhahood". The great Orgyan said, "If there is no compassion, the root of dharma rots", so this is extremely important. "Non-self not functioning" refers to meditation having been produced but not maintained, so having been discarded.

---

[49] In Tibet, one's bed was usually also one's meditation seat, so the meaning here is "put yourself on your meditation seat".

Therefore, summon up your meditation within rational mind then put yourself into meditation. Sometimes "setting yourself not functioning" will happen; meditation sometimes will come and sometimes will not come, but that's just how it is. You set yourself there anyway, whether it is coming or not and practise. "Functioning around the clock" is to the point that keeping it up it all day means that it will also come at night; this is when meditation makes an inner restriction. "Supreme yoga" in Great Completion is referred to as "the time of separation from conceived efforts for achievement" and in Mahamudra as the level called "non-meditation".

Outside of those three types divided into nine, there are also the "persons of cut-off family" who are not fit vessels for Thorough Cut and Direct Crossing. It has been taught that, if people of that type are empowered and purify the channels and winds, then have a consort, a karmamudra, given to them, then join the two faculties so that the four joys come on, allowing the bliss factor to be introduced as empty, then they, like the others above, can be brought into mind instruction.[50] Those for whom that is not possible can be brought in through the approach of gradual liberation using the methods of liberation by signs, liberation by sight, liberation by taste, and so on.

Generally, the mind side[51] and Mahamudra are called "wisdom generally visible", which is explained to mean that "until they have been finalized, they entail a type of view in which there is the grasping that goes with mental analysis". Nevertheless, if a Great Completion practitioner of that sort additionally receives the introduction and then meditates accordingly, the external objects that

---

[50] Here, he goes quickly through the steps of the first three empowerments. These are the preparations for the introduction to the nature of mind, which is the fourth empowerment.

[51] "Mind side" here means the Mind Section of the three sections of Great Completion. As he says in the colophon, this text is based on a text concerning Mind Section Great Completion.

appear and the internal grasping mind with all of its proliferations and abidings will shine forth as wisdom—Great Completion, referred to as "the unbiassed mind of own appearance", has the ability to produce great intelligence in a person. It is fine all around: mind is met in the introduction then practice is done in relation to appearance; then Direct Crossing is entered and the darkness instructions or visible instructions are provided; then, if practice is done in relation to the empty forms of luminosity, self-arising wisdom will become manifest in direct perception and there is no doubt that the person will be liberated in the dharmata bardo.[52]

In regard to someone like myself who has no meditative experience and no experience in the foremost instructions due to having heard but mostly forgotten them, as Lord Barawa[53] said,

> Having no experience in meditation,
> I have given the meditation instructions
> Based on the letters in books; you might understand them intellectually but
> There is a danger that you could practise them the wrong way.

and,

> Through that, there has been no attainment of levels and none of good qualities either,
> But through gaining Patience, the four will be accomplished,[54]

---

[52] This is the phase immediately after death of the bardo in which a person is fully immersed in the condition or dharmata of reality. For dharmata and bardo, see the glossary.

[53] Lord Barawa was another of the great, early Drukpa Kagyu masters.

[54] Patience is the name of the first of the four levels of the Path of Connection, the third of the five paths taught in the Prajnaparamita sutras. It is generally considered in Buddhism that it is not all right to

(continued ...)

And by making the root of compassion firm,
Works done for the sakes of migrators will be all right.

This means that my giving this instruction can be all right even when Patience has not been attained as long as there is a little compassion in mind. This is especially true if mind has been mixed with dharma and a workable concentration has been produced and one then writes down what one recalls of the words of holy gurus who are like buddhas. Master Saraha said,

First, meet at the meeting point!
Next, set yourself in the resting place!
Finally, let go into the destination!

The first line means that you meet a guru who knows how to give the instructions then, having honed in on mind, you meet it in a refined way. The next one means to set yourself without any manufacture or alteration in what shines forth. Finally, without clinging to the play of the concentrated state of experience, let go into absence of grasping!

This was extracted from an instruction manual on Mind Section Great Completion. May it benefit all.

❁ ❁ ❁

Furthermore, here are various pieces of instruction that I have heard in person from various gurus and which are important to understand.

---

[54] (... continued)
teach others until the Path of Seeing, which is the path after the Path of Connection, has been attained. So his meaning here is that, if one is on the way to the path of seeing and has compassion, it can still be all right to teach.

Having various experiences and realization shine forth is a good sign of meditation, one which increases one's certainty of it, but there is the important key point that it does not last and one should not enter into clinging at truth because of it. To have what shines forth continue on, in the present and without relying on a grasping thought process, to naked self-liberation should be understood as the good path to complete purity.

Appearance of the guru's form, the yidams of development stage, and the like should also be a case of non-appearance, with the recitations and so forth being done in naked stillness.[55] Those bodily forms will appear but without nature; they will be illuminated by mind but in that luminosity there will be no-thought; and there will be no clinging to the bliss aspect of it. If, while possessing the three characteristics like that, the recitations and so forth are done within the state of the clear-presence[56] appearance which is the unstopped self-output of the emptiness, it will not be necessary to meditate on the guru on the crown of the head, and so on, with great vigour and importance attached to doing so.

The defining features of the path-time's ground, path, and fruition are as follows. Even at path-time, mindness[57] root-free, unbiassed, and all-pervasive[58] is the ground. In its state, preserving the objectless self-illumination without subtraction or addition is the path. Thereby, the fruition's completion stage deity form self-shines forth being

---

[55] Tib. hrig ge rjen ne. These are special words of the system which indicate aspects of the presence of rigpa. Stillness was mentioned in a previous footnote.

[56] Tib. sa ler. This is a special word of the system which indicates an aspect of the presence of rigpa.

[57] For mindness, see the glossary and the very nice explanation of it on page 73.

[58] If you look carefully, you will see the three characteristics taught in Foremost Instruction Great Completion here.

equivalent to melting bliss, so goes on to being counted as the fruition of the path.

Moreover, the texts of Great Completion speak of "recognition over oneself"[59] which means that, while not creating any spoilage of contrivance in this present awareness that is free from thoughts of the three times, within the state of the innate an identification of the vivid, cleared out, totally spread-out rigpa[60] is rapidly imposed on a person, resulting in the person being introduced to self-arising wisdom.

With that completed, there is then "decision on one thing" which is that, with past thought process and thinking stopped and the future one not yet arisen, the present awareness has all the cogitation and thought process of rational mind stopped, then the fourth-part-freed-of-the-three rigpa brings the presence of fresh, no-discursive-thought wisdom which is knowing, cleaned-out, standing up, vividly present, and there[61]—and that's it!

"The fourth part freed of the three" is as follows. There is the time of the three times of past, present, and future, a time which has thought associated with it. There is freshness—the absence of spoilage that comes with the contrivance done by the thought process and cogitation connected with the three times—found in the present

---

[59] From here to the end of this section, the instruction is a very brief but fine instruction on Garab Dorje's Three Lines that Strike the Key Points teaching. More complete instructions on it can be found in Dza Patrul's *Feature of the Expert Glorious King* and in the writings of Dodrup III Tenpa'i Nyima such as *About the Three Lines that Strike Key Points*, both of which have been published by PKTC.

[60] These three are special qualities used to identify the immediate direct experience of rigpa.

[61] These five are special qualities used to identify the immediate direct experience of rigpa.

moment which has no thought. That is the fourth part. It is a time of no engagement in discursive thinking, so is freed of the three times that go with discursive thought. It is mind beyond rational mind, the fourth-part-freed-of-the-three dharmakaya mind.

"Assurance built on liberation" is as follows. Looking directly and without the spoilage of alteration at the face of what shines forth then relaxing in the state of that causes thought process and thoughts to vanish without trace, so that, like waves vanishing into water, what shines forth self-liberates without something to be abandoned and an antidote to it. Building one's assurance in that state of self-liberation is what is being referred to here.

Here is the way that the key points of Great Completion's Mind and Space Sections are incorporated in the Foremost Instruction Section. With equipoise in the state of alpha purity, all appearances of containers and contents are decided on as mindness, self-arising wisdom, expression-free dharmakaya, which incorporates the key points of Mind Section. That, decided on as the in-space of dharmata free of conceived efforts to achieve something incorporates In-Space Section.[62]

---

[62] There are several types of space taught in these teachings. Space itself, with no word used to modify it, is the idea of uncompounded space, the metaphysical space that accommodates all things. "In-space" (Tib. klong) is the space of a person's direct experience. It is a space which you feel you are immersed within, similar to the experience of a parachutist floating down who feels that he is at the centre of a vast, surrounding space. The original Sanskrit means the "interior space", so it is not merely a sense of space all around but conveys the sense that one is completely immersed within it. This is one of several particularly important terms in Great Completion. If it is translated simply as space, the actual meaning intended is lost. There is a problem here. The second section of Great Completion teachings has been called "Space Section" for a long time but should be understood as In-Space Section.

(continued ...)

Thus, all the practices of both Mind and In-Space Sections are included within Foremost Instruction Section's practice of Thorough Cut, which means that the pinnacle, the supreme among Great Completion's paths is Foremost Instruction Section. In it, the method of coming down right on the key point of how it is, free of the abandoning and accepting of samsara and nirvana, is used to make beyond-rational-mind self-arising wisdom shine forth for an instant. Through that, within the actual fact of it, the dharmata of all dharmas is determined in direct perception of the self-illuminating actuality and in that way there is the unsurpassed supreme method for introduction to the wisdom-luminosity spontaneous-existence that resides in the ground.

Thus the abilities both to carry appearances of the sixfold group[63] that shine forth onto the path via self-liberation and to seal with the deity and mantra are greatly increased indeed. There is the point though that the self-liberating appearances of the innate's liveliness are carried onto the path as the self-output of deity and its mantra absent of conceived efforts otherwise used to create them, with the result that the awareness proceeds down a very special path of unification.

Rigpa nakedly shines forth in various doors of shining forth but everything that shines forth could be produced without wavering from mindfulness yet without an identification of what shines forth. That would be similar in the Great Completion system to the abiding experience of the four steps of producing experience and in the Mahamudra system to abiding in the Yoga of One Pointedness, so it is definitely nothing more than just seeing the side of mind's entity.

---

[62] (... continued)
When you understand that the name is actually "In-Space Section" and put that together with the meaning of "in-space" just described, the meaning of "In-Space Section" as he has just defined it becomes very clear. See the glossary for a more complete explanation of in-space.

[63] The sixfold group is the set of six consciousnesses of humans.

One might have the thought, "Taking simply the issue of whether finality has been obtained or not, is there still something more than this to be seen or is there nothing else to be realized?" Both intellectual understanding and experience which are consistent with how reality is may well be in accord with wisdom that has none of the confusion of rational mind, however, such understanding and experience has turned into a discursive thought type of thing which has with it rational mind grasping at a self in dharmas and which is thinking, "Is there nothing more than this?" Therefore, it is necessary to know the details both of experience that is not grasping at anything with rational mind in the elaboration-free innate disposition that appears at the time of looking directly, nakedly at one's own rigpa and of experience of the intellectually-understood emptiness.

Now, in relation to this "seeing of mind's entity" there is the skilful means for being self-introduced to simile wisdom which sees merely a generic image and what it leads to, the self-knowing wisdom of self-characterized entity[64] of no discursive thinking which arises only in the meditation of those who have attained the level of a noble one. If those who are developing certainty on the Path of Connection—the path of connecting to the attainment of mastery—do not have it, then why bother to mention the mindstreams having dhyana absorption of those who are on and those who have not yet entered the path of accumulation?

Therefore, a differentiation must be made. In the state of mindfulness which has self-recognized a dream, without a mindful consciousness which thinks, "I must train here in this dream", a greater level of purity can happen than with daytime training. The early phase

---

[64] Anything can be either generally characterized or self-characterized. The former points at a conceptual understanding of the thing and the latter at the actual thing itself.

of identifying, training, developing, and transforming a dream[65] involves stabilization and no change—enhancement comes later. The latter types mentioned above only get as far as appearances which come due to the day's activities, so there are few who arrive at the key points that come once dream identification and training having been stabilized. The majority are capable, within a deep sleep, of freeing luminous-empty rigpa from the grime of discursive thoughts and preserving its face. The capability of having its liveliness appearances arise as controlled manifestations of a dream experience can occur; this is counted as identification of the sleep luminosity, and, should that sort of thing happen within a dream, if there is also no seizing upon it by a thought-process consciousness at the time of the dream, that is considered as having arrived at the key point.

Direct Crossing is a system which leads the practitioner along the path of viewing visual appearances, where the appearances viewed are the signs of empty forms. The practitioner sets himself in a state without discursive thinking and does the familiarization within that because of which many people think that it is nothing more than shamatha giving rise to an individually discriminating prajna not having analysis, in which case it does not turn into vipashyana. However, it is explained in the Kalachakra and other tantras that familiarization with a concentration in which there is no discursive thinking leads to the production of no-thought wisdom which itself is the production of individually discriminating prajna's vipashyana. It is explained especially in Great Completion's own system where, with a basis consisting of the three body postures, three gazes, and winds not moving, the key points of channels and winds are worked in stages, causing discursive thought to stop. The object is visible in direct perception, so the practitioner is freed from the exaggerations that go with the words of mental analysis. Because of abiding in

[65] These are the four steps described in the Great Completion teachings of becoming adept at using dreams to increase one's ability to know that all dharmas are like an illusion, and so on.

dharmata itself, mother and son merge, which means that the practitioner crosses over into the primal situation's dhatu. Then the practitioner focusses his gaze on the appearances of the bindu with vajra chains. It is the settling without distraction and without manufacture in the state of the nature of just those appearances vividly present[66] itself that gets to the key point.

The length of a dhyana day at the time of the dharmata bardo goes beyond the measure of a practice session of merged equipoise and post-attainment; it is very difficult indeed to assess the production of the experiences of wisdom's spontaneous existence as "They are this". Very generally speaking, we can say that a dhyana absorption lasts for the period from entering the equipoise to the point when it is interrupted by discursive thought.

The degree to which a person will be able to liberate himself in the dharmata bardo depends on how well he, starting now, prepares the four appearances of luminosity for his own use. This being very important, the assessment of whether it has been achieved or not can be done through dream practice.

Proliferation appears on the surface of the equipoise and each thought process simply going through its complete cycle might shine forth together with the bliss-luminosity experience, nonetheless, for as long as there is no engagement in the grasping of wanting to have the experiences, that will get to the key point. What shines forth is decided on as one's own mind and mindness shines forth root-free luminous and empty without grasping; because of that, the grasping at a separated body, mind, and so on that comes from the surface of the equipoise self-purifies and, abiding in an absence of outer, inner, and in-between in naked pure knowing, discursive thought as discursive thought does not shine forth. The appearance shines forth

---

[66] Vividly present is a special wording which indicates the presence of rigpa.

but in merely being recognized it is all right; it is appearance merged with mind, appearance continuously shining forth as meditation. However, there is still the need to differentiate whether the grasping thought process is needed or not. Therefore, we have to say that, if this fresh appearance-rigpa, this self-knowing self-illumination, occurs as something divorced from conceived efforts to achieve and from suppression and furtherance, because the appearance is shining forth as meditation, it is not put together through grasping thought process. Following on from that, even with conceived effort yet no engagement in grasping, if it shines forth in self-liberation and vastness, it does get to the key point.

Generally speaking, a practitioner continuously maintains his spiritual practices via the three approaches to Being Just So.[67] He views in stark liberation the entity which has been realized. Externally, in viewing the phenomena made by dualistic mind, confusion's appearances appear without truth and he enters into being without clinging and grasping in the state of realizing those appearances to be illusory. Internally, in viewing the dharmata of those phenomena, he enters into being without grasping in the state of realizing absence of objects, like space. Secretly, in viewing the entity of rigpa, he realizes it as empty, luminous, and non-stop then enters being without conceived effort and achievement in that state. By staying in equipoise like that, he is able to gain control over unfathomable good qualities—the eyes, extra-sensory perceptions, and so on—and has no difficulty with liberating afflictions in their own place. Moreover, I heard from the holy lord guru's mouth many times that, "Beginners, meaning those who have thoroughly cleansed themselves, and those who have the good qualities of their familiarization coming forth as in-space due to having gone through the developmental stages, all arrive at the profound method of accomplishing buddha-

[67] Tib. chog zhag. Being Just So or Chog Zhag is defined in the glossary and also in the next teaching in the root text and also in the commentary to that where it is more extensively explained.

wisdom." Having trust in what he said, I gained the full extent of what that indicates and now offer it as advice to others; please keep it in mind!

Due to everything of the two entities of view[68] appearing as phenomena not being individually referenced but being realized as self-knowing, primordially-liberated, spontaneously-existing, empty-luminous elaboration-free, delimitation-and-falling-into-sides-free many-in-one-taste, everything also appears without the slightest concern or anxiety. However, there is the arising over and again of desire, aversion, and so on that occurs in reliance on those objects and until the self-grasping of rational mind has subsided, even though there might be a good intellectual understanding of the view, in actual experience what appears will be in contradiction to it. For a dharmata person[69] though, because at that point what shines forth is carried onto the path via naked self-liberation, it gets to the key point. Thus, preserving the state of this sort—primordially abiding in the nature which is beyond the coarse and subtle mental analysis that comes with tenet systems, beyond clinging's appearing objects, and beyond mental mind's domain, in the great vast in-space liberated from extremes—is the key point.

Whatever else might be the case, a yogin's experience has a pattern of good and bad thoughts that is just like the grass sprouting all over the ground in summer time and which cannot simply be assessed as one point on a scale of good and bad. For him, there is the view free of extremes in the liveliness of the self-output of no-thought, the meditation not bound by antidotes, the conduct in which what shines forth is left to self-liberate, and the fruition which is free of hopeful and fearful dualistic grasping. In relation to those, appearances shine forth, but if they involve the rational mind which wants experiences,

---

[68] … emptiness and luminosity …

[69] A dharmata person is one who is abiding in the dharmata of dharmas, which starts with the sense of emptiness.

they become like undigested medicine turning to poison, so at that time, if, in the state of just that fact which has been decided on, not being bound by grasping and clinging, the practitioner sustains himself perpetually with the natural style of proceeding which is one of being not distracted and not meditating, he will be satisfied.

Merely to identify dreams in the same way as people always identify their coarse dreams is not all right. Still, as long as you do not become involved in grasping at daytime appearances—the appearances of the sixfold group—if you adjust them with conceived efforts when you go to sleep, then, not automatically becoming lost in the thought process of the day, when you do fall asleep, experience, realization, and luminosity will gradually shine forth.

No matter how temporary experiences arise, do not spoil them with thoughts of suppression and furtherance, adoption and rejection. Instead, preserve just whatever shines forth, because that will cause the entire mass of grasped-grasping's thoughts to clear away, like clouds disappearing in the sky, and the seeds of samsara to be exhausted. There is the dhatu whose nature is complete purity and one's own in-space of immersion into it; rigpa, which is naturally a complete purity, dissolves into it, and mother and son have merged. Wisdom without the duality of grasped-grasping has been determined as the changeless dhatu. Discursive thoughts purify into the dhatu like waves disappearing into water, causing the barrier between samsara and nirvana to drop. The gradual path of the five paths and ten levels is traversed all of a sudden and you are liberated!

"Lamp for a Dim Room" The Meanings of the Key Points of The Secret, Quintessential Great Completion's Tantras, Protected with the use of Thorough Distinctions by Dza Patrul

I prostrate with respectful three doors to the dharma kings the All-Knowing One and his father-son succession[70] and take refuge in them.

Here, to explain the meaning of the great tantras of the quintessence level of the secret, the tantras of Nature Great Completion, the first of the eleven topics of the *Word's Meaning*[71] will be explained, a topic

---

[70] "All-knowing One" is a common epithet for Longchen Rabjam. His father-son succession is the succession of father-like gurus and son-like disciples who transmitted his system of teaching and realization. In the case of Dza Patrul, this is a prostration made to his lineage of Longchenpa followed by Jigmey Lingpa followed by Jigmey Gyalway Nyugu.

[71] *The Treasury of the Word's Meaning* is the pinnacle treasury of the *Seven Treasuries* of Longchenpa. It deals with Thorough Cut and Direct Crossing, with an emphasis on the latter, in eleven topics. The first topic is an extensive exposition of the ground. Given that view and ground are closely connected, the words here tell us that this text will primarily be an explanation of the view in relation to the ground according to the explanations given by Longchenpa in his *Treasury of the Word's Meaning*.

(continued ...)

concerned with "what the primal situation, the ground's actuality, is like at the time when neither realization—buddhas—nor non-realization—samsara—has arisen".[72]

Nowadays, presentations of that view are too often laced with the Bon tradition's various mistaken claims about it. Therefore, I am, like deliberately setting a lamp in a dim room, setting up needed protection for it. This protection consists of making thorough-going distinctions in regard to the meanings of the key points. Setting up this protection has three topics: identifying the ground, establishing it according to what the experts accept, and eliminating opposing arguments.

1. Identifying the ground

The profound, secret level of the speech of our teacher—the sugata gone easily to ease[73]—is found in the extremely vast sutra section of the Great Vehicle in the explanations of the element,[74] the sugatagarbha.[75] It is found in the main texts in general of the Secret Mantra

---

[71] (... continued)
This is useful because this chapter of *The Treasury of the Word's Meaning* is regarded as the most difficult chapter in that treasury, though few commentaries on it are available.

[72] The quotation given comes from Longchenpa's *Treasury of the Supreme Vehicle*, which was written before *The Treasury of the Word's Meaning*. Later, Longchenpa used it to introduce the first topic of *The Treasury of the Word's Meaning* and Dza Patrul follows suit here.

[73] For sugata see the glossary. He is referring to Buddha Shakyamuni here.

[74] See the element in the glossary.

[75] See sugatagarbha in the glossary.

Vajra Vehicle under the heading "the nature, ground tantra".[76] It is found in the uncommon Secret Mantra[77] that concerns us here under the heading "the primal situation's primordial ground". All of them are referring to exactly the same thing, despite their different names for it.

It is expressed in the *Treasury of Abhidharma*[78] using these words:

> The beginningless time's dhatu
> Is the abode of all dharmas;
> Because there is such, all migrators
> And nirvana happen.

And a doha says,

> I prostrate to mindness, alone the seed of all—
> Where becoming[79] and nirvana come on—
> A mind which, like a wish-fulfilling jewel,
> Fully dispenses all desired results.

And the *Garbha of the Secret*[80] says,

> E MA HO! From the sugata's garbha
> One's own discursive thoughts manifest via karma.
> A variety of bodies and possessions and
> Self and mine are individually grasped.

---

[76] Where tantra has the meaning of continuum and so refers to a mind.

[77] … the quintessential Great Completion teaching …

[78] The *Abhidharmakosha* of Vasubhandu.

[79] For becoming, see the glossary. It is an alternative name for samsara that focusses on migrators taking rebirth and *becoming* one sort of sentient being after another.

[80] Skt. *Guhyagarbha*. The name of the root tantra of the Mahayoga tantra section.

And the *Contained Understanding*[81] says,

> The appearance in the primal sugatagarbha of
> Adventitious discursive thoughts will cause obscuration through karmas.

And also,

> The unfathomable situation's conquerors
> Arise from the cause, samsara's sentient beings.

And Guardian Nagarjuna said,[82]

> Bowing down, I prostrate to
> That which when it does not know the totality
> Of everything is the three becomings,[83]
> The dharmadhatu which is certainly present in all sentient beings.

And also,

> That which has become the cause of samsara,
> Just that through having been cleansed is
> Purity—nirvana,
> And the dharmakaya too.

And the *All Creator*[84] says,

---

[81] Tib. bla ma dgongs 'dus. A tantra revealed by Sangyay Lingpa.

[82] … in his *Praise to the Dharmadhatu* …

[83] The three becomings are the three places of becoming, the three realms of samsara.

[84] Tib. kun byed. The abbreviated name of the root tantra of the Mind Section of Great Completion teachings.

> I am the teacher, the all-creator, enlightenment mind.[85]
> Enlightenment mind is the All-Creating King:
> The buddhas of the three times were made by
> enlightenment mind,
> The sentient beings of the three realms were made by
> enlightenment mind.

And so on; there have been extensive explanations of this point. This is the place where sutra and tantra arrive at the same understanding.

"Well", you query, "There are the Yogacharin Mind Only followers for whom the alaya consciousness is truly established and if they assert that as sugatagarbha, will that be the same as this?"[86] It would indeed not be the same! Asserting true existence for the sugatagarbha is a fault of rational mind involved with tenets. Besides, it does not matter if it is not fully consistent with what is being presented here because the way that the topmost level that goes beyond that understanding, the Middle Way, posits the ground is fully consistent with this.[87]

---

[85] For enlightenment mind, see the glossary. The Mind Section primarily teaches Great Completion through the concept of a mind. The mind taught is not the mind of samsara but the mind of enlightenment, bodhichitta, hence the use of the term here.

[86] For alaya, see the glossary. Alaya here means fundament. The person is thinking that for the Yogacharin followers of Mind Only, the fundament, which is similar to saying the ground, is the alaya consciousness. However, they declare that it is truly established, which is usually taken to mean that it is truly existent. Could their fundament and this ground you are speaking of be the same?

[87] It does not matter if the alaya of the Mind Only level of understanding the Buddha's teaching has the problem that it is taken to be truly existent because the topmost level of understanding the Buddha's teaching, called the Middle way, posits the ground in a manner fully consistent with what has been presented so far and all Tibetan Buddhists accept the Middle

(continued ...)

Going back to what is being discussed here, when its characteristics are presented, it is explained in the tantra sections of Nature Great Completion as that which has threefold entity, nature, and compassionate activity; the *Sound Breakthrough*[88] says,

> It resides as the beginning's three aspects of
> Entity, nature, and compassionate activity.

Consistent with that, the *Highest Continuum*[89] also presents it as threefold, defining it as:

> The element or type[90] of entity suchness, nature
> dharmakaya, and compassionate activity ...

Let us evaluate this first from the aspect of its entity, being empty. Being divorced from all of elaboration's extremes—the is and is nots of existence and non-existence—it resides as a region of space. In regard to this, the *Highest Continuum Commentary*[91] says,

> Suchness, because it is a not changing into something else
> is, via the characteristic of its own entity, to be known to
> be analogous to space.

And the *Precious Garland*[92] says,

---

[87] (... continued)
Way as their view.

[88] Tib. sgra thal 'gyur. This is the root tantra of Quintessence Great Completion.

[89] Tib. rgyud bla ma. The fifth of the Five Dharmas of Maitreya which many Tibetan Buddhists, including the Nyingma School as a whole, regard as the most profound presentation of all the sutra presentations. The "highest continuum" in the name refers to the sugatagarbha.

[90] See "the element" in the glossary for both element and type.

[91] This is Asaṅga's commentary to Maitreya's *Highest Continuum*.

[92] The *Ratnavali* of Nagarjuna.

The entity, if it is utterly non-dwelling,
Is not existent, is not non-existent, is not both,
Is not empty, is not not empty,
Is not without cause, is not the authentic,
Is not true, is not false,
Is not pure, is not impure,
Is without acceptance, is without rejection; just that.

And the *Treasury of the Birthless*[93] says,

Emptiness is the core of samsara and nirvana,
The birthless ground, path, and fruition which is
Without the ground and root of thought process,
    beyond rational mind,
Without mind and also without mind's events,
Activity-free, the fetter of a continuity of hope and fear
    cut.

And *The Middle Way Becoming's Transference* says,

Every nature is equal to space:
Causeless, fruition-less,
Karmic-things-less[94]
And similarly all-things-less.
This world and the next
Are birthless in their entityness.[95]

---

[93] Tib. skye med rin po che mdzod. A text by Nagarjuna.

[94] "Things" here and in the next line means the phenomena created by dualistic mind.

[95] Entityness is not the same as entity. In this sort of discussion, the entity is the empty quality. However, it is not a mere vacuity, for the empty quality only exists in relation to phenomena. Therefore, the empty entity is an entityness because, grammatically speaking, the -ness added to "entity" says that the entity has an existence to it, that of all phenomena.

And the *Pearl Strings*[96] says,

> In the alpha purity of the beginning,
> There is no expression even of "confusion".
> Similarly, what could there be of non-confusion?

Many other quotes could be given here as there have been extensive explanations of this point.

Then, from the aspect of its nature, dharmakaya, it is taught to be good qualities coming spontaneously into existence; the *Highest Continuum Commentary* says,

> In regard to that, in this instance, the tathagata's dharmakaya is, via the characteristic of an ultimate entityness of accomplishing the wishes of others, to be known to be analogous to a wish-fulfilling jewel.

And the doha cited earlier says,

> Mindness, alone the seed of all ...

And the *King of Samadhis Sutra* says,

> The pristine pure, luminous,
> Undisturbed, uncompounded,
> Sugatagarbha is
> The primordially abiding dharmata.

And, the *Words of Manjushri*[97] says,

> Great Completion wisdom's general form,
> The total purity kaya great Vajradhara ...

And *Illusion*[98] says,

---

[96] Tib. mu tig 'phreng ba. This is one of the seventeen root tantras of Quintessence Great Completion.

[97] Tib. 'byams pa'i dbyang zhal lung. A sutra.

[98] The *Net of Illusion* is the *Garbha of the Secret* mentioned earlier.

> Self-arising wisdom enlightenment mind:
> The uncompounded enlightenment core[99]
> Adorned with a blaze of spontaneously-complete good qualities
> Is the unsurpassed mandala of spontaneous existence.

And *Praise to the Dharmadhatu*[100] says,

> Just as a lamp inside a vase
> Does not illuminate anything outside,
> So this dharmadhatu also
> Does not illuminate samsara.
> If that vase were broken,
> As all would be totally illuminated,
> At some point the Vajra Concentration[101]
> Will defeat all obscurations
> And at that point will illuminate the limits of space.

And the *All Creator* says,

> This enlightenment mind the essence of all
> Primordially has its own nature spontaneously existing,

---

[99] Tib. snying po. This is the Tibetan translation of the Sanskrit term "garbha". Where garbha means "seed contained in a husk", nyingpo means "core", which was the Tibetan translator's understanding of this word for the buddha nature. In this book, it will be given as "garbha" because I think it can make the meaning clearer. See also sugatagarbha in the glossary.

[100] A text by Nagarjuna that explains the meaning of other emptiness according to the third turning of the wheel.

[101] This quotation is about wisdom. The pure wisdom of a buddha is co-present with the dharmadhatu so the dharmadhatu in that case illuminates itself. The Vajra-Like Samadhi as it is more fully called is one of the four concentrations that typify a buddha. At the attainment of buddhahood, a buddha achieves a vajra-like or indestructible samadhi on the wisdom of enlightenment.

> So does not need to be sought out then accomplished
> through the ten natures.[102]

Many other quotes could be given here as there have been extensive explanations of this point.

Then, compassionate activity is defined as the rigpa-wisdom of the tathagata family; the *Highest Continuum Commentary* says,

> The tathagata family is, due to its characteristic of having a self-entity of being moistened with compassion and love for sentient beings, to be known as analogous to water.

And *The Condensed*[103] says,

> If there were no wisdom, there would be no
> development of good qualities, no enlightenment
> mind,
> And also no ocean-like buddha dharmas.

And *The Words of Manjushri* says,

> If the chief of all things, one's own mind's
> Entity-ness, realizes itself,
> That is buddha, that is enlightenment,
> And that also is the three worlds.[104]

and also,

---

[102] The ten natures are ten features of the path to enlightenment which are explained in the tantras in general. The ten natures are part of a path in which enlightenment is achieved through conceived efforts and striving. Great Completion is not like that. Longchenpa makes a strong point about this in his *Treasury of the Dharmadhatu*.

[103] The name here is an abbreviation of the name of the sutra called *The Condensed Prajnaparamita in Verse*. It is the second shortest of the Prajnaparamita sutras, summing up the subject in fifty-two verses.

[104] The three worlds are the three realms of samsara.

> Buddhahood is the place without misery,
> The birthless vajra of manifest enlightenment,[105]
> The most excellent sugatagarbha,
> The non-dual, thought-free, great fact.[106]

And *Hevajra*[107] says,

> Sentient beings are buddha itself
> But are obscured by adventitious stains.
> If that is removed, they are buddha itself.

And *Sound Breakthrough* says,

> From the all-pervading compassionate activity wisdom
> The door of shining forth of the not deeds
> Appearing as deeds is complete in the entity.[108]

---

[105] Vajra here is a synonym for unchanging wisdom.

[106] This is a case where fact means superfact, the actual fact of that just mentioned seen in direct perception by wisdom. One way to know that that is so is to note the use of "great". Great is used in the higher tantras not only to mean that something is big, grand, etcetera, but that it is the greater version of something, the version known by wisdom rather than dualistic mind. The "great fact" is the highest or superior spiritual fact known by wisdom.

[107] The Hevajra Tantra.

[108] These three lines are difficult to understand without a deep knowledge of Quintessence Great Completion. Not deeds are the deeds done by the nirmanakaya. They are deeds which are not deeds because they are not done by anyone to anyone and without any action being involved. The eight doors of shining forth are the special explanation in Quintessence Great Completion of how appearances come out from the ground into the worlds of samsara and nirvana. While there is no explanation of the eight doors themselves in this book, there is some clarification of how ground appearances come out from the ground according to the explanation of Quintessence Great Completion contained in the text in this book called "*Luminosity's Appearance Aspect*",

(continued ...)

> From the empty dharmakaya's nature
> The factor of wisdom with a buddha's knowing complete
> Automatically shines forth for sentient beings.
> If it were not that way, the hub of samsara and nirvana
> would be cut,
> So, through the knowing involved, there is knowledge
> and illumination.
> From this personage of self-knowing illumination,
> The nature's automatic compassionate activity
> Unstopped is non-stop.[109]

Many other quotes could be given here as there have been extensive explanations of this point.

Their meanings were taught in the sutras of the middle turning of the wheel as "the three doors of complete emancipation" which defines the sugatagarbha's nature of entity emptiness, nature characteristiclessness, and compassionate activity wishlessness. *The Sutra Petitioned by Brahma Special Mind*[110] says,

> "What is the nature of all phenomena?" you ask. All phenomena have a nature of emptiness; they are reference-free. All phenomena have a nature of being without characteristics; they are thought-free. All phenomena have a nature of being wishless; they have a nature of being without adoption, without rejection—they do not have the ability to think discursively, they are

---

[108] (... continued)
The Ultimate Key Points in the Practice of Great Completion: Root Text and Commentary. After that is read, this section here will make a little more sense.

[109] Unstopped and non-stop are key terms of Quintessence Great Completion and point at profound experiences. Longchenpa gives some explanation of these terms in his *Dharmadhatu Treasury*, but Ontrul Tenpa'i Wangchug's commentary to it is more revealing.

[110] This is a sutra of the second turning of the wheel.

> extremely free of entityness, they are the nature's luminosity. That which is samsara's nature is nirvana's nature. That which is nirvana's nature is all phenomena's nature; therefore, mind is the nature's luminosity.[111]

And *Descent Into Langka*[112] says:

> Mahamati, the tathagatagarbha teaching is not equivalent to the self propounded in the works of the Tirthikas. Mahamati, the tathagata, arhat, truly complete buddhas have given the teaching, within the meanings of the words emptiness, the authentic's limit, nirvana, the unborn, characteristicless, wishlessness, and so on, of the tathagatagarbha ...

Those and other quotes could be given in order to explain it.

Thus, there is not the slightest discrepancy between the teaching of the characteristics of the ground that is found in the sutras and tantras of the Great Vehicle; it is the same key point in each case of threefold entity, nature, and compassionate activity.

2. Establishing it According to What the Experts Accept

The primordial ground as explained in the words of the Great Completion tantras, which is the prior ground[113] on which generally

---

[111] Note that this is not saying "Mind is naturally luminous" or some other variation on that. It is saying that mind is the luminosity which is the nature of its very entity, suchness.

[112] Skt. laṅkāvatara sutra. This is a sutra of the third turning of the wheel. In the previous paragraph, he showed how the ground described in Quintessence Great Completion is the same as what is taught in the sutras of the second turning of wheel and now he shows how it is the same as what is taught in the sutras of the third turning of the wheel.

[113] The prior ground means the ground prior to samsara and nirvana.

(continued ...)

characterized samsara and nirvana[114] depend, is not the same as the sugatagarbha explained in other main systems.[115] "Well then, is this something you made up yourselves?" you ask. No, this point is the un-mistaken acceptance of the All-Knowing Dharma King,[116] and to say a little more about that at this point,[117] the *Wish-fulfilling Treasury* explains just this issue of the beginning in these words:

> The beginning's luminosity sugatagarbha,
> The factual basis of all,[118] is in nature uncompounded,

---

[113] (... continued)
This relates back to the quotation given at the very beginning of this text "what the primal situation, the ground's actuality, is like at the time when neither realization—buddhas—nor non-realization—samsara—has arisen". The original words are slightly mis-quoted—a common occurrence in Tibetan texts and one that mostly does not matter because anyone involved will know the original words off by heart. The original wording is "the primal ground's actuality in the prior situation before realization—buddha—and non-realization—samsara—arose".

[114] Anything can be either generally characterized or self-characterized. The former points at a conceptual understanding of the thing and the latter at the actual thing itself.

[115] This is the subject explained at length in the third part of the commentary of the other text in this book "*Luminosity's Appearance Aspect*", *The Ultimate Key Points in the Practice of Great Completion: Root Text and Commentary*. After reading that, it will be easier to understand what he is getting at here and vice versa.

[116] Longchenpa.

[117] He now gives quotes from most of Longchenpa's *Seven Treasuries* in order to prove this view.

[118] "The factual basis of all" or "factual alaya"; here is another usage of "fact" where the meaning is the actual one known in direct perception by wisdom. In this case, factual is an abbreviation of superfactual. Alaya here indicates "fundament to all that there is".

> Primordially complete purity[119], like the sun in space.[120]
> If it is shrouded in ignorance's latencies,[121]
> Then it is what confusion for sentient beings is.

And the *Tenet's Treasury*, in the context of explaining the vehicle of Luminosity Vajragarbha,[122] sets out five main headings—the way that the confusion of a sentient being comes from the nature ground's actuality, and so on. Under the first heading, this is said:

> First, the primal situation's ground, self-arising wisdom without delimitation and falling into bias,[123] resides having an entity which, being empty, is like space, a nature which, being luminous, is like the sun, and a compassionate activity which, being all-pervading, is like

---

[119] Complete purity here is the same meaning as alpha purity, the utter absence of all dualistic, conceptual stuff, of all elaborations. That it is primordially so means that it always has been, is right now, and always will be so.

[120] The sun is the example because it is brilliantly luminous like the wisdom nature of the sugatagarbha. That it is in space indicates that it is within the space-like utter purity which is the primordial complete purity, free of all samsaric traces.

[121] Latencies are karmic seeds. This ignorance is the co-emergent not-rigpa which is at the root of samsaric existence.

[122] Nature Great Completion, Luminosity Great Completion, and Luminosity Vajra Garbha Great Completion are all names for Great Completion. Luminosity Vajra Garbha as a name is explained in Longchenpa's *Dharmadhatu Treasury*. The nature aspect is luminosity, the knowing quality of wisdom. That is the luminosity of superfactual sugatagarbha. That nature luminosity is indestructible, therefore is "vajra garbha".

[123] Delimitation is the pigeon-holing that occurs when dualistic mind knows something. Non-dual wisdom is an unending space without any boxing, that is delimitation, anywhere within that space. A bias occurs when dualistic mind knows what it knows because it automatically puts what it knows on one side or another of a dualistic equation.

> its light rays. The three reside as a dhatu which is primordially, perpetually without shift and change in which they are of inseparable entity and are the three kayas whose nature is wisdom. This dhatu, which essentially speaking is an entity empty, the dharmakaya, a nature luminosity, the sambhogakaya, and a compassionate activity pervasive, the nirmanakaya, is not samsara and nirvana at all, nevertheless, to be able to understand it, it is designated "the dhatu whose nature is complete purity".
>
> This approach is also found in the sutra section:[124]
>
> > The beginningless time's dhatu
> > Is the abode of all dharmas;
> > Because there is such, all migrators and
> > Nirvana have come about.

Moreover, it becomes the ground from which the two, samsara and nirvana, are elaborated. This is also clearly shown in the doha cited earlier that says, "Mindness, alone ..." It is also clearly shown in the commentary to the *Dharmadhatu Treasury*[125] during the explanation of the meaning of its title, which includes a statement taken from the *Self-Shining Forth*:[126]

> The beginning's dhatu is referred to as the buddha which is the spontaneously-existing nature, the sugatagarbha, and there is no samsara and nirvana other than realizing

---

[124] This is the same verse from the *Treasury of Abhidharma* quoted earlier, though it has been quoted a little differently here. As mentioned before, this is very common in Tibetan texts, where authors usually wrote a quotation from memory, without checking the exact wording in the original. Doing so usually suffices to convey the meaning intended.

[125] Longchenpa's own commentary to the treasury.

[126] Tb. rang shar gyi rgyud. The name of one of the seventeen root tantras of Quintessence Great Completion.

> and not realizing just that. In this prior time, there is no establishment ever of the convention "buddha and sentient being" because, if there were no rigpa, neither what ascertains it as samsara and nirvana nor the general ground of liberation and confusion would exist at all.
>
> That being so, rigpa self-arising wisdom is the "dharmadhatu" and, given that every single one of the phenomena of samsara and nirvana arises from its dhatu, it is very fittingly expressed with the term "treasury".

Moreover, the *Actuality Treasury*[127] says,

> The primordially, spontaneously-existing nature
> Is, unmade by anyone at all, primordially present;
> Comparable to a gem which is the source of all, the enlightenment mind
> Exists as the ground which is the source of all phenomena of samsara and nirvana.
> From the state of space, as the appearances of appearance and becoming,
> From enlightenment mind samsara and nirvana shine forth non-stop.
> The myriad variety, like a dream arising from sleep,
> Of the six migrators and three realms, shines forth from the state of mind.
> From the very time they shine forth, all phenomena are the state of rigpa,
> Empty spontaneous existence, the great ground appearances.

That elegantly explains rigpa enlightenment mind dharmata sugatagarbha as the primal situation's primordial ground. However, it does not end there, for the *Supreme Vehicle Treasury*[128] extensively

---

127 Tib. gnas lugs mdzod.

128 Tib. theg mchog mdzod.

explains the enumerations of ground and ground appearances and then, in its conclusion, says:

> Thus, both the ground of confusion and the ground of liberation can be nicely understood by connecting them with the doors of spontaneous existence.[129]

And it says,

> Third, setting out agreement with the rising and subsiding modes of appearance has two parts. For the person of great perseverance, either during the time of the bardo or the time of practise in this life, the factor of ground appearance which is the self-output of that ground abiding at the heart centre, the light channels, and the appearance in the outer sky …

which is explaining the vast mode of shining forth of the eight doors of spontaneous existence. It also says,

> Buddhas and sentient beings are simply about self-recognition and not appearances; samsara and nirvana in having a single cause in rigpa are like the front and back of the hand.
>
> This present appearance also is merely appearance occurring in impurity's door, the eight analogies of illusion in which there are no outer and inner objects, just a ground-free equality, a single flatness, because of which, without needing to abandon and without needing to accept them, when other appearance shines forth, if the sleep dissolves in the great groundless self-waking, then, like coming out of a dream, they self-waken into the ground of liberation. If, through all of them being

---

[129] The "doors of spontaneous existence" is more fully known as the "eight doors' mode of shining forth of spontaneous existence". As mentioned in earlier footnotes, this topic is partially covered in *"Luminosity's Appearance Aspect"*, *The Ultimate Key Points in the Practice of Great Completion: Root Text and Commentary*.

> liberated in the one emptiness of primordial emptiness, there is a good realization of the one key point, then all the seals[130] will be released without hardship.[131]

That explains rigpa enlightenment mind as the primal situation's primordial ground and teaches that this appearance of the present also is the play of ground appearance.

Then, the matter can also be understood by these words which appear in the *Word's Meaning Treasury* when its headings are being set out:

> First is the teaching on the primal ground's actuality in the prior situation before realization—buddha—and non-realization—samsara—arose.[132] Second is the way that sentient beings become confused from that. Third is the way that, at the time of confusion, it is pervaded by that ground …

And especially, the *Sun, Moon, Planets, and Stars*, which is the support text for *Yangthig Wish-fulfilling Gem*'s Direct Crossing explanations, says:

> Three headings are defined: the nature ground's actuality; how sentient beings' confusion occurs from it; and distinguishing mind and wisdom. Then, when explaining the first one, nature primal situation's general ground's element, natural complete purity, sugatagarbha, luminosity's dhatu abides as the threefold entity, nature, and compassionate activity.

---

[130] Seals are the knots which bind our psycho-physical structure, keeping it in dualistic becoming.

[131] Without hardship here does not mean without difficulty exactly; it means without the hardship of progressive practice that has to go through many levels and stages.

[132] As mentioned in an earlier footnote, this is the actual wording of the text. Note the words "in the prior situation before".

And the text *nam mkha' klong gsal*[133] says,

> First is the primal situation's general ground of
> Threefold entity, nature, compassionate activity.
> Being empty, luminous, and an unstopped basis of shining forth,
> It is like space, sun and moon, and a mirror.
> Primordially, it abides as great spontaneous existence.
> It is a basis of shining forth in which there is no division into two, samsara and nirvana,
> That shines forth in an indeterminate way.
> Called "the ground which is the source of all phenomena",
> It is self-knowing itself, without meeting and parting.
> Because it is good qualities spontaneously coming into existence,
> It is explained as "the sugatagarbha".
> Because of the empty entity, it never knows permanence;
> Because of the nature luminosity, it never knows nihilism;
> Because of the compassionate-activity rigpa, it is not physical matter;
> Because it is free from one and many,
> It is the inseparable three kayas without meeting and parting.
> It is the nature ground's buddha.
> It has been designated as the buddha Maker of Light,
> And the Primal Guardian Unchanging Light,
> And Fathomless Light;
> That is the primal situation's actuality;
> The way that ground appearances shine forth from it
> Is for example like the way that light shines forth from a crystal.[134]

---

[133] One of the tantras of Quintessence Great Completion.

[134] Tibetans consider that the light emerging from a crystal, such as the (continued ...)

And the *nam mkha' klong chen*[135] says,

> Of ground dhatu, path, and complete liberation fruition,
> Dhatu is luminosity nature spontaneously existing
> Which, empty, luminous, and having a core of rigpa,
> Possesses many masses of good qualities which are totally inseparable from it.
> It is sun-like spontaneous existence with a nature of completely purity.
> Primordially empty of the stains which are totally separable from it,[136]
> It is primally complete purity, luminosity, dharmata's fact.[137]
> It is explained that, because this exists, from rigpa and not-rigpa[138]

---

[134] (... continued)
rainbow from a prism, is light that exists within the crystal but only appears when circumstances allow it. In that way, the light of a crystal becomes a suitable analogy for what is being discussed.

[135] This is one of the one hundred thousand tantras of Space Section Great Completion.

[136] These are the adventitious stains of the afflictions, grasped-grasping, and so on, all the stuff of dualistic mind. There is a pair of lines in the *Highest Continuum Commentary* which indicate the key point that "the stains are entirely separable from this ground of being called the sugata-garbha, but the good qualities of enlightenment which number more even than the sands of the Ganges are not ever separable from it", and which are the source of the words here.

[137] This is another case where "fact" refers the actual fact known in direct perception by wisdom.

[138] Here "space dhatu" simply means the expanse of physical space. "Not-rigpa" is usually translated as "ignorance", but when that is done, the crucial connection between rigpa and not-rigpa is lost. See the glossary for more.

> The appearances of nirvana and the sixfold migrators respectively appear.
> Right upon their shining forth, in that dhatu of the garbha,
> There is no shift or change to better or worse, purity or impurity.
> The shift and change of the space dhatu into
> The four elements' appearances[139] does not result in its being covered over,
> In accordance with which it is called "the source dhatu providing the opportunity for all".
> The basis for stain-filled mind, the nature spontaneous existence,
> Grasps strongly at mind, therefore, in that there is becoming.[140]

The following nicely explains it:[141]

> Similar to the sun and clouds, adventitious stains
> Cause obscuration and because of that "the element" has been present for the duration of time;
> Because of that it is expressed as "the beginning's virtuous element";[142]

---

[139] The four elements are the earth, water, fire, and wind that were regarded as the base elements from which the world is constructed.

[140] This is simply saying that the nature, wisdom, is the basis for the mind of samsara, a transformation that occurs when it grasps at itself, with the result that the mind enters samsaric existence in which it is always becoming one thing or another due to the force of karma latencies.

[141] This is the point here where the bottom half of the Tibetan text was switched with the bottom half of the *Luminosity's Appearance Aspect* text as explained in the introduction to this book.

[142] This line can be translated, using the wording made famous by the vidyadhara Chogyam Trungpa's system of teachings called Shambhala as "because of which it is called basic goodness".

Because it is actuality it is named "superfactual truth";[143]
Because it is beyond being an object of thought it is
Prajnaparamita;
Because it is uncompounded it is the spontaneous
existence mandala;
Because it is a warehouse of the oceanic good qualities,
the strengths and so on,
It was taught[144] as "the sugatagarbha totally pervading all
migrators".
The examples of its being obscured in that it exists
within oneself but is not seen are:[145]
Treasure under the ground, a lamp inside a vase,
Seed in its husk, sugata in a bad lotus,[146]
Valuables in an old rag, a jewel in mud,
Honey in a lotus, precious minerals within rock,
Jewel of a champion in rottenness,[147] something golden
within mud,[148]
Seed of a tree, butter of milk,
The third order world in an immense bolt of cloth, and
so on,
All of which illustrate it well. In accordance with those
examples taught in the scriptures,

---

[143] For superfactual truth, see the glossary.

[144] … by the Buddha …

[145] This list contains the nine examples of the sugatagarbha being hidden in beings given in the *Highest Continuum* with some added examples first given by the Buddha in the sutras.

[146] Lotus here is a synonym for the womb of a woman. The example is explained to mean the womb of a poor-quality low-grade woman holding the jewel-like being of a buddha.

[147] Jamgon Kongtrul explains it like this: "a ruler of men, (a chakravartin emperor) in the belly of a woman of bad appearance".

[148] This refers to a golden image of a buddha hidden in the muck of muddy manure.

This type element garbha[149] completely pervading all migrators
Is called "the heart definitive meaning ground".[150]
From that sort of dhatu self-knowing rigpa is completely liberated and
Its details all are exposed in an instant, resulting in buddhahood
With the primal guardian's good qualities gone to the other shore.[151]
In accordance with how that is seen internally, in relation to the complete purity,
Original buddha, dharma, and sangha are defined.
In the beginningless—a time whose duration is hard to fathom—dhatu,
Under the influence of ignorance the six migrators have been confused ...

---

[149] These are three names the Buddha frequently used when referring to the sugatagarbha. "Type", or lineage or family as it has been translated, is defined in the scriptures to mean that thing which is of the same type as some other thing and therefore could turn into that other thing. The sugatagarbha, because it is exactly the same type of thing as enlightenment mind can become enlightenment mind. See also "the element" and "garbha" in the glossary.

[150] There is a group of twenty sutras of the third turning of the wheel called "the heart definitive-meaning sutras"; these are the core sutras in which the Buddha gave the definitive-meaning teachings on sugatagarbha. The verse is saying that the type of ground being considered is not a conventional presentation of ground but is this ultimate type of presentation of ground.

[151] "Gone to the other shore" is the literal translation of the Sanskrit "paramita". There is a play on words here: firstly, they have become complete at the level of a buddha, and secondly, they are ultimate paramita.

There is also an explanation of it in the Khadro Yangthig's *Lamp of the Three Key Points*[152] which is consistent with the preceding explanation and exceptionally clear. Between these two definitive explanations, the meaning is nicely settled.

Following on from that, there also have been attempts to show that the explanation of Samantabhadra being liberated over the ground is mistaken and that it is not in agreement with other main approaches, but these are the outcome of not having understood the key points.[153] Given that there is buddha, it is not possible that there could not be liberation over the beginning ground: in accordance with the quotation from the *Supreme Vehicle Treasury* given earlier, the luminosity of the four appearances shining forth in this life and the appearance factor of the bardo are explained as ground appearance and it is the primal situation's sugatagarbha that is the subject of discussion here, therefore, what is being realized is the sugatagarbha's nature, and it is impossible for that, which is buddhahood, to be not buddhahood. There is more, too; in line with the explanation of Samantabhadra's way of liberation, it says in the support text for Direct Crossing[154] *Sun, Moon, Planets, and Stars* that "the entirety of the degrees of liberation from dhatu appearances are just this" and, in particular, that "the system of extent of liberation from the bardo's ground appearances is just this". And, in line with the primal guardian's mode of liberation explained in both the *Supreme Vehicle Treasury* and *Word's Meaning Treasury*, there is the scripture of the *Highest Continuum Commentary*, which says in the same way that it is:

---

[152] *Lamp of the Three Key Points* by Padma Laydray Tsal is found in the *Nyingthig Yazhi* compiled by Longchenpa, in the Dakini or Khadro Yangthig section, which is in the HŪṂ section of Adzom Drukpa's edition of the *Nyingthig Yazhi.*

[153] ... of being liberated over the Samantabhadra ground.

[154] Tib. Thogal.

> … an exceptionally amazing and inconceivable type of buddhahood. Not heard about from anyone except one's own master, it is manifest complete buddha whose nature of self-arising wisdom cannot be verbally expressed …[155]

From this quotation it is clearly evident that their respective understandings are the same. Furthermore, *Expressing the Names of Manjushri* says:

> original buddha without bias.

And the *Kalachakra* says:

> supreme original buddha.

And another tantra, too, says:

> Buddha: earliest buddha buddha.

And the *White Lotus Sutra* says:

> From an inconceivable ten billion aeons ago,
> A point in the past which has no measure,
> I sought the ease of supreme enlightenment;
> I perpetually fully explain the dharma, too.

These quotations show with no inconsistency the one, same key point, so do not give thought to there being some contradiction within the sugata's excellent speech.

In connection with that, it also has to be comprehended that there are lower levels of understanding whose ways of expressing these subjects are less than complete and higher levels above them in which there are definitions of special features that are subtle and require clarification. In line with that, the ground of samsara and nirvana as explained earlier and the sugatagarbha element should never be thought of as the same sort of thing, and you must know, by carefully

---

[155] The Tibetan for this quotation is slightly misquoted in this text; I have corrected it to follow the original scripture, which has the advantage of enhancing the meaning.

distinguishing them, the coarse and subtle features of ultimate ground appearances, rigpa residing and not residing in a house of light, and so on.

3. Eliminating Opposing Arguments

Those whose approach to the view is shackled by clinging and dualistically grasping at good and bad say that the superfactual dharmata sugatagarbha, being none other than the nature of buddha exhausted of all faults and complete in all good qualities, can only be a basis for liberation.[156] Thus we have to point out that "The other explanation of it as the general ground of both samsara and nirvana is not the same" then ask, "Are these differing presentations in complete disagreement?"[157]

---

[156] This refers to those who are absorbed in the rights and wrongs of the various levels of the vehicles that explain the path to enlightenment. Caged by their dualistic approach to dharma they are not connecting with innate wisdom. They in particular have argued against the profound teachings of Great Completion, including the special presentations of ground found in Great Completion. Dza Patrul is now going to expose their objections in relation to ground and ground appearances and show why they are wrong. It starts with pointing out that they assert ground only to be a ground of being liberated into enlightenment, not a ground which can function both as a ground for liberation and a ground for falling into the confusion of samsara.

[157] In the first section, Dza Patrul established the essential idea of the ground. In the second section he established the details of that view according to Great Completion by presenting what the experts of Great Completion—primarily Longchen Rabjam—accept. In this section, he points out that there are objections to some of the details of the Great Completion view of the ground, then shows those objections to be wrong. The objections mainly concern the presentation of what is called "ground and ground appearances" in the Great Completion system.

In relation to this, note how he went to pains in the previous section to

(continued ...)

To answer that, the following explanation has to be given. The sugatagarbha from its own side does not primordially have samsara's confused appearances in its spontaneous existence, yet at the time of ground appearances shining forth from it, the two things of liberation and confusion arise due to self-recognizing and not self-recognizing, so there is not the slightest contradiction in explaining sugatagarbha as the general ground. The root text of *Wish-Fulfilling Treasury* and the commentary to it say:

> That ground, moreover, in relation to samsara is, like space, primally empty of a supporting basis. And it is, in terms of what it actually is, without a self and luminous like the sun and moon and spontaneously existing; present beginninglessly, it is without shift, beyond the extremes of elaborations, so, naturally being itself, it is the sugatagarbha present as the region of luminosity, kayas and wisdoms without meeting and parting, the actuality which supports the phenomena of samsara and nirvana. Called "the factual alaya[158]", it resides as a great

---

[157] (... continued)

show that the full definition of the ground in Great Completion involves a ground itself of complete purity and the possibility for that ground to function as a ground of both liberation and confusion through the appearances of the ground itself.

There are some who, because of their rational-minded approaches to the view, remain entrenched in clinging to the presentations of the various vehicles and, because of that, insist that the more general presentations of ground found in the vehicles other than the Great Completion vehicle of Maha Ati must be correct. In other words, they argue against the presentation of ground and ground appearances as given in Great Completion.

[158] Here, "factual" means fact of something existence known in direct perception by wisdom, not a fact known by rational mind. Here, factual can also be taken to mean "superfactual", the actually existing meaning beyond the fictions of dualistic, rational mind. Alaya is a region which

(continued ...)

> uncompounded situation, a great primordial complete purity.[159]
>
> Moreover, samsara's phenomena produced by karma and afflictions are supported on it in the mode of there being no support for them: as clouds are supported on the surface of a sun-filled sky, the ground not being conjoined with ignorance is present in that state. The ground not having a nature in actual fact, it appears, supporting while no support and supported are established, and so is designated. The phenomena of nirvana are supported as being inseparable with it, like the sun and its rays, because they are present primordially without meeting and parting.

In particular, it says in the *Supreme Vehicle Treasury* that there is no confusion in the beginning ground but at the time when it shines forth as ground appearances, an indeterminate awareness not recognizing its own face that is the root of non-rigpa's ignorance cuts the ground appearances up into biasses whereby it becomes confused into a sentient being. The following quotes illustrate this. The *Pearl Strings*[160] says,

> The great differentiation into appearance
> Gives rise to dual existent and non-existent
> And the general one is named "ground of confusion"
> Because it has become saturated with what is not-rigpa.

---

[158] (... continued)
acts as a basis for everything above it. Thus, the sense here is 'the *actually existing fact* which is the *basis for all* of samsara and nirvana".

[159] Here, "great" conveys the sense of something which is not the conceptually known idea of uncompounded, complete purity but the greater version of it, which is the actually experienced space which is uncompounded and completely pure.

[160] Tib. mu tig 'phreng ba. One of the seventeen root tantras of Quintessence Great Completion.

> That which is knowable appears as its outer layer.

and *The Vajrasatva Garbha's Mirror*[161] says,

> All of these sentient beings of the three realms
> Are confusion which arose from that which is not at all
> the ground.

and,

> Vajrasatva possess no confusion but
> Shows, in sentient beings, the mode of confusion.

Especially though, it is taught in that treasury[162] as something which can be either faulty or helpful depending on the circumstance, like this, which explains it clearly:

> Camphor is seen to be a beneficial substance for the treatment of heat sicknesses and a faulty substance for cold sicknesses, though camphor itself has neither benefit nor fault in it. Similarly, the ground and the way that ground appearances shine forth appear as a liberating circumstance for those who self-recognize it, because of which it comes out as a good quality, and appears for those who do not recognize it to be a faulty thing which creates the ground of confusion, even though that ground and the appearances made by it have no good or fault in them …

That is not all, for at the time of appearing as the confused appearances of samsara, there is also not the slightest movement away from being the primordial situation's ground itself to being something else, nor the slightest distinction into good and bad, faulty and helpful, despite the duality of samsara and nirvana which is shining forth in

---

[161] This is a tantra of Great Completion.

[162] This quote comes a little further on in the *Supreme Vehicle Treasury* from what was mentioned at the beginning of the previous paragraph.

the ground appearances, the liveliness of the dharmata. The determination of those as elaboration-free equal-purity is the uncommon Great Vehicle view of the authentic. The *Sutra Showing All Phenomena to be Without Origination*[163] says,

> View and not view both have one mode;
> Equal and not equal likewise are equal.
> There is no buddha and there is no dharma and
>   saṅgha—
> Who understands it like that is expert.

And the *All Creator* explains it extensively with,

> Buddha, sentient being, karma, latencies;
> There are no phenomena except for what comes from
>   enlightenment mind.

And other quotations could be given.

Thus it is that, in the liveliness and play of the one primal situation's ground, sugatagarbha, shining forth as the two, samsara and nirvana, there is not the slightest distinction into good and bad, that to be abandoned and that to be adopted.

When it is not understood like that, if there is assertion only of the primordial ground that depends on a generally characterized samsara and nirvana which are not the dharmata sugatagarbha, this question has to be asked: "Does that sort of ground pervade all sentient beings or not?" If it does and so if there is a general ground other than the sugatagarbha which functions as the pervader, then all sentient beings would come to have one mindstream. Moreover, each sentient being would come to have two mind streams, and in the liberation of one, all would be liberated, and so on. There would be those faults and, on top of that, it would come to be not the slightest bit different from the space having nine features asserted by the practitioners of the Tirthika secret mantra. Now, if it did not pervade, there would be

---

[163] This is a sutra of the second turning of the wheel.

no opportunity for the sentient beings who do abide wherever space pervades to abide pervasively in it, and also, on having become confused, their liberation would not be tenable! There also would be no agreement with the explanation of ground appearances shining forth in the bardo and the like. Thus, a ground explained like that would come to have contradictions such as not going far enough to contact the actual thing, and so on.

Well then, given that sort of explanation of the ground, is there the slightest difference between what other main systems and Great Completion say about it? There is not the slightest difference in their explanations of the primal situation's primordial ground itself. Yet, the very detailed explanation given in relation to the time when samsara and nirvana appear from it, of the ground appearance being the preciousness of spontaneous existence having the eight doors' mode of shining forth, which is there but exceedingly hidden in other sutras and tantras, is brought to life in Great Completion, so there is that difference.

Due to that key point, in terms of actually practising the path to gain experience, there are these special features in this system: the very best practitioners gain liberation in this life using the oral instructions of Direct Crossing; the middling ones gain liberation in the bardo using the self-appearances of the bardo, the mode of shining forth of the ground appearances; the least ones gain liberation in the becoming bardo in the ground appearances which are the field of a nature nirmanakaya; and so on. These special features which exist in this system and not in any other are what has to be known.

Phenomena-ended dharmakaya mind shiftless
Perpetually views the appearances of luminosity, sambhogakaya's fields, and
Manifests compassionate activity to enact the sake of migrators in becoming;
I respectfully prostrate at the feet of the kind guru.

With heartfelt respect, I supplicate you that I may
In all my successive lives meet with a totally incomparable guru,
Then accomplishing what he says and serving him with respect,
Perform the service of guiding migrators with enlightened activity.

The topic of the profound whose words have a meaning difficult to realize
Is something that I am not very good at unravelling,
But by hearing and contemplating the texts of the All-Knowing One's lineage
I have developed a little familiarity with it and with that have recorded this here.

I dedicate this merit so that migrators without exception
Will, through relying on this profound path, effortlessly
Obtain complete liberation, the wealth of the conquerors,
And while they are on the way have their minds of desire and anger alleviated.

Virtue!

"Luminosity's Appearance Aspect" The Ultimate Key Points in The Practice of Great Completion

The Root Text

With highly respectful three doors I prostrate at the feet of the buddhas of the three times in person, lord of the families, the kind Jigmey Gyalway Nyugu.

On the twenty-fifth lunar day of the first month of the water hare year, I with the tulku name Tshogdrug Rangdrol,[164] on the occasion of doing the longevity practice of the Sakyong King, while in the luminosity of the earliest period of the morning,[165] found that I had arrived at the Bliss-Making Stacked Stupa. I was sitting inside the vase section[166] when dakas and dakinis appeared in the space before me accompanied by the sounds of many musical instruments and a wave of perfume that wafted through the whole area. One dakini said to me, "The great vidyadhara Gyalway Nyugu over there has left this

---

[164] This is the tulku name of Mingyur Namkha'i Dorje, the fourth Dzogchen Rinpoche of Dzogchen Monastery. He uses it here rather than his common name because of the unique circumstances involved.

[165] This is the first of three watches of the morning prior to sunrise, which runs from about three a.m. to four a.m. His being in luminosity means that he was sleeping during this time which in turn means that he is about to describe a dream-like occurrence.

[166] The vase section is the bulbous middle section of a stupa.

world of humans and gone to the chief of the Orgyan dakinis".[167] Four dakinis in the centre of the assembly of dakas and dakinis were bearing a palanquin of white silks, each silk extending in one of the four directions and ending in a half vajra. The palanquin supported a lion throne with lotus, sun, and moon seat on which the kind root guru, wearing a yogin's accoutrements and more brilliant than ever before, sat with his two hands holding a vajra and bell crossed at his heart centre. The dakinis at the ends of the four silks, to the east, south, west, and north respectively, had their right hands appropriately coloured white, yellow, red, or green and their left hands holding up the vajra at the end of the silk. These four dakinis rode an elephant, supreme steed, peacock, and shang shang[168] respectively. With them, the other dakas and dakinis carried victory umbrellas and victory banners and sang and danced and played many different types of musical instrument in a grand way, all of them within a mass of the five lights and clouds of rainbows. At that time, I petitioned the guru to work for the sake of migrators in this human world and received this reply:

> Lord Srongtsen[169] to those of the present
> Have worked for the taming of the six migrators.
> In particular, within this human realm
> They have, for the sake of all sentient beings of the three realms,
> Taught adoption and rejection corresponding to karmic fruition good and bad
> And Great Completion's special feature Ati
> As their way of working for all migrators' sakes.
> All of my followers, my son disciples,

---

[167] Chief of the Orgyan dakinis is Guru Rinpoche.

[168] The shang shang is a being with bird-like top half and human-like bottom half.

[169] Srongtsen Gampo, the first king of Tibet, the one who initiated Buddhism within Tibet.

Follow the dharma of our own system, not found
elsewhere,
The teaching of my great vidyadhara.[170]

Now I will give you some un-mistaken advice.[171]
Primal complete purity is an in-space beyond an object
of thought,
The mindness king, the nature which is a greater
completion,[172]
The no-abandonment-at-all-beyond-all fact.
What shines forth without clinging is the in-space of the
spontaneous zone of rigpa,
Being just so,[173] self-liberation nakedly seen, objects of
thought absent.
It is the nature left untouched, so do not engage in the
spoilage of contrivance!
The ones who are stupid reject that entity,
Then, caging the innate mind in their cleverness,

---

[170] He means that his disciples follow the particular practice of Longchen Nyingthig Great Completion, which at that time was only found in a small area of Tibet and which was taught to him by his guru, the great vidyadhara Jigmey Lingpa. The advice, which continues to the end of the text, is amply explained in the commentary following the root text.

[171] Now, he will give some teaching of that Longchen Nyingthig system to his heart son Mingyur Namkha'i Dorje.

[172] Greater completion conveys the sense of a nature which really includes everything. This is of course why Great Completion is so named. It is the system of inclusion of all things. Interestingly, as pointed out in the introduction, the original name for Great Completion, Mahāsaṅdhi, means the great juncture point, that is, the place of great inclusion.

[173] Tib. cog zhag. Pronounced Chog Zhag. The teachings on Being Just So or Chog Zhag are one of the several key teachings of Great Completion.

It becomes contrived and contrived and the fact of the garbha is obscured.
That, which has no liberation, only binds them further.

If there is relaxation towards whatever is included in rational mind,
That naturalness will do, there being no need to contrive it.
Movement seen self-purifies—not spoiled by an antidote and
Not changed by abandonment, the innate disposition is a greater completion.
Existence is non-existent and in non-existence there is existence to the limit.
All things having collapsed, there is an emptiness of greater completion.
For persons who assert liberation through contriving and contriving
What emancipation from both permanence and nihilism could there be?
Groundless, root-free, it is a primordial greater completion!
They have meditations of emptiness, appearance, existence, and non-existence but
Where there is meditation, there is view and conduct,
And in that there is becoming, so there is samsara's unsatisfactoriness.
Where there is dharma, there is clinging to and desire for vehicles,
And in that there are antidotes to afflictions, so there is bondage.
There is no staying at all in clinging to a ground-freed, path-ceased fruition,
Nor in clinging that desires for the beginning,

And in that, there is no karma, so no shroud of full-ripening.[174]
Thus, not staying in becoming or peace,[175] a yogin proceeds within the state of space.
In the space of objects, rigpa's liveliness is floating about,
So the yogin is one for whom the focus-less king,[176] grasping-less, shines forth
And phenomena are in self-liberation from subject-object becoming.
For the yogin who stays in the state without shift in the three times
There is the output of the empty-luminous dharmakaya—the rigpa king
And the output of unchanging spontaneous existence that is free of ground and root.
The yogin has the in-space of the primal situation that has this output, AḤ.

After saying that, the vidyadhara guru switched places in an instant to the centre of the city on Ngayab Glorious Mountain where he arose as the azure-blue body of Chemchog Heruka with three faces, six arms, four feet spread apart, the nine moods of dance, the eight charnel-ground accoutrements, and a retinue of seven hundred and twenty-five deities, all appearing with complete clarity. I felt I should supplicate for empowerment. The assemblies of the seven hundred and twenty-five deities dissolved back into the principal deity, the Great Glorious One, Palchen, who transformed into blue light and dissolved into the heart centre of Guru Rinpoche upon which the

---

174 "Full-ripening" is the ripening of karma, which is one of the bases of continuing on in samsara.

175 Becoming is samsara and peace is the personal peace of nirvana.

176 "Focus" is a name for the conceptual references that samsaric mind uses to know phenomena. The focus-less king is rigpa, the enlightened kind of mind that knows everything without the use of foci.

dakas and dakinis recited the Vajra Guru mantra with a tremendous sound. I woke me up, lying in my own bed. Now, as a way of remembering the great vidyadhara guru, I offer on each twenty-fifth day an extensive *Summation of the Vidyadharas*[177] feast for accomplishing the guru.

May there be virtue!

[177] Tib. rig 'dzin bsdus pa.

"Luminosity's Appearance Aspect" The Ultimate Key Points in The Practice of Great Completion

The Commentary

I prostrate to the kind root guru who is all the buddhas in person.

There were the great masters Garab Dorje and the others who in the past gained attainment through the path of Nature Great Completion and who, after having passed away, gave advice to their senior-most son-disciple in the form of a testament that showed the ultimate key points in the practice of the meaning to be realized. By this, the disciple realized the meaning and was liberated at the same time and his mind became equal in every way to that of his master.

Similarly in this time too, the unparalleled owner of all turnings of the wheel of dharma, the famous guardian Jigmey Gyalway Nyugu did, at the time when his mind had dissolved into dharmadhatu, appear in luminosity to his unparalleled heart son, the precious nirmanakaya tulku Mingyur Namkha'i Dorje[178], and teach him the ultimate key points in the practice of Great Completion in the form of an after-passing testament. I will explain its meaning in a short commentary, which has three topics: showing the ground, the un-

---

[178] Mingyur Namkha'i Dorje was the fourth Dzogchen Padma Rigdzin emanation. He was a contemporary of Dza Patrul and, in the Dzogchen Monastery system, is counted with Dza Patrul and others as a principal lineage holder of Longchen Nyingthig.

confused dharmata, the innate; showing how to practise the path, uncontrived mindness, naked rigpa-emptiness; and showing the fruition, the place of being liberated from confused thought in the state divorced from adoption and rejection.

1. Showing the ground, the unconfused dharmata, the innate

This what the primal situation, the actuality that is your own innate disposition, wisdom freed of all elaborations, sugatagarbha is. It is simply that time when realization—buddha—has not occurred and non-realization—sentient being—has not occurred, the general ground[179] of samsara and nirvana; it is the dharmata's own entity, a ground which never knows spoilage by the stains of the two obscurations, the great alpha purity, which he refers to with the words "*primal complete purity*".[180] It not being possible to know that sort of dharmata through rational mind's process of examination and analysis, verbal expressions of words, and the like, it is beyond the reach of mind's thought, so it is immersion in an *in-space*. And the fact of that in-space, which is the internal emptiness dhatu freed of all extremes of elaboration, he shows to be *beyond being an object of thought* and verbal expression.

That sort of dharmata moreover is not anything else than your own mind's nature of luminosity. It is inseparable with it. Therefore it

---

[179] Tib. spyi gzhi. "General ground" is the particular name used in this system; it has the sense of the "ground that covers everything".

[180] In this commentary, the words of the root text are highlighted by preceding them with "therefore". They have been italicized as well in the translation to make them unmistakably clear.

is your own *mind-ness*.[181] That, your mind's innate condition,[182] is the creator of all the phenomena of samsara and nirvana and, because it rules over all phenomena, it is *king*. When immersed in an in-space of the dhatu of that dharmata—the superfactual state—which is our *nature*, appearance and becoming are complete while not moving from the ground, therefore, it *is a greater completion*.

For example, just as for all "things" there is pervasion by space and no abandonment of them by it, so, for all phenomena, the dharmata of great completion does not abandon phenomena at all, therefore, for it there is *no abandonment at all*. Just as all characteristics of things—shape, colour, and so on—do not exist in space and space is beyond such objects, so, all conceived things, concept labels, verbal expressions, and so on, that exist for all dharmins[183] do not exist in dharmata great completion and great completion is beyond it, therefore, it is the *beyond-all fact*ual situation.

Having shown what the actuality of the ground, dhatu dharmata great completion, the innate wisdom, is, its dharmakaya of non-dual shining forth and liberation, the view of alpha-purity's Thorough Cut has to be decided, as follows. When the sudden flashes of discursive thought shine forth as objects, looking at the entity of what has shone forth without engaging in the slightest in the adoption and rejection that goes with clinging and grasping to either the object shining forth or the discursive thought shining forth, causes the discursive thought to purify itself and to shine forth as uncontrived self-knowing rigpa,

---

[181] Here, we get a neatly stated definition of the word "mindness"; it is the *-ness* meaning nature or essence of your own samsaric *mind*.

[182] And here we get a neatly stated definition of the term "the innate". The innate is the inner nature of your own mind that you do have inside you.

[183] Dharmin is a Sanskrit term. See the glossary. Dharmins here means the samsaric minds having the conceived-of dharmas or phenomena just mentioned.

which is rigpa in the state of the spontaneously existing three kayas, the great in-space of wisdom, therefore, *what shines forth without clinging is the in-space of the spontaneous zone of rigpa.*

By setting yourself with mind uncontrived into being just so[184] in the state like that of seeing the view's own face, discursive thought self-purifies and you abide in the absorption of the nature left untouched, therefore, *being just so.*[185] At that time, the birthless state will give rise to the non-stopped situation of rigpa's liveliness shining forth in a variety of ways, but it will be liberated in the state without clinging, therefore, there is *self-liberation.* When, by looking nakedly[186] at the entity of the discursive thought which has been produced, discursive thought self-vanishes and the entity of the innate is distinctly seen with the insight of vipashyana, therefore, it is *nakedly seen.* That sort of meditation, moreover, is free of all clinging to the experiences of bliss, luminosity, and no-thought, and so on; it is beyond the objects thought of by rational mind such as "the nature is this sort of thing", therefore, *objects of thought* are *absent.*

This uncontrived mind, which is arrived at through that mere preservation of itself recognizing itself, is the central issue of practice, therefore, it is the nature *left untouched, so* if you insist upon apprehending it with rational mind, you will be manufacturing and contriving it, and as much as you contrive it, you deviate from the path, therefore, *do not engage in the spoilage of contrivance!*

Those who do not self-recognize the dharmata which is, like that, uncontrived, are stupid in regard to Great Completion's path, there-

---

[184] Being just so is Chog Zhag.

[185] Chog Zhag.

[186] Looking nakedly means that you look right at something so that you see it nakedly. We would normally say "look directly" in English but then the connection to the words of the root text "nakedly" would be lost.

fore it says *the ones who are stupid.* The ones who are stupid in that way reject the uncontrived entity of mind and make contrivance into the path, therefore, they *reject that entity.* Trying to achieve an abiding in the primordial liberation of the innate mind using the various types of mental examination and analysis of their clever intellects, they put it into the cage of hope and fear, therefore, *then caging the innate mind in their cleverness...* Having been put in the cage of hope and fear, *it becomes contrived and contrived* again and again by rational mind thinking, "It is this. It is not this", and then, as much as there is this contrivance of it, the fact of the garbha is not seen and this rational-mind-made view and meditation does not achieve the levels of the path *and the fact of the garbha is obscured.*

Just as a knot could never be made in space and therefore also could not be untied, mindness which resides as primordial liberation from the outset could not be liberated by the determined strivings of concept, therefore, *that, which has no liberation...* Those who desire for liberation through the contrivance that comes from striving like that bind themselves again and again through their heartfelt wish to be free. Like a silk-worm who binds itself with the excretions of its own mouth,[187] what they do *only binds them further.*

If the meaning of those key points is distilled right down, exactly this common awareness of the present which has not gone into rational mind's manufacture and contrivance at all, whether we call it "rigpa resident in the ground" or "great completion", or similarly "great seal",[188] "great middle way",[189] "freedom from elaboration", "birthlessness", or some other name, exactly this common awareness

---

[187] This is how Tibetan culture thinks the silk-worm produces silk.

[188] Skt. mahamudra.

[189] Skt. mahamadhyamaka.

in actual fact is naked rigpa,[190] so the self-recognition of that is called "the view", and that brings the first topic to a close.

2. The way to practise the path, uncontrived mindness, naked rigpa-emptiness

To set yourself at ease free of mind's contrivance in the state exactly of that uncontrived situation which is that sort of view of self-recognition is the meditation, therefore, *if there is relaxation towards whatever is included in rational mind...* If you put yourself simply undistracted in the state that like of what has been left untouched, a self-occurring dwelling that is absorption in rigpa will come on, therefore, *that naturalness will do, there being no need to contrive it.*

When you put yourself in just that left it untouched, its liveliness will come on as various discursive thoughts that are emitted as both objects and movement. In relation to that, first the movement of discursive thought is self-recognized and then, having put yourself in the state of seeing what it is, the discursive thought will purify itself in its own place—it will proceed into shining forth and liberating without trace, therefore, *movement seen self-purifies.*

Moreover, any good thoughts—ones having a virtuous aspect—that shine forth should not be tied with clinging and grasping with the thought, "This is good", but should, by putting yourself into an absence of clinging, be allowed to vanish of themselves, therefore, it is *not spoiled with an antidote. And*, for bad thoughts such as

---

[190] This nicely explains the meaning of common awareness. Common awareness does not mean "ordinary awareness" as it is usually translated. The original Sanskrit term does not mean common in the sense of nothing special, vulgar, but common in the sense of that which is the common denominator. This common awareness is the one connected with the innate, with mindness; it is the nature of all awareness and is common to all them.

attachment and anger and thoughts of the eight dharmas[191] that shine forth you should not think, "This is bad", then regret them, stop them, and so on, but should put yourself into your innate disposition in which they self-liberate, therefore, they are *not changed by abandonment*. In that way, even though good thoughts with a virtuous aspect shine forth, the surface of mind is not changed to something better and even though bad thoughts with a non-virtuous aspect shine forth, it is not changed to something worse; from sentient beings through to buddhas there is no difference in mind's innate disposition, therefore, *the innate disposition is a greater completion*.

If that sort of nature is realized, there is equal taste within the state without any abandoning and accepting. The acceptance-rejection, hope-and-fear-driven suppression and furtherance, and the attachment and aversion that we currently have entails phenomena being bound by clinging at truth whilst thinking, "This is; this is not". With that, phenomena are taken to be existent as one class of thing or another. However, all of them are not existent; in the state of all-encompassing rigpa in full view, all of them are purified in absence of abandonment and acceptance, therefore, *existence is non-existent. And*, moreover, at that time of the practise of naked self-knowing rigpa, there is no saying at all that its nature is "like this and like this" with words like "it is blissful, cleared out luminosity, flashing on and off in the state of no-thought", because it is not present as an object of verbal expression or rational-minded thinking. For the yogin, the nature at all times shines forth distinctly in self-knowing rigpa of full transparency, something that exists in the domain of personal self-knowing wisdom, therefore, *in non-existence there is existence to the limit*.

In the state of uncontrived mindness, all factors of clinging at truth in things has, like that, self-collapsed, therefore, *all things having collapsed…* Exactly that condition of being freed of the bonds of grasping at truth is the emptiness of non-dual knowing and being

191 … the eight worldly dharmas …

empty, so it is not necessary to confuse the issue with an emptiness apart from that, one which has been made as an object of rational mind, therefore, *there is an emptiness of greater completion.*

Those who, not knowing that, put their hopes in a mental analysis type of emptiness, seek it apart from emptiness over appearance; having been bound by the clinging of grasping at emptiness, they contrive and contrive, they assert an intellectually-known emptiness thought of as "an emptiness which is arrived at through mental examination", therefore, *for persons who assert liberation through contriving and contriving...* With that sort of approach, they fall into the extreme of nihilism due to over-stating the importance of appearance or fall into the extreme of permanence due to taking emptiness as supreme then clinging to truth in it; for them there is no emancipation from the abyss of permanence and nihilism, therefore, one wonders *what emancipation could there be from both permanence and nihilism?*

For example, all of the containers and contents constituted by the four elements are present supported by space, but there is no basis for their support anywhere in space and, likewise, all phenomena are supported by dharmata great completion, but dharmata great completion provides no support for them anywhere at all, there being no supporting ground, therefore, it is *ground-less.* While all the groundless phenomena of samsara and nirvana have no production from causes and conditions, dharmata great completion has no root for the creation of anything at all, therefore, it is *root-free.* That ground and root-less dharmata resides at all times primordially without the spoilage of contrivance, therefore, *it is a primordially residing greater completion.*

There are those who do not know that sort of primordially-resident, innate dharmata which is present as itself untouched. Among them, one group of people who think that all phenomena are emptiness pursue their meditation on the basis of a grasped-at emptiness. Another group grasp at the form of the appearance aspect, taking that to be the actual fact, and meditate on deities, spheres of light, and so on, with conceptualized characteristics. Another group, saying that the superfactual dharmata described above "is like this and like that", strongly solidify it, making it true and permanent, then hold on to it in their meditation on the foci of rational mind; they exaggerate it so that it is existent. Another group, because of their idea that all phenomena are emptiness, meditate on the nihilism of no samsara and no nirvana, no karma and effect, nothing existing at all, and go into the exaggeration of non-existence. The people who in those various ways have not realized the actual situation grasp at the superfactual meaning in accordance with their own wants and meditate accordingly, therefore, *they have meditations of emptiness, appearance, existence, and non-existence*. Those who have that sort of rational-mind-made dualistically-grasping meditation also have a view of tenets accompanied by wanting.[192] They also have a conduct with the biasses of adoption and rejection, therefore, *but where there is meditation, there is view and conduct*.

Those who put their hopes in view and meditation which is an artefice made by rational mind do not have the key point of primordial liberation free from abandonment and acceptance,[193] they grasp strongly at mind, therefore, *in that there is becoming*.[194] Having, like that, grasped at becoming as true, they attempt to get rid of it but that cannot work; just as they cannot get rid of their shadows unless

---

[192] They engage in religious systems of tenets because of wanting liberation, but there is no liberation can be gained directly in that, only an alignment towards it.

[193] This is the point where the bottom half of the Tibetan text was switched with the bottom half of the *Lamp for a Dim Room* text as explained in the introduction to this book.

[194] This is simply saying that the nature, wisdom, is the basis for the mind of samsara, a transformation that occurs when it grasps at itself, with the result that the mind enters samsaric existence in which it is always becoming one thing or another due to the force of karma latencies.

they get rid of their bodies, so they cannot get rid of samsara's unsatisfactoriness unless they get rid of the root of samsara, clinging at truth. Therefore, it says, *so there is* for them *samsara's unsatisfactoriness.*

Similarly with the clinging associated with each side of dualistic grasping:[195] bound by their wanting dharma and its vehicles, they have thoughts of "This is good. This is bad. This is my own tradition. This is another's tradition. Mine is best. Theirs is inferior". With such thoughts their attachment and aversion, and argumentativeness visibly increase, therefore, *where there is dharma, there is wanting which clings to vehicles.*[196] That sort of thing, because it follows on from dualistic clinging to oneself and other, traps them in the cage of the afflictions and binds them with all of the fetters of samsara, therefore, *in that there is a cage of afflictions, so there are fetters*[197]. This sort of thing leads to what Guardian Nagarjuna said in his middle way's *Precious Garland*,

> For as long as there is grasping at the aggregates
> For that long there will grasping at an I.
> If there is grasping at I, then also karma ...

and that is how it is.

In the state of the innate disposition, alpha purity, its being primordially empty, root-free keeps it cleared of grasping at the ground. With self-knowing naked and in full view, the shackle of concept-driven striving is released and a path that proceeds in stages is

[195] Each side of dualistic grasping means the subjective mind that grasps and the objects which are grasped at by it. The pair is summed up in the name grasped-grasping which is explained in the glossary.

[196] The commentary quotes this line a little differently from the root, though there is no substantial change in meaning.

[197] The commentary quotes this line a little differently from the root, though there is no substantial change in meaning.

stopped. Everything being known as primordial liberation, there is no desire for something to be accomplished, which in turn puts an end to wanting a fruition. Therefore, *one remains ground-free, path stopped, and wanting a fruition ended.*[198]

Phenomena-ended rigpa[199] is beyond demonstration and expression. The words used in the vehicles cannot demonstrate it exactly as it is, yet, if the yogin evaluates it with the partial understandings that the words of the vehicles provide, he will find that it agrees with every one of the vehicles. Because of that, he will separate from the desire and clinging connected with the ideas of superior and inferior that happen when establishing the views of the vehicles and their tenets. Therefore, *he does not have even a speck of wanting and clinging to a vehicle.*[200]

That yogin realizes full-view rigpa, through which all of his discursive thoughts are purifying themselves in simultaneous shining-forth-liberation; they are collapsing instantly, like a drawing on water, so do not accumulate karma, therefore, *and in that, there is no karma.* He has similes of the thoughts of desire and anger which appear in this view that does not accumulate karma, but they have neither positive nor negative effects. Therefore, it says, *so no shroud of full-ripening.*[201]

---

[198] The commentary quotes this line a little differently from the root, though there is no substantial change in meaning.

[199] This means "rigpa with all of the phenomena of dualistic mind exhausted".

[200] The commentary quotes this line a little differently from the root. There is a change in meaning though both lines work.

[201] Full-ripening is one of the several types of karmic cause and effect taught by the Buddha; it refers to the cause and effect of a karma ripening into a samsaric existence. The point here that he does not engage in the karmic process the way that an ordinary being would with

(continued ...)

Because that yogin has known samsara to be non-existent, appearance for him does not abide in the extreme of becoming and because he completes the three kayas as path appearance, he does not fall into a one-sided peace, therefore, *not staying in becoming or peace* ... Being in the state of space-like dharmata there is an uninterrupted flow of the innate, therefore, *a yogin proceeds within the state of space*. For this yogin, every one of the external objects that seemingly appear—confusion's containers and contents—shine forth as empty forms, the superficies of illusion, therefore, *in the space of objects*, rigpa's liveliness, the discursive thoughts of mind, is floating about flickering on and off here and there, but is shining forth and liberating continuously. In that way, *rigpa's liveliness is floating about* and becomes trained.

This yogin has these appearances shining forth like that within the in-space of the rigpa king which is divorced from foci such as "It is this", but they are mere un-grasped liveliness, *so the yogin is one for whom the focus-less king, grasping-less, shines forth* ... Because they shine forth without rational mind's grasping like that at objects with a focus, the yogin is completely liberated from the discursive thoughts of grasped-grasping—the grasped-at objects and grasping subject which are the source of all of becoming's confused appearances—therefore, ... *and phenomena are in self-liberation from subject-object becoming.*[202] At all times and in all circumstances the yogin never knows separation from the actuality of the self-liberation that has been manifested like that and has the innate shining forth without interruption, therefore, *for the yogin who stays in the state without shift into the three times* ...[203] That yogin is staying in, without shifting

---

[201] (... continued)
his real discursive thoughts.

[202] This means "the becoming in samsara in which there is the duality of the objects grasped at and the subject grasping at them".

[203] "Without shift into the three times" means that the yogin has arrived at the end of meditation. He does not sometimes meet with and

(continued ...)

from, the state of the uncontrived innate, the in-space of the dharmakaya naked and in full view, which is the meditation. And he conducts himself in self-liberation, which is the fruition. With that, the second topic is completed.

3. Showing the fruition, the place liberated from confused thought in the state divorced from adoption and rejection

The empty entity's alpha purity has an output of rigpa. The rigpa in turn has an output of liveliness and that in turn manifests as play. The play blazing up from that yogin's uncontrived mind of empty-luminous dharmakaya is coming forth as the nirmanakaya manifestations. Therefore, the yogin has *the output of the empty-luminous dharmakaya*. And, the basis for the shining forth of the appearance factor of spontaneous existence being free of ground and root, the light output, sambhogakaya's appearance, also shines forth, therefore, *and there is the unchanging spontaneous-existence ground-and-root-free output*. The yogi has seized the stronghold which is the basis for the shining forth of every output, the primal situation's dharmata elaboration-free and beyond expression, the dharmakaya mind changeless and birthless, the innate, therefore, the yogin resides *in the in-space of the primal situation that has this output AḤ*.

Spoken by the Expert, Glorious King.[204]

Virtue! Virtue! Virtue!

---

[203] (... continued)
sometimes part from the in-space of enlightenment. He has reached the fruition of the meditation in which he never falls into samsara, which only operates in the three times of past, present, and future.

[204] The Expert, Glorious King is a name that Patrul used to refer to himself when teaching and writing about Great Completion.

Glossary of Terms

Accomplishing and Stopping: same as furtherance and suppression *q.v.*

Actuality, Tib. gnas lugs: A key term in both sūtra and tantra and one of a pair of terms, the other being "apparent reality" (Tib. snang lugs). The two terms are used when determining the reality of a situation. The actuality of any given situation is how (lugs) the situation actuality sits or is present (gnas); the apparent reality is how (lugs) any given situation appears (snang) to an observer. Something could appear in many different ways, depending on the circumstances at the time and on the being perceiving it but, regardless of those circumstances, it will always have its own actuality of how it really is. This term is frequently used in Mahāmudrā and Great Completion teachings to mean the fundamental reality of any given phenomenon or situation before any deluded mind alters it and makes it appear differently.

Adventitious, Tib. glo bur: This term has the connotations of popping up on the surface of something and of not being part of that thing. Therefore, even though it is often translated as "sudden", that only conveys half of the meaning. In Buddhist literature, something adventitious comes up as a surface event and disappears again precisely because it is not actually part of the thing on whose surface it appeared. It is frequently used in relation to the afflictions because they pop up on the surface of the mind of buddha-nature but are not part of the buddha-nature itself.

Affliction, Skt. kleśha, Tib. nyon mongs: This term is usually translated as emotion or disturbing emotion, etcetera, but the Buddha was very specific about the meaning of this word. When the Buddha referred to the emotions, meaning a movement of mind, he did not refer to them as such but called them "kleśha" in Sanskrit, meaning exactly "affliction". It is a basic part of the Buddhist teaching that emotions afflict beings, giving them problems at the time and causing more problems in the future.

Alaya, Skt. ālaya, Tib. kun gzhi: This term, if translated, is usually translated as all-base or something similar. It is a Sanskrit term that means a range that underlies and forms a basis for something else. In Buddhist teaching, it means a particular level of mind that sits beneath all other levels of mind. However, it is used in several different ways in the Buddhist teaching and changes to a different meaning in each case. In the Great Completion teachings, an important distinction is made between ālaya alone and ālaya consciousness.

All-Knowing One, Tib. kun mkhyen: Every century in Tibet, there were just a few people who seemed to know everything so were given the title "All-Knowing One". One of them was Longchen Rabjam and throughout this text All-Knowing One always refers to him. Moreover, of all the All-Knowing ones, Longchenpa was regarded as the greatest, therefore, he is also frequently referred to as the "great" or "greatest" All-Knowing One. Note that "All-Knowing" does not mean "omniscient one" even though it is often translated that way.

Alpha purity, Tib. ka dag: A Great Completion term meaning purity that is there from the first, that is, primordial purity. There are many terms in Buddhism that express the notion of "primordial purity" but this one is unique to the Great Completion teaching. The term "alpha purity" matches the Tibetan term both literally and in meaning.

Alteration, altered: Same as contrivance *q.v.*

Appearance and becoming, Tib. snang srid: This is a stock phrase in which "appearance" refers to the worlds that appear to the senses of beings and "becoming" refers to the beings born into those worlds. "Becoming" actually means "a birth taken somewhere with the result that a being becomes one type of migrator or another". This phrase "appearance and becoming" is equivalent in meaning to another stock phrase "containers and contents" with the containers being the appearances of their worlds and contents being the beings in those worlds. The phrase often is used indicate all of samsāra and nirvana, though it can be used to indicate only one or the other.

Assurance, Tib. gdeng: Although often translated as confidence, this term means assurance with all of the extra meaning conveyed by that term. A bird might be confident of its ability to fly but, more than that, it has the assurance that it will not fall to the ground because it knows it has wings and it has the training to use them. Similarly, a person might be confident that he could liberate the afflictions but not be assured of doing so because of lack of training or other causes. However, a person who has accumulated the causes to be able to liberate afflictions is assured of the ability to do so.

Awareness, Skt. jñā, Tib. shes pa: "Awareness" is always used in our translations to mean the basic knower of mind or, as Buddhist teaching itself defines it, "a general term for any registering mind", whether dualistic or non-dualistic. Hence, it is used for both samsaric and nirvanic situations; for example, consciousness (Tib. rnam par shes pa) is a dualistic form of awareness, whereas rigpa, wisdom (Tib. ye shes), and so on are non-dualistic forms of awareness. See under rigpa.

It is noteworthy that the key term "rigpa" is often mistakenly translated as "awareness", even though it is not merely an awareness; this creates considerable confusion amongst practitioners of the higher tantras who are misled by it.

Bardo, Tib. bar do: Literally, "interval" or "in-between place". The general teachings of Buddhism explain this as the interval between one life and the next. However, Nature Great Completion teaches that the cycle of samsaric life consists of four intervals, with the interval between lives consisting of two of the four.

Becoming, Skt. bhāvanā, Tib. srid pa: This is another name for samsaric existence. Beings in samsara have a samsaric existence but, more than that, they are constantly in a state of becoming—becoming this type of being or that type of being in this abode or that, as they are driven along without choice by the karmic process that drives samsaric existence.

Bliss, Skt. sukha, Tib. bde: The Sanskrit term and its Tibetan translation are usually translated into English as "bliss" but refer to the whole range of possibilities of everything on the side of good as opposed to bad. Thus, the term will mean pleasant, happy, good, nice, easy, comfortable, blissful, and so on, depending on context.

Bliss, luminosity, and no-thought, Tib. bde gsal mi rtog pa: A person who actually practises meditation will have signs of that practice appear as various types of temporary experience. Most commonly, three types of experience are met with: bliss, luminosity, and no-thought. Bliss is an ease of body or mind or both, luminosity is the knowing factor of mind, and no-thought is an absence of thought that happens in the mind. The three are usually mentioned when discussing the passing experiences that arise because of practising meditation but there is also a way of describing them as final experiences of realization.

Note that this has often been called "bliss, clarity, and no-thought" but that makes the mistake that the word for luminosity has been abbreviated in this phrase and mistaken by translators to mean something else.

Bodhichitta, Tib. byang chub sems: See under enlightenment mind.

Bodhisatva, Tib. byang chub sems dpa': A bodhisatva is a person who has engendered the bodhichitta, enlightenment mind, and with that as a basis has undertaken the path to the enlightenment of a truly complete buddha specifically for the welfare of other beings. Note that, despite the common appearance of "bodhisattva" in Western books on Buddhism, the Tibetan tradition has steadfastly maintained since the time of the earliest translations that the correct spelling is bodhisatva; see under satva and sattva.

Chog Zhag, Tib. cog bzhag: The teaching on four Chog Zhag is part of the Thorough Cut teaching of Great Completion. The four Chog Zhag are four ways of being in which the practitioner has put himself "chog zhag", meaning "set just so". The four are mountain, ocean, appearances, and rigpa. They show the way of being that is taught in the Thorough Cut practice; they can be used as an introduction to that practice but also to give profound instruction on the details of the practice.

Clinging, Tib. zhen pa: In Buddhism, this term refers specifically to the twofold process of dualistic mind mis-taking things that are not true, not pure, etcetera as true, pure, etcetera and then, because of seeing them as highly desirable even though they are not, attaching itself to or clinging to those things. This type of clinging acts as a kind of glue that keeps a person joined to the unsatisfactory things of cyclic existence because of mistakenly seeing them as desirable.

Common awareness, Tib. tha mal gyi shes pa: One of several path terms used to indicate mind's essence. It is equivalent to "mindness" and "rigpa". These terms are used by practitioners as a code word for their own, personal experience of the essence of mind. These words are secret because of the power they are connected with and should be kept that way.

This term is often referred to as "ordinary mind", a term that was established by Chogyam Trungpa Rinpoche for his students. However, there are two problems with that wording. Firstly, "tha mal" does not mean "ordinary". It means the awareness which is common to all parts of samsaric mind and also which is common to all beings. It is glossed in writings on Mahāmudrā to mean "nature". In other words, it refers to that part of mind which, being common to all events of mind, is its nature. This is well attested to in the writings of the Kagyu forefathers. Secondly, this is not "mind", given that mind is used to mean the dualistic mind of beings in cyclic existence. Rather this is "shes pa", the most general term for all kinds of awareness.

Compassionate activity, Tib. thugs rje: This does not mean compassionate activity in general. Rather, it is a specific term of the most profound level of teachings of Mahāmudrā and Great Completion. These teachings describe innate wisdom as having three characteristics. The third characteristic is this compassionate activity. It refers to the fact that wisdom spontaneously does whatever needs to be done, throughout all reaches of time and space, for all beings. Although it includes the word "compassion" in its name, it is more primordial than that. It is the dynamic quality of enlightenment which choicelessly, ceaselessly, spontaneously, and pervasively acts to benefit others. The term is often used in discussions of Great Completion and essence Mahāmudrā.

Complete purity, Tib. rnam dag: This term refers to the quality of a buddha's mind, which is completely pure compared to a sentient being's mind. The mind of a being in samsara has its primordially pure nature covered over by the muck of dualistic mind. If the being practises correctly, the impurity can be removed and mind can be returned to its original state of complete purity.

Conceived effort, Tib. rtsol ba: In Buddhism, this term usually does not merely mean effort but has the specific connotation of effort that is driven by the concepts of dualistic mind. For example, the term "mindfulness with effort" specifically means a type of mindfulness that is occurring within the context of dualistic mind and its various operations. The term "effortless" is often used in Mahāmudrā and Great Completion teachings to mean a way of being in which dualistic mind has been abandoned and, therefore, in which there is none of the endeavouring of ordinary people.

Conceived-of thing, Tib. dngos po: In Buddhist texts, "thing" refers specifically to a conceived-of thing. Dualistic mind creates things as concepts and then relates to the concepts whereas non-dualistic wisdom does not create them to begin with because it does not have dualistic mind's conceptual process. What does wisdom know then, if it does not know things? Wisdom knows all phenomena in direct perception; these phenomena are not called things because if they were, that would immediately imply the presence of dualistic mind in wisdom, something which by definition is impossible. Wisdom knows phenomena in direct perception whereas dualistic mind knows "things" in a specific conceptual process called "identification". Identification is a dualistic process and therefore that process does not exist in wisdom.

Concept label, Tib. mtshan ma: This is the technical name for the structures or concepts which function as the words of conceptual mind's language. They are the very basis of operation of the third aggregate and hence of the way that dualistic mind communicates with its world. For example, a table seen in direct visual perception will have no concept labels involved with knowing it. However, when thought becomes involved and there is the thought "table" in an inferential or conceptual perception of the table, the name-tag "table" will be used to reference the table and that name tag is the concept label.

Although we usually reference phenomena via these concepts, the phenomena are not the dualistically referenced things we think of them as being. The actual fact of the phenomena is quite different from the concept labels used to discursively think about them and is known by wisdom rather than concept-based mind. Therefore, this term is often used in Buddhist literature to signify that dualistic samsaric mind is involved rather than non-dualistic wisdom.

Confusion, Tib. 'khrul pa: In Buddhism, this term mostly refers to the fundamental confusion of taking things the wrong way that happens because of fundamental ignorance, although it can also have the more general meaning of having lots of thoughts and being confused about it. In the first case, it is defined like this: "Confusion is the appearance to rational mind of something being present when it is not" and refers, for example, to seeing an object, such as a table, as being truly present, when in fact it is present only as mere, interdependent appearance.

Consciousness, Skt. vijñāna, Tib. rnam shes: The term literally means "awareness of superficies". A consciousness is a *jñā* dualistic type of knowing which simply registers *vi* a certain type of superfice, for example, an eye consciousness by definition registers only the superficies of visual form. A very important point is that the addition of the "vi" to the basic term "jñā" for knowing conveys the sense of a less than perfect way of being aware. This is not a wisdom awareness which knows every superfice in an utterly uncomplicated way but a limited type of awareness which is restricted to knowing one kind of superfice or another and which is part of the complicated—and highly unsatisfactory process—called (dualistic) mind. Note that this definition, which is a crucial part of understanding the role of consciousness in samsaric being, is fully conveyed by the Sanskrit and Tibetan terms but not at all by the English term.

Also note that occasionally the term is used in a very general way to mean simply "knowing mind". It used in this book once with that sense.

Containers and contents, Tib. snod bcud: Containers are the outer worlds and environment and their contents are the beings living in them. This phrase is sometimes extended to "outer and inner, containers and contents" with the same meaning. It usually means "the entirety of samsara", though sometimes means "the entirety of samsara and nirvana".

Contrivance, contrived, Tib. bcos pa: A term meaning that something has been altered from its native state and is now artificial rather than the actual thing itself. See also manufacture and contrivance.

Cyclic existence: See under samsara.

Dharmadhatu, Skt. dharmadhātu, Tib. chos kyi dbyings: See the explanation of dhatu first. As explained there, a dhatu is a place or region within which something comes into being. Dharma dhatu is the region in which all dharmas, meaning phenomena, can and do come into being. If a flower bed is the place where flowers grow and are found, the dharmadhatu is the bed in which all phenomena come into being and are found. The term is used in all levels of Buddhist teaching with that general meaning, though the explanation of it becomes more profound as the teaching becomes more profound. For example, in Great Completion and Mahāmudrā, it is the all-pervading sphere of empty luminosity-wisdom, given that empty luminosity is where phenomena arise and luminosity is none other than wisdom.

Dharmakaya, Skt. dharmakāya, Tib. chos sku: In the general teachings of Buddhism, this refers to the mind of a buddha, with "dharma" meaning reality and "kāya" meaning body. In the Thorough Cut practice of Great Completion it additionally has the special meaning of being the means by which one rapidly imposes liberation on oneself.

Dharmata, Skt. dharmatā, Tib. chos nyid: This is a general term meaning the way that something is, and can be applied to anything at all; it is similar in meaning to "actuality" *q.v.* For example, the dharmatā of water is wetness and the dharmatā of the becoming bardo is a place where beings are in a samsaric, or becoming mode, prior to entering a nature bardo. It is used frequently in Tibetan Buddhism to mean "the dharmatā of reality" but that is a specific case of the much larger meaning of the term. To read texts which use this term successfully, one has to understand that the term has a general meaning and then see how that applies in context.

Dharmin, Tib. chos can: A dharmin is defined as an awareness having, meaning knowing, a dharma or phenomenon. The awareness can either be a dualistic or a non-dualistic awareness, that is, it can either be a samsaric consciousness or wisdom knower, though it is mostly used to indicate a samsaric knower of a phenomenon.

Dharmin and dharmata, Tib. chos can, chos nyid: Each term starts with *dharma*, meaning a phenomenon. Each term has a suffix that gives it a more specific meaning. The *in* on dharmin makes a term meaning "that possessing a dharma or phenomenon"; it is referring to the mind that has a phenomenon for its object. The *tā* on dharmatā makes a term meaning "dharma-ness"; it is referring to the quality of a dharma or phenomenon. For example, you have water, which is a dharma, a phenomenon. A samsaric consciousness that has water for its object is called the dharmin for the water. The property or dharmatā of water is that it is wet, liquid, transparent, and so on. Another property or dharmatā of every dharma is that it is empty, therefore terms like "emptiness of the dharmatā" or "dharmatā emptiness" are seen.

It is important to understand that dharmatā is a general term that refers to the property or quality of any given phenomenon. In Buddhist discussions of reality, it is often used in relation to the empty quality of phenomena. Because of that, many Western students have come to think that dharmatā means the empty quality of phenomena in general and have translated dharmatā as reality, and so on. However, as just explained, dharmatā has a more general meaning than that. Understanding all of this will give you a better and possibly quite different sense of what dharmatā actually means.

Dhatu, Skt. dhātu, Tib. dbyings: The Sanskrit term has twenty-two meanings. The most basic one is the meaning of a source or a basis from which something comes. The difficulty of translating it can be seen from the fact that the Tibetan translators were not able to come up with one term in Tibetan that would cover all meanings but had to use three different words for the term. Of the three the one listed just above, dbyings, is the term used in the texts in book.

Dhatu in the case of dbyings means a region or zone in which something occurs and then other words can be joined with it to indicate the specific things that happen in that region. For instance, a flower bed is a region to begin with and more specifically is a region in which flowers happen.

When dhatu is seen alone in the texts in this book, it conveys the sense of emptiness, not as the philosophical or mental idea of emptiness, but the actual space-like region of emptiness. When dhatu is joined with dharma to give "dharma dhatu", the term refers to the space-like region in which all dharmas, meaning all phenomena, happen. A complication to watch out for is that dhatu by itself, as is often found in writings on Great Completion and other tantras, rather than implying the empty space-like region, can be an abbreviation of "dharma dhatu". In that case, the emphasis is still on the empty space-like region but with the added understanding that it is the region in which all phenomena can and do occur.

It is essential to understand all of these points and to read carefully so that the fullness of what is being expressed by "dhatu" can be understood.

Dhyana, Skt. dhyāna, Tib. bsam gtan: This is a general term meaning all types of mental absorption. Mental absorptions cultivated in the human realm generally result in births in the form realms which are deep forms of mental absorption in themselves. The practices of mental absorption done in the human realm and the godly existences of the form realm that result from them both are named "dhyāna". The Buddha repeatedly pointed out that the dhyānas were a side-track to emancipation from cyclic existence.

In a more general way, the term also means meditation in general where one is concentrating on something as a way of developing oneself spiritually. Texts on Great Completion often use the word in this sense when making the point that attempts to meditate on anything are the very opposite of the Great Completion practice and will inevitably keep the practitioner within samsara.

Direct Crossing, Tib. thod rgal: The name of one of the two main practices of the unsurpassed, extra-secret level of Great Completion. The other one is Thorough Cut *q.v.*

Discursive thought, Skt. vikalpa, Tib. rnam rtog: This means more than just the superficial thought that is heard as a voice in the head. It includes the entirety of conceptual process that arises due to mind contacting any object of any of the senses. The Sanskrit and Tibetan literally mean "(dualistic) thought (that arises from the mind wandering among the) various (superficies *q.v.* perceived in the doors of the senses)".

Doha, Skt. dohā, Tib. mgur; A dohā is a song sung spontaneously from spiritual realization. Dohās are popular in the tantric traditions because they are enjoyable to listen to and go right to the heart of the matter.

Effort, Tib. rtsol ba: See under conceived effort.

Elaboration, Tib. spro ba: This is a general name for what is given off by dualistic mind as it goes about its conceptual business. The term is pejorative in that it implies that a story has been made up, unnecessarily, about something which is actually nothing, which is empty. Elaborations, because of what they are, prevent a person from seeing emptiness directly.

Freedom from elaboration or being elaboration-free implies direct sight of emptiness. It is important to understand that these words are used in a theoretical or philosophical way in the second turning sutra teachings but are used in an experiential way in the final teachings of the third turning sutras and in the tantras of Great Completion and Mahāmudrā. In the former, being free of elaborations is a definition of what could happen according to the tenets of the Middle Way, and so on; in the latter it is a description of a state of being, one which, because it is empty of all the elaborations of dualistic being, is the actual sphere of emptiness.

Emptiness having the excellence of all superficies, Tib. rnam kun mchog ldan gyi stong pa nyid: This term is taught in the *Kālachakra Tantra* to emphasize the fact that emptiness is always unified with appearance. The tantra teaches, in conjunction with this term, that emptiness always has the excellence of all superficies, that is, always has the fullness of appearance with it. The term is employed in philosophical writings to imply that emptiness is never the bare kind of emptiness that can come from mistakenly understanding the Prajñāpāramitā teachings on emptiness.

The term is usually mistakenly translated as "emptiness endowed with the supreme of all aspects" because of mistaking the Tibetan term "mchog" to mean the buddha qualities. However, the translation as given is the correct understanding of the term, an understanding which is standard throughout Tibetan literature. Furthermore, grammatically speaking, this is emptiness which is not "endowed with" anything but simply "has" or "possesses" something.

Enlightenment mind, Skt. bodhichitta, Tib. byang chub sems: This is a key term of the Great Vehicle. It is the type of mind that is connected not with the lesser enlightenment of an arhat but with the enlightenment of a truly complete buddha. As such, it is a mind which is connected with the aim of bringing all sentient beings to that same level of buddhahood. A person who has engendered this mind has by definition entered the Great Vehicle and is either a bodhisatva or a buddha.

It is important to understand that "enlightenment mind" is used to refer equally to the minds of all levels of bodhisatva on the path to buddhahood and to the mind of a buddha who has completed the path. Therefore, it is not "mind striving for enlightenment" as is so often translated, but "enlightenment mind", meaning that kind of mind which is connected with the full enlightenment of a truly complete buddha and which is present in all those who belong to the Great Vehicle. The term is used in the conventional Great Vehicle and also in the Vajra Vehicle. In the Vajra Vehicle, there are some special uses of the term where substances of the pure aspect of the subtle physical body are understood to be manifestations of enlightenment mind.

Entity, Tib. ngo bo: The entity of something is just exactly what that thing is. In English we would often simply say "thing" rather than entity. However, in Buddhism, "thing" has a very specific meaning rather than the general meaning that it has in English. It has become common to translate this term as "essence" *q.v.* However, in most cases "entity", meaning what a thing is rather than an essence of that thing, is the correct translation for this term.

It is important to understand that in Buddhist teachings and especially in Mahāmudrā and Great Completion teachings, "entity" is frequently used to refer to the empty quality of something. In that case, entity is correct and essence incorrect.

Equipoise and post-attainment, Tib. mnyam bzhag and rjes thob: Although often called "meditation and post-meditation", the actual term is "equipoise and post-attainment". There is great meaning in the actual wording which is lost by the looser translation.

Exaggeration, Tib. sgro 'dogs: In Buddhism, this term is used in two ways. Firstly, it is used in general to mean misunderstanding from the perspective that one has added more to one's understanding of something than needs to be there. Secondly, it is used specifically to indicate that dualistic mind always overstates or exaggerates whatever object it is examining. Dualistic mind always adds the ideas of solidity, permanence, singularity, and so on to everything it references via the concepts that it uses. Severing of exaggeration either means removal of these un-necessary understandings when trying to properly comprehend something or removal of the dualistic process altogether when trying to get to the non-dualistic reality of a phenomenon.

Expressions, Tib. brjod pa: According to Sanskrit and Tibetan grammar following it, expressions refers to mental and verbal expressions. Thus, for example, the phrase seen in translation of "word, thought, and expression" is mistaken. The phrase is actually "expressions mental and verbal".

Fact, Skt. artha, Tib. don: "Fact" is that knowledge of an object that occurs to the surface of mind or wisdom. It is not the object but what the mind or wisdom understands as the object. Thus there are two usages of "fact": fact known to dualistic and non-dualistic minds. The higher tantras especially use "fact" to refer to the actual fact known in direct perception of actuality. Thus, there are phrases such as "in fact" which do not mean that the author is speaking truly about something but that whatever is about to be said is referring to actual fact as known to wisdom. A further complexity is that phrases such as "in fact" in those contexts are often abbreviations of "in superfact" *q.v.* This brings a further difficulty for the reader because "superfact" can be used in a general way to indicate directly perceived non-samsaric fact or can be used according to its specific definition (for which see superfact). In Buddhist tradition, problems like this are solved by having the text explained by one's teacher. That might not be possible for some readers, so uses of the word "fact" should be looked at carefully to see whether they are indicating fact in general or the factual situation of knowing reality in direct perception.

Familiarization, Tib. goms pa: Familiarization is similar to but not the same as meditation (Tib. sgom pa). Where meditation is the process of creating then cultivating a certain quality which was not there before, habituation is the process of re-familiarizing yourself with a quality that is already present, even if it has become temporarily unavailable due to being covered over.

Fictional, Skt. saṃvṛiti, Tib. kun rdzob: This term is paired with the term "superfactual" *q.v.* In the past, these terms have been translated as "relative" and "absolute" respectively, but those translations are nothing like the original terms. These terms are extremely important in the Buddhist teaching so it is very important that they be corrected, but more than that, if the actual meaning of these terms is not presented, then the teaching connected with them cannot be understood.

The Sanskrit term saṃvṛiti means a deliberate invention, a fiction, a hoax. It refers to the mind of ignorance which, because of being obscured and so not seeing suchness, is not true but a fiction. The things that appear to that ignorance are therefore fictional. Nonetheless, the beings who live in this ignorance believe that the things that appear to them through the filter of ignorance are true, are real. Therefore, these beings live in fictional truth.

Fictional and superfactual, Skt. saṃvṛiti, paramārtha: Fictional and superfactual are our greatly improved translations for "relative" and "absolute" respectively. Briefly, the original Sanskrit word for fiction means a deliberately produced *fiction* and refers to the world projected by a mind controlled by ignorance. The original word for superfact means "that *superior fact* that appears on the surface of the mind of a noble one who has transcended samsara" and refers to reality seen as it actually is. Relative and absolute do not convey this meaning at all and, when they are used, the meaning being presented is simply lost.

In more detail, the Sanskrit term behind "fictional", saṃvṛiti, is a common word that was used in ordinary language in India. It means "a fiction", "a deliberate coverup". This word was used in a variety of Indian religions, including Buddhism, to refer to the reality of ordinary beings, ones who are not spiritually advanced. The reality that these beings experience is a trumped up one, a big fiction, made up by their delusion.

The term fictional was paired with another term that was also widely used amongst Indian religions. This other term was used for talking about the reality of beings who are spiritually advanced enough to see things as they really are. The term, "paramartha", means "the spiritually superior (parama) fact known by mind (artha)". It refers to the fact of reality known by spiritually advanced beings and includes a sense of comparison with the fictional reality made up by sentient beings. There is no equivalent for this in English so I have coined the new term "superfactual", which is not only a very accurate translation of both the Sanskrit and Tibetan terms but also conveys the meaning correctly, as shown in this paragraph.

The two terms "fictional" and "superfactual" are used in any discussion of the two levels of reality that exist for beings as a whole: the fictional level of reality that sentient beings create for themselves by means of their delusion and the superior, factual level of reality that undeluded beings know as a fact. The terms "relative" and "absolute" sound nice but do not convey either the meanings of the original words nor the meanings that the Buddha gave to them when explaining these two levels of reality. The terms fictional and superfactual not only translate the original terms accurately but also convey the sense of the terms as used by the Buddha. Note the difference in feeling that you get when you use "fictional" and "superfactual" as opposed to relative and absolute.

Field, Field realm, Tib. zhing, zhing khams: This term is often translated "buddha field" though there is no "buddha" in the term. There are many different types of "fields" in both samsara and nirvana. Thus there are fields that belong to enlightenment and ones that belong to ignorance. Moreover, just as there are "realms" of samsara—desire, form, and formless—so there are realms of nirvana—the fields of the dharmakāya, saṃbhogakāya, and nirmāṇakāya and these are therefore called "field realms".

Finality obtained, Tib. gtan pa thob ba: The path of a Thorough Cut practitioner proceeds in a three step process of introduction, followed by training, followed by attaining finality. This term is sometimes translated as stability but that does not capture the full meaning. The original term means that one has gone to the point where the whole training is finalized; it has been taken its finish.

Five paths, Tib. lam lnga: In the Prajñāpāramitā teachings of the Great Vehicle, the Buddha explained the entire Buddhist journey as a set of five paths called the paths of accumulation, connection, seeing, cultivation, and no more training. The first four paths are part of journeying to enlightenment; the fifth path is that one has actually arrived and has no more training to undergo. There are a set of five paths that describe the journey of the Lesser Vehicle and a set of five paths that describe the journey of the Greater Vehicle. The names are the same in each case but the details of what is accomplished at each stage are different.

Foci, focus, focus on, Tib. gtad so: A focus is any given thing that a dualistic mind has focussed on using its concepts. Having a focus is equivalent to having a reference *q.v.*, and focussing on a focus entails referencing a reference. All of these terms imply the presence of dualistic mind.

Foremost instruction, Skt. upadeśha, Tib. man ngag: There are several types of instruction mentioned in Buddhist literature: there is the general level of instruction which is the meaning contained in the words of the texts of the tradition; on a more personal and direct level there is oral instruction which has been passed down from teacher to student from the time of the buddha; and on the most profound level there are foremost instructions which are not only oral instructions provided by one's guru but are special, core instructions that come out of personal experience and which convey the teaching concisely and with the full weight of personal experience.

Furtherance and suppression, Tib. rnam pa: This term is used to express the way that dualistic mind approaches the path to enlightenment. In that case, some states of mind are regarded as ones to be discarded, so the practitioner takes the approach of attempting to suppress or stop them, and some are regarded as ones to be developed, so the practitioner takes the approach of trying to go further with and develop them. These two poles represent the way that dualistic mind always works with itself. Thorough Cut practice goes beyond that duality.

Garbha, Skt. garbha, Tib. snying po: see under sugatagarbha.

Generic image, Tib. spyi don: Generic image is the technical name for one type of conceptual structure used in the operation of conceptual mind. A generic image is a concept that conceptual mind takes and uses instead of having a direct perception of the actual thing. For example, a person can have a concept of a table, a complicated operation one aspect of which is a generic image, or can have direct sight of a table, which has no operation of concept with it. Thus, for example, the process of rational, dualistic mind with its generic images can never get at something like rigpa which lies outside the reach of dualistic mind.

Grasped-grasping, Tib. gzung 'dzin: When mind is turned outwardly as it is in the normal operation of dualistic mind, it has developed two faces that appear simultaneously. Special names are given to these two faces: mind appearing in the form of the external object being referenced is called "that which is grasped at" and mind appearing in the form of the consciousness that is registering it is called the "grasper" or "grasping" of it. Thus, there is the term "grasped-grasper" or "grasped-grasping" which is a convenient abbreviation for the mode of operation of dualistic mind. Moreover, when these two terms are used, it alerts one to the fact that a Mind Only style of presentation is being discussed. This pair of terms pervades Mind Only, Middle Way, and tantric writings and is exceptionally important in all of them.

Note that one could substitute the word "apprehended" for "grasped" and "apprehender" for "grasper" or "grasping" and that would reflect one connotation of the original Sanskrit terminology. The solidified duality of grasped and grasper is nothing but an invention of dualistic thought; it has that kind of character.

Great Vehicle, Skt. mahāyāna, Tib. theg pa chen po: The Buddha's teachings as a whole can be summed up into three vehicles where a vehicle is defined as that which can carry a person to a certain destination. The first vehicle, called the Lesser Vehicle, contains the teachings designed to get an individual moving on the spiritual path through showing the unsatisfactory state of cyclic existence and an emancipation from that. However, that path is only concerned with personal emancipation and fails to take account of all of the beings that there are in existence. There used to be eighteen schools of Lesser Vehicle in India but the only one surviving nowadays is the Theravāda of south-east Asia. The Greater Vehicle is a step up from that. The Buddha explained that it was great in comparison to the Lesser Vehicle for seven reasons. The first of those is that it is concerned with attaining the truly complete enlightenment of a truly complete buddha for the sake of every sentient being where the Lesser Vehicle is concerned only with a personal liberation that is not truly complete enlightenment and which is achieved only for the sake of that practitioner. The Great Vehicle has two divisions: a conventional form in which the path is taught in a logical, conventional way, and an unconventional form in which the path is taught in a very direct way. This latter vehicle is called the Vajra Vehicle because it takes the innermost, indestructible (vajra) fact of reality of one's own mind as the vehicle to enlightenment.

Ground, Tib. gzhi: This is the first member of the formulation of ground, path, and fruition. Ground, path, and fruition is the way that the teachings of the path of oral instruction belonging to the Vajra Vehicle are presented to students. Ground refers to the basic situation as it is.

Guardian, Skt. nātha, Tib. mgon po: This name is a respectful title reserved for the buddhas and highly-developed bodhisatvas. It means that they both protect and nurture sentient beings who they oversee, like a child who, having no parents has been given or has found a guardian. It is often translated as "protector" but that correctly translates another Sanskrit term to start with and on top of that is insufficient because it does not include the aspect of nurturing. It is also given to other beings such as bodhisatvas who have a similar quality, for example, Guardian Nāgārjuna and Guardian Maitreya.

Ground and root free, Tib. gzhi rtsa bral: The terms ground and root are often combined in terms like "ground and root free", "groundless, rootless", "without ground or root" to give the fullest possible sense of there being nothing from which something is produced. Ground-free specifically means that there is no ground for supporting the production of something and root-free specifically means that there is no root from which something could grow.

Identification, Tib. ngos bzung ba: This is the technical name for a process belonging only to dualistic mind. It is the process that uses concepts to identify this and that item of consciousness and pigeon hole it so that it can be dealt with in the general perceptual process.

Ignorance: See under not-rigpa.

Illumination, Skt. vara, Tib. gsal ba: The Tibetan term is an abbreviation of the parent Tibetan term, "'od gsal ba", which is translated with luminosity *q.v.* Illumination is not another factor of mind distinct from luminosity but merely a convenient abbreviation in both Indian and Tibetan dharma language for luminosity.

In-space, Tib. klong: This term has no equivalent in English. It is used to refer to physical and mental things. In the case of physical things, it refers to the full extent of something, for example the *klong* of an ocean refers to the entirety of the ocean but in the sense of the volume of the ocean. For example, it refers to the interior space of a room where a person sitting in the room has the experience of being within the space of the room. In the case of mind, it refers to having the experience of something in the sense of being fully immersed in it. The standard example for the latter is of a parachutist who is floating down within space and who has the experience of being at the centre of a vastness that goes on and on. This term is used frequently in Great Completion and other tantras to indicate that the yogin-practitioner has gained sufficient realization that he is no longer looking at the realization from outside, but is immersed, to a greater or lesser degree in it. For example, the Tibetan term "dgongs pa'i yangs klong" is often used in Great Completion teachings to indicate the experience of immersion in the vast and un-constricted (*yangs*) interior space (*klongs*) of (*pa'i*) the realization mind of enlightenment (*dgongs*) that is had by a yogin who has reached fruition.

This term has, to date, often been translated simply as space, but that totally fails to indicate the exceptionally important meaning of this term. I am not suggesting that "in-space" is sufficient but, it is a step forward. "In-space" is, like *klong*, unique and immediately distinguishable from the many other terms that refer to one space or another—such as dhatu or space in the sense of a region or area and akasha or metaphysical space. That combined with the explanation just given enables the reader to understand the meaning involved. Thus, the sense of being immersed in the space of realization, no matter what the degree of the realization, is unmistakenly conveyed by "in-space".

Innate, Tib. gnyug ma: This is a standard term of the higher tantras used to mean the inner situation of samsaric mind, which is its in-dwelling or innate wisdom.

Introduction and To Introduce, Tib. ngos sprad and ngos sprod pa respectively: This pair of terms is usually mistakenly translated today as "pointing out" and "to point out". The terms are the standard terms used in day to day life for the situation in which one person introduces another person to someone or something. They are the exact same words as our English "introduction" and "to introduce".

In the Vajra Vehicle, these terms are specifically used for the situation in which one person introduces another person to the nature of his own mind. There is a term in Tibetan for "pointing out", but that term is never used for this purpose because in this case no one points out anything. Rather, a person is introduced by another person to a part of himself that he has forgotten about.

Kagyu, Tib. bka' brgyud: There are four main schools of Buddhism in Tibet—Nyingma, Kagyu, Sakya, and Gelug. Nyingma is the oldest school dating from about 800 C.E. Kagyu and Sakya both appeared in the 12th century C.E. Each of these three schools came directly from India. The Gelug school came later and did not come directly from India but came from the other three. The Nyingma school holds the tantric teachings called Great Completion (Dzogchen); the other three schools hold the tantric teachings called Mahāmudrā. Kagyu practitioners often join Nyingma practice with their Kagyu practice and Kagyu teachers often teach both, so it is common to hear about Kagyu and Nyingma together.

Kaya, Skt. kāya, Tib. sku: The Sanskrit term means a functional or coherent collection of parts, similar to the French "corps", and hence also comes to mean "a body". It is used in Tibetan Buddhist texts specifically to distinguish bodies belonging to the enlightened side from ones belonging to the samsaric side.

Enlightened being in Buddhism is said to be comprised of one or more kāyas. It is most commonly explained to consist of one, two, three, four, or five kāyas, though it is pointed out that there are infinite aspects to enlightened being and therefore it can also be said to consist of an infinite number of kāyas. In fact, these descriptions of enlightened being consisting of one or more kāyas are given for the sake of understanding what is beyond conceptual understanding so should not be taken as absolute statements.

The most common description of enlightened being is that it is comprised of three kāyas: dharma-, saṃbhoga-, and nirmāṇa-kāyas. Briefly stated, the dharmakāya is the body of truth, the saṃbhoga-kāya is the body replete with the good qualities of enlightenment, and the nirmāṇakāya is the body manifested into the worlds of samsara and nirvana to benefit beings.

Dharmakāya refers to that aspect of enlightened being in which the being sees the truth for himself and, in doing so, fulfils his own needs for enlightenment. The dharmakāya is purely mind, without form. The remaining two bodies are summed up under the heading of rūpakāyas or form bodies manifested specifically to fulfil the needs of all un-enlightened beings. "Saṃbhogakāya" has been mostly translated as "body of enjoyment" or "body of rapture" but it is clearly stated in Buddhist texts on the subject that the name refers to a situation replete with what is useful, that is, to the fact that the saṃbhogakāya contains all of the good qualities of enlightenment as needed to benefit sentient beings. The saṃbhogakāya is extremely subtle and not accessible by most sentient beings; the nirmāṇakāya is a coarser manifestation which can reach sentient beings in many ways. Nirmāṇakāya should not be thought of as a physical body but as the capability to express enlightened being in whatever way is needed throughout all the different worlds of sentient beings. Thus, as much as it appears as a supreme buddha who shows the dharma to beings, it also appears as anything needed within sentient beings' worlds to give them assistance.

The three kāyas of enlightened being is taught in all levels of Buddhist teaching. It is especially important in Mahāmudrā and

Great Completion and is taught there in a unique and very profound way.

Key points, Tib. gnad: Key points are those places in one's being that one works, like pressing buttons, in order to get some desired effect. For example, in meditation, there are key points of the body; by adjusting those key points, the mind is brought closer to reality and the meditation is thus assisted.

In general, this term is used in Buddhist meditation instruction but it is, in particular, part of the special vocabulary of the Great Completion teachings. Overall, the Great Completion teachings are given as a series of key points that must be attended to in order to bring forth the various realizations of the path.

Latency, Skt. vāsanā, Tib. bag chags: The original Sanskrit has the meaning exactly of "latency". The Tibetan term translates that inexactly with "something sitting there (Tib. chags) within the environment of mind (Tib. bag)". Although it has become popular to translate this term into English with "habitual pattern", that is not its meaning. The term refers to a karmic seed that has been imprinted on the mindstream and is present there as a latency, ready and waiting to come into manifestation.

Liveliness, Tib. rtsal: This is a key term in both Mahāmudrā and Great Completion. The term is sometimes translated as "display" or "expression" but neither is correct. The primary meaning is the ability of something to express itself but in use, the actual expression of that ability is also included. Thus, in English it would not be "expression" but "expressivity", but that is too dry. This term is not at all dry; it is talking about the life of something and how that life comes into expression; "liveliness" fits the meaning of the original term very well.

Luminosity or illumination, Skt. prabhāsvara, Tib. 'od gsal ba: The core of mind has two aspects: an emptiness factor and a knowing factor. The Buddha and many Indian religious teachers used "luminosity" as a metaphor for the knowing quality of the core of mind. If in English we would say "Mind has a knowing quality", the teachers of ancient India would say, "Mind has an illuminative quality; it is like a source of light which illuminates what it knows".

This term has been translated as "clear light" but that is a mistake that comes from not understanding the etymology of the word. It does not refer to a light that has the quality of clearness (something that makes no sense, actually!) but to the illuminative property which is the nature of the empty mind.

Note also that in both Sanskrit and Tibetan Buddhist literature, this term is frequently abbreviated just to Skt. "vara" and Tib. "gsal ba" with no change of meaning. Unfortunately, this has been thought to be another word and it has then been translated with "clarity", when in fact it is just this term in abbreviation.

Maha Ati, Skt. mahāti, Tib. shin tu chen po: Mahā Ati or Ati Yoga is the name of the ninth and last of the nine vehicles taught in the Nyingma system of nine vehicles. The name "ati" literally means that it is the vehicle at the end of the sequence of all other vehicles. It is not only the final vehicle at the end of the sequence but the peak of all vehicles given that it presents reality more directly than any of the vehicles below it. It is therefore also called the king of vehicles.

"Mahāsaṅdhi"—"Dzogpa Chenpo" in the Tibetan language and "Great Completion" in the English language—is the name of the teachings on reality contained in the Maha Ati vehicle and also of the reality itself. Great Completion and Maha Ati are often used interchangeably even through their references are slightly different.

Mahamudra, Skt. mahāmudrā, Tib. phyag rgya chen po: Mahāmudrā is the name of a set of ultimate teachings on reality and also of the reality itself. This is explained at length in the book *Gampopa's Mahamudra: The Five-Part Mahamudra of the Kagyus* by Tony Duff, published by Padma Karpo Translation Committee, 2008, ISBN 978-9937-2-0607-5.

Manufacture and contrivance, Tib. bzos bcos: A pair of terms that work together to give the full meaning of leaving something just as it is. The first term of the pair, "manufacture", means to create something new that was not already there. The second, "contrivance", which could also be translated as "alteration" or "modification", means to make a modification in order to correct something that is already there and in doing so to make it artificial.

Meeting and parting, Tib. 'du bral. This is usually seen in the phrase "without meeting and parting" which means without change of degree of occurrence. For instance, in Mahāmudrā and Great Completion, it is used in reference to the ground situation where it indicates that innate wisdom, etcetera, is not sometimes with and sometimes without the good qualities of the ground. It is also used in reference to the path situation to indicate that a practitioner has gone past the training stage in which sometimes he was connected with and sometimes disconnected from wisdom. However, it is not restricted to discussions of wisdom but can be used in regard to anything.

Migrator, Tib. 'gro ba: Migrator is one of several terms that were commonly used by the Buddha to mean "sentient being". It shows sentient beings from the perspective of their constantly being forced to go here and there from one rebirth to another by the power of karma. They are like flies caught in a jar, constantly buzzing back and forth. The term is often translated using "beings" which is another general term for sentient beings, but doing so loses the meaning entirely. Buddhist authors who know the tradition do not use the word loosely but use it specifically to give the sense of beings who are constantly and helplessly going from one birth to another, and that is how the term should be read. The term "six migrators" refers to the six types of migrators within samsaric existence—hell-beings, pretas, animals, humans, demi-gods, and gods.

Mind, Skt. chitta, Tib. sems: There are several terms for mind in the Buddhist tradition, each with its own, specific meaning. This term is the most general term for the samsaric type of mind. It refers to the type of mind that is produced because of fundamental ignorance of enlightened mind. Whereas the wisdom of enlightened mind lacks all complexity and knows in a non-dualistic way, this mind of un-enlightenment is a very complicated apparatus that only ever knows in a dualistic way.

The Mahāmudrā and Great Completion teachings use the terms "entity of mind" and "mind's entity" to refer to what this complicated, samsaric mind is at core—the enlightened form of mind.

Mindness, Skt. chittatā, Tib. sems nyid: Mindness is a specific term of the tantras. It is one of many terms meaning the essence of mind or the nature of mind. It conveys the sense of "what mind is at its very core". It has sometimes been translated as "mind itself" but that is a misunderstanding of the Tibetan word "nyid". The term does not mean "that thing mind" where mind refers to dualistic mind. Rather, it means the very core of dualistic mind, what mind is at root, without all of the dualistic baggage.

Mindness is a path term. It refers to exactly the same thing as "actuality" or "actuality of mind" which is a ground term but does so from the practitioner's perspective. It conveys the sense to a practitioner that he has baggage of dualistic mind that has not yet been purified but that there is a core to that mind that he can work with.

Nature Great Completion, Tib. rang bzhin rdzogs pa chen po: This is one of several names for Great Completion that emphasizes the path aspect of Great Completion. It is not "natural great completion" nor is it "the true nature Great Completion" as commonly seen. In terms of grammar, the first term is the noun "nature" not the adjective "natural". In terms of meaning, the noun nature is used because it refers to the nature aspect in particular of the three characteristics of the essence of mind—entity, nature, and unstopped compassionate activity—used to describe Great Completion as experienced by the practitioner. Thus, this name refers to the approach taken by Great Completion and does not refer at all to Great Completion being a "natural" practice or its being connected with a "natural reality" or any of the many other, incorrect meanings that arise from the mistaken translation "natural Great Completion".

Noble one, Skt. ārya, Tib. 'phags pa: In Buddhism, a noble one is a being who has become spiritually advanced to the point that he has passed beyond cyclic existence. According to the Buddha, the beings in cyclic existence were ordinary beings, spiritual commoners, and the beings who had passed beyond it were special, the nobility.

Non-stop, Tib. 'gags pa med pa: An important path term in the teaching of both Mahāmudrā and Great Completion. There are two ways to explain this term: according to view and to practice. The following explanation is of the latter type. The core of mind has two parts—emptiness and luminosity—which are in fact unified so must come that way in practice. However, a practitioner who is still on the path will fall into one extreme or the other and that results in a stoppage of the expression of the luminosity. When emptiness and luminosity are unified in practice, there is no stoppage of the expression of the luminosity that comes from having fallen into one extreme or the other. Thus "non-stop luminosity" is a term that indicates that there is the luminosity with all of its appearance yet that luminosity, for the practitioner, is not mistaken, is not stopped off. "Stopped luminosity" is an experience like luminosity but in which the appearances have, at least to some extent, not been mixed with emptiness.

Not-rigpa, Skt. avidya, Tib. ma rig pa: Rigpa *q.v.* is a key term in these discussions. It refers to the enlightened kind of knowing. Its opposite, not-rigpa, which refers to the unenlightened way of knowing, is equally important. As it says in the *Abhidharmakoṣha*, "not-rigpa is not merely a discordance with rigpa but is its very opposite". Not-rigpa is usually translated as ignorance but this masks the all-important opposing relationship between rigpa and not-rigpa. Therefore, in this book, this term is usually translated as "not-rigpa" rather than "ignorance".

Output, Tib. gdangs: Output is a general term for that which is given off by something, for example, the sound that comes from a loudspeaker. In Mahāmudrā and Great Completion, it refers to what is given off by the emptiness factor that is the very entity of mind. Emptiness is the empty condition, like space, that is also referred to as the entity of mind. However, that emptiness has liveliness which comes off the emptiness as compassion and all the other qualities of enlightened mind, and, equally, all the apparatus of dualistic mind. All of this is called its output. All of this is called its output.

Note that the Great Completion teachings have a special word that is a more refined version of this term (Tib. mdangs); see under lustre for that.

Own Appearance, Tib. rang snang: This is regarded as one of the more difficult terms to explain within Buddhist philosophy. It does not mean "self-appearance" in the sense of something coming into appearance of itself. Suffice it to say that it refers to a situation that is making its own appearances in accord with its own situation.

Post-attainment, Tib. rjes thob: See under equipoise and post-attainment.

Prajna, Skt. prajñā, Tib. shes rab: The Sanskrit term, literally meaning "best type of mind" is defined as that which makes correct distinctions between this and that and hence which arrives at correct understanding. It has been translated as "wisdom" but that is not correct because it is, generally speaking, a mental event belonging to dualistic mind where "wisdom" is used to refer to the non-dualistic knower of a buddha. Moreover, the main feature of prajñā is its ability to distinguish correctly between one thing and another and hence to arrive at a correct understanding.

Preserve, Tib. skyong ba: This term is important in both Mahāmudrā and Great Completion. In general, it means to defend, protect, nurture, maintain. In the higher tantras it means to keep something just as it is, to nurture that something so that it stays and is not lost. Also, in the higher tantras, it is often used in reference to preserving the state where the state is some particular state of being. Because of this, the phrase "preserve the state" is an important instruction in the higher tantras.

Primal Guardian, Skt. ādinātha, Tib. gdod ma'i mgon po: Primal Guardian is one of many names for the *primal* state of enlightenment innate to each person personified as the *guardian* who in Nyingma tradition is Samantabhadra and in new translation schools is Great Vajradhara.

Proliferation, Tib. 'phro ba: A term meaning that the dualistic mind has become active and is giving off thoughts. This is actually the same word as "elaboration" but is the intransitive sense.

Provisional and definitive meaning, Skt. neyartha and nitartha, Tib. drangs don and nges don: This is a pair of terms used to distinguish which is an ultimate or final teaching and which is not. A teaching which guides a student along to a certain understanding where the understanding led to is not an ultimate understanding is called "provisional meaning". The teaching is not false even though it does not show the final meaning; it is a technique of skilful means used to lead a student in steps to the final meaning. A teaching which shows a student the final meaning directly is called "definitive meaning". The understanding presented cannot be refined or shown in a more precise way; it is the final and actual understanding to be understood. These terms are most often used in Buddhism when discussing the status of the three turnings of the wheel of dharma.

Rational mind, Tib. blo: Rational mind is one of several terms for mind in Buddhist terminology. It specifically refers to a mind that judges this against that. It is mainly used to refer to samsaric mind, given that samsaric mind only works in the dualistic mode of comparing this versus that. Because of this, the term is mainly used in a pejorative sense to point out samsaric mind as opposed to a non-dualistic enlightened type of mind. However, it is occasionally used to refer to the discriminating wisdom aspect of non-dualistic mind, for example, in the case of a buddha. In that case it is a mind making distinctions between this and that but within the context of non-dualistic wisdom.

This term has been commonly translated simply as "mind" but that fails to identify it properly and leaves it confused with the many other words that are also translated simply as "mind". It is not just another mind but is specifically the sort of mind that creates the situation of this and that (*ratio* in Latin). Therefore, the term "rational mind" fits perfectly. This is a key term which must be understood as a specific term with a specific meaning and should not be just glossed over as "mind".

Realization, Tib. rtogs pa: Realization has a very specific meaning: it refers to correct knowledge that has been gained in such a way that the knowledge does not abate. There are two important points here. Firstly, realization is not absolute. It refers to the removal of obscurations, one at a time. Each time that a practitioner removes an obscuration, he gains a realization because of it. Therefore, there are as many levels of realization as there are obscurations. Maitreya, in the *Ornament of Manifest Realizations*, shows how the removal of the various obscurations that go with each of the three realms of samsaric existence produces realization.

Secondly, realization is stable or, as the Tibetan wording says, "unchanging". As Guru Rinpoche pointed out, "Intellectual knowledge is like a patch, it drops away; experiences on the path are temporary, they evaporate like mist; realization is unchanging".

A special usage of "realization" is found in the Essence Mahāmudrā and Great Completion teachings. There, realization is the term used to describe what happens at the moment when mindness is actually met during either introduction to or self-recognition of mindness. It is called realization because, in that glimpse, one actually directly sees the innate wisdom mind. The realization has not been stabilized but it is realization.

Reference and Referencing, Tib. dmigs pa: Referencing is the name for the process in which dualistic mind references an actual object by using a conceptual label instead of the actual object. Whatever is referenced is then called a reference. Note that these terms imply the presence of dualistic mind and their opposites, non-referencing and being without reference, imply the presence of non-dualistic wisdom.

Rigpa, Tib. rig pa: This is the singularly most important term in the whole of Great Completion and Mahāmudrā. In particular, it is the key word of all words in the Great Completion system of Thorough Cut. Rigpa literally means to know in the sense of "I see!" It is used at all levels of meaning from the coarsest everyday sense of knowing something to the deepest sense of knowing something as presented in the system of Thorough Cut. The system of Thorough Cut uses this term in a very special sense, though it still retains its basic meaning of "to know". To translate it as "awareness", which is common practice today, is a poor practice; there are many kinds of awareness but there is only one rigpa and besides, rigpa is substantially more than just awareness. Since this is such an important term and since it lacks an equivalent in English, I choose not to translate it.

This is the term used to indicate enlightened mind as experienced by the practitioner on the path of these practices. The term itself specifically refers to the dynamic knowing quality of mind. It absolutely does not mean a simple registering, as implied by the word "awareness" which unfortunately is often used to translate this term. There is no word in English that exactly matches it, though the idea of "seeing" or "insight on the spot" is very close. Proof of this is found in the fact that the original Sanskrit term "vidyā" is actually the root of all words in English that start with "vid" and mean "to see", for example, "video", "vision", and so on. Chogyam Trungpa Rinpoche, who was particularly skilled at getting Tibetan words into English, also stated that this term rigpa really did not have a good equivalent in English, though he thought that "insight" was the closest. My own conclusion after hearing extensive teaching on it is that rigpa is best left untranslated. Note that rigpa has both noun and verb forms.

Ríshí, Skt. ṛiṣhi, Tib. drang srong: A rishi is a holy man. The Sanskrit itself means one who has a sufficient level of spiritual accomplishment and knowledge to bring others along the path of spirituality properly. It was a common appellation in ancient India where there were many rishis. The Buddha was often referred to as "the rishi" meaning the rishi of all rishis or as the "great ṛiṣhi" meaning the greatest of all ṛiṣhis.

Samsara, Skt. saṃsāra, Tib. 'khor ba: This is the most general name for the type of existence in which sentient beings live. It refers to the fact that they continue on from one existence to another, always within the enclosure of births that are produced by ignorance and experienced as unsatisfactory. The original Sanskrit means to be constantly going about, here and there. The Tibetan term literally means "cycling", because of which it is frequently translated into English with "cyclic existence" though that is not exactly the meaning of the original Sanskrit term.

Satva and sattva: According to the Tibetan tradition established at the time of the great translation work done at Samye under the watch of Padmasambhava not to mention one hundred and sixty-three of the greatest Buddhist scholars of Sanskrit-speaking India, there is a difference of meaning between the Sanskrit terms "satva" and "sattva", with satva meaning "an heroic kind of being" and "sattva" meaning simply "a being". According to the Tibetan tradition established under the advice of the Indian scholars mentioned above, satva is correct for the words Vajrasatva and bodhisatva, whereas sattva is correct for the words samayasattva, samādhisattva, jñānasattva, and mahāsattva and is also used alone to refer to any or all of these three sattvas.

All Tibetan texts produced since the time of the great translations conform to this system and all Tibetan experts agree that this is correct, but Western translators of Tibetan texts have for the last few hundred years claimed that they know better and have changed "satva" to "sattva" in every case, causing confusion amongst Westerners confronted by the correct spellings. Recently, publications by Western Sanskrit scholars have been appearing in which it is admitted that the Tibetan system is and always has been correct.

Secret Mantra, Skt. guhyamantra, Tib. gsang sngags: Another name for the Vajra Vehicle or the tantric teachings.

Self-arising wisdom, Tib. rang byung ye shes: The words "self-arising" are added to wisdom *q.v.* to indicate that it is not caused, that it is outside the samsaric process of cause and effect. As the vidyādhara Chogyam Trungpa said, it is self-existing.

Seven Dharmas of Vairochana, Tib. rnam par snang mdzad chos bdun: These are the seven aspects of Vairochana's posture, the posture used for formal meditation practice. The posture for the legs is the one called "vajra posture" or vajrāsana. In it, the legs are crossed one on top of the other, right on top of left. The advantage of this posture is that, of the five basic winds of the subtle body, the Downward-Clearing Wind is caused to enter the central channel. The posture for the hands is called the equipoise mudrā. The right palm is placed on top of the left palm and the two thumbs are just touching, raised up over the palms. The advantage of this posture is that the Fire-Accompanying Wind is caused to enter the central channel. The posture for the spine is that the spine should be held straight. The advantage of this posture is that the Pervader Wind is caused to enter the central channel. The posture for the shoulders is one in which the shoulders are held up slightly in a particular way. The advantage of this posture is that Upward-Moving Wind is caused to enter the central channel. The neck and chin are held in a particular posture: the neck is drawn up a little and the chin slightly hooked in towards the throat. The advantage of this posture is that the Life-Holder Wind is caused to enter the central channel. The tip of the tongue is joined with the forward part of the palate and the jaws are relaxed, with the teeth and lips allowed to sit normally. The eyes are directed down past the tip of the nose, into space. Placing the gaze in this way keeps the clarity of mind and prevents sinking, agitation, and so on.

Shamatha, Skt. śhamatha, Tib. gzhi gnas: This is the name of one of the two main practices of meditation used in the Buddhist system to gain insight into reality. This practice creates a one-pointedness of mind which can then be used as a foundation for development of the insight of the other practice, vipaśhyanā. If the development of śhamatha is taken through to completion, the result is a mind that sits stably on its object without any effort and a body which is filled with ease. Altogether, this result of the practice is called "the creation of workability of body and mind".

Shifting events, Tib. yo lang: This refers to the events of a practitioner's life being seen as the shifting events of the dharmakāya. The dharmakāya has an outpouring of display which comes out not as a nice, rationally-ordered experience but as the random and higgledy-piggledy events experienced by the practitioner of that state.

Shiftless, Tib. 'pho ba med pa: Shiftless is in reference to a buddha's wisdom. It means that the wisdom does not shift from being itself to being samsaric mind. For example, the common phrase "without shift into the three times" means "without shift from non-dual wisdom into the dualistic mind of samsara which operates within the context of there being past, present, and future.

Shine forth, shining forth, Tib. shar ba: This term means "to dawn" or "to come forth into visibility" either in the outer physical world or in the inner world of mind.

It is heavily used in texts on meditation to indicate the process of something coming forth into mind. There are other terms with this specific meaning but most of them also imply the process of dawning within a samsaric mind. "Shine forth" is special because it does not have that restricted meaning; it refers to the process of something dawning in any type of mind, un-enlightened and enlightened. It is an important term for the higher tantras of Mahāmudrā and Great Completion where there is a great need to refer to the simple fact of something dawning in mind especially in enlightened mind but also in un-enlightened mind.

In the Tibetan language, this term stands out and immediately conveys the meaning explained above. There are words in English like "to appear" that might seem easier to read than "shine forth", but they do not stand out and catch the attention sufficiently. Moreover, terms such as "appear" accurately translate other Tibetan terms which specifically indicate an un-enlightened context or a certain type of sensory appearance, so they do not convey the meaning of this term. There will be many times where this term's specific meaning of something occurring in any type of mind is crucial to a full understanding of the expression under consideration. For example, "shining-forth liberation" means that some content of mind, such as a thought, comes forth in either un-enlightened or enlightened mind, and that, on coming forth, is liberated there in that mind.

Solidification, Tib. a 'thas: This term could also be translated as "concretization". It is a very strong term that has the full weight of "the deep stupidity of ignorance which solidifies empty actuality into concrete existence". This is how samsaric mind operates. It does not merely live in dualistic ways of knowing but solidifies all of what it knows into the perception of a very concrete existence.

Spontaneous existence, Tib. lhun grub: Spontaneous existence is a key term in Essence Mahamudra and Nyingthig Great Completion. The term "grub" refers to something coming into existence. The term "lhun" means that it is happening spontaneously, though note that spontaneous here has the specific meaning of being without karmic cause and effect. Thus, spontaneous existence in these teachings has two, equally important connotations: presence as opposed to absence and a type of existence occurring of itself, outside the process of karmic cause and effect.

State, Tib. ngang: This is a key term in Mahāmudrā and Great Completion. Unfortunately it is often not translated and in so doing much meaning is lost. Alternatively, it is often translated as "within" which is incorrect. The term means a "state". A state is a certain, ongoing situation. In Buddhist meditation in general, there are various states that a practitioner has to enter and remain in as part of developing the meditation.

Sugata, Tib. bde bar gshegs pa: This term is one of many names for a buddha. It has the twofold meaning of someone who has gone on a good, pleasant, easy journey and someone who has arrived at a place which is good, pleasant, and full of ease. The meaning in relation to buddhahood is explained at length in *Unending Auspiciousness, the Sutra of the Recollection of the Noble Three Jewels* by Tony Duff, published by Padma Karpo Translation Committee, 2010, ISBN: 978-9937-8386-1-0.

Sugatagarbha, Tib. bde bar gshegs pa'i snying po: This is one of a pair of terms for the potential existing in all sentient beings that makes the attainment of buddhahood possible, also called the buddha-nature. The other term is tathāgatagarbha. The Sanskrit term "garbha" primarily means something which is potent but contained in an outer shell, like a seed, and is also used to mean a matrix or womb from which something can be produced. Both meanings are applicable. Tibetans translated garbha with "snying po" which has many meanings but in this case means "an essence or core", which was their take on the meaning of buddha-nature. The meaning altogether is a seed contained within the obscurations of samsaric being, which makes it possible to become a sugata or tathāgatha, that is, a buddha.

Sugatagarbha has the same basic meaning as tathāgatagarbha but is a practical way of talking where tathāgatagarbha is theoretical. Sugatagarbha is used when an author is talking about the practical realities of an essence that can be or is being developed into enlightened being. For example, in the sutras of the third turning of the wheel, the Buddha speaks of tathāgatagarbha when laying out the theory of buddha-nature but switches to sugatagarbha when speaking of wisdom as what is to be actually attained. Similarly, the tantras, which are mainly concerned with the practical attainment of wisdom use the term sugatagarbha and rarely use the term tathāgatagarbha. See also under sugata.

Superfactual, Skt. paramārtha,Tib. don dam: This term is paired with the term "fictional" *q.v.* In the past, the two terms have been translated as "relative" and "absolute", but those translations are nothing like the original terms. These terms are extremely important in the Buddhist teaching so it is very important that their translations be corrected but, more than that, if the actual meaning of these terms is not presented, the teaching connected with them cannot be understood.

The Sanskrit term paramārtha literally means "the fact for that which is above all others, special, superior" and refers to what is known to the wisdom mind possessed by those who have developed themselves spiritually to the point of having transcended samsara. That wisdom is *superior* to an ordinary, un-developed person's consciousness and the *facts* that appear on its surface are superior compared to the fictions that appear on the ordinary person's consciousness. Therefore, it is superfact or, more colloquially, the highest thing that could be known. What this wisdom knows is true for the beings who have it, therefore what the wisdom sees is superfactual truth.

Superfactual truth, Skt. paramārthasatya, Tib. don dam bden pa: See under superfactual.

Superfice, superficies, Tib. rnam pa: In discussions of mind, a distinction is made between the entity of mind which is a mere knower and the superficial things that appear on its surface and which are known by it. In other words, the superficies are the various things which pass over the surface of mind but which are not mind. Superficies are all the specifics that constitute appearance—for example, the colour white within a moment of visual consciousness, the sound heard within an ear consciousness, and so on.

Six-fold group, Tib. tshogs drug. "Tshogs" means a group, a single collection, and, because of the Sanskrit original, can also simply be a plural-making particle in English. "Tshogs drug" means the six different consciousnesses, taken as a group, of beings in this human realm. There is a second description of the consciousnesses given by the Buddha in which he explains eight consciousnesses, and these taken as one group are correspondingly called "the eight-fold group".

Tathagatagarbha, Skt. tathāgatagarbha, Tib. de bzhin gshegs pa'i snying po: This means the garbha or seed of a tathāgata; see under sugatagarbha.

The authentic, Tib. yang dag: This is a term commonly used in the sūtras as a synonym for reality. For example "view of the authentic" means "view of reality". The sutras also often have the Sanskrit term "bhūtakoṭi" literally meaning "limit of the authentic" referring to the final or utmost reality, that is, nirvana.

The element, Skt. dhātu, Tib. khams. The Sanskrit term has many meanings; the meaning here is "a fundamental substance from which something else can be produced". When the Buddha explained the tathāgatagarbha or buddha nature in the third turning of the wheel, he used several names for it, each one showing a specific aspect of it. He called it the element with the meaning "that basis substance from which buddhahood can be produced". He called it "the type" meaning that it was the same sort of thing as buddhahood and therefore could lead to buddhahood; this term is also translated as "family" and "lineage". He also called it "the seed" meaning the seed of enlightenment. He also called it "the garbha"; see under sugatagarbha for the meaning.

The nature, Tib. rang bzhin: The nature is one of the three characteristics—entity, nature, and un-stopped compassionate activity—of the core of mind. Using this term emphasizes that the empty entity does have a nature. In other words, its use explicitly shows that the core of mind is not merely empty. If you ask "Well, what is that nature like?" The answer is that it is luminosity, it is wisdom.

Third order thousandfold world system, Tib. stong gsum 'jig rten: Indian cosmology has for its smallest cosmic unit a single Mt. Meru with four continents type of world system; an analogy might be a single planetary system like our solar system. One thousand of those makes a first order thousandfold world system; an analogy might be a galaxy. One thousand of those makes a second order thousandfold world system; an analogy might be a region of space with many galaxies. One thousand of those makes a third order thousandfold world system (1000 raised to the power 3); an analogy would be one whole universe like ours. The Buddha said that there were countless numbers of third order thousandfold world systems, each of which would be roughly equivalent to a universe like ours.

Thorough Cut, Tib. khregs chod: The extra-secret level of Great Completion has two main practices, the first called Thregcho which literally translates as Thorough Cut and the second called Thogal which translates as Direct Crossing. The meaning of Thorough Cut has been misunderstood. The meaning is clearly explained in the *Illuminator Tibetan-English Dictionary*:

> Thorough Cut is a practice that slices through the solidification produced by rational mind as it grasps at a perceived object and perceiving subject. It is done in order to get to the underlying reality which is always present in the core of mind and which is called Alpha Purity in this system of teachings. For this reason, Thorough Cut is also known as Alpha Purity Thorough Cut.

Three kayas: See under kāya.

Tirthika, Skt. tīrthika, Tib. mu stegs pa: This is a very kind name adopted by the Buddha for those who did not follow him but who, because they followed some other spiritual path, had at least arrived at the brink of the true path back to enlightenment. The Sanskrit name means "those who have arrived at the steps at the edge of the pool" and comes to mean those on the brink of actually crossing the river of samsara. A lengthy explanation is given in the *Illuminator Tibetan-English Dictionary* by Tony Duff and published by Padma Karpo Translation Committee.

Vajra Vehicle, Skt. vajrayāna, Tib. rdo rje'i theg pa: See under Great Vehicle.

View, meditation, and conduct, Tib. lta sgom spyod: This set of three is a formulation of the teachings that contains all of the meaning of the path.

Vipashyana, Skt. vipaśhyanā, Tib. lhag mthong: This is the Sanskrit name for one of the two main practices of meditation needed in the

Buddhist system for gaining insight into reality. The other one, shamatha, keeps the mind focussed while this one looks piercingly into the nature of things.

Wisdom, Skt. jñāna, Tib. ye shes: This is a fruition term that refers to the kind of mind—the kind of knower—possessed by a buddha. Sentient beings do have this kind of knower but it is covered over by a very complex apparatus for knowing, that is, dualistic mind. If they practise the path to buddhahood, they will leave behind their obscuration and return to having this kind of knower.

The Sanskrit term has the sense of knowing in the most simple and immediate way. This sort of knowing is present at the core of every being's mind. Therefore, the Tibetans called it "the particular type of awareness which is there primordially". Because of the Tibetan wording it has often been called "primordial wisdom" in English translations, but that goes too far; it is just "wisdom" in the sense of the most fundamental knowing possible.

Wisdom does not operate in the same way as samsaric mind; it comes about in and of itself without depending on cause and effect. Therefore it is frequently referred to as "self-arising wisdom" *q.v.*

About the Author, Padma Karpo Translation Committee, And Their Supports for Study

I have been encouraged over the years by all of my teachers to pass on the knowledge I have accumulated in a lifetime dedicated to study and practice, primarily in the Tibetan tradition of Buddhism. On the one hand, they have encouraged me to teach. On the other, they are concerned that, while many general books on Buddhism have been and are being published, there are few books that present the actual texts of the tradition. Therefore they, together with a number of major figures in the Buddhist book publishing world, have also encouraged me to translate and publish high quality translations of individual texts of the tradition.

My teachers always remark with great appreciation on the extraordinary amount of teaching that I have heard in this life. It allows for highly informed, accurate translations of a sort not usually seen. Briefly, I spent the 1970's studying, practising, then teaching the Gelugpa system at Chenrezig Institute, Australia, where I was a founding member and also the first Australian to be ordained as a monk in the Tibetan Buddhist tradition. In 1980, I moved to the United States to study at the feet of the Vidyadhara Chogyam Trungpa Rinpoche. I stayed in his Vajradhatu community, now called Shambhala, where I studied and practised all the Karma Kagyu, Nyingma, and Shambhala teachings being presented there and was a senior member of the Nalanda Translation Committee. After the vidyadhara's nirvana, I moved in 1992 to Nepal, where I have been continuously involved with the study, practise, translation, and teaching of the Kagyu system and especially of the Nyingma system of Great Completion. In recent years, I have spent extended times in Tibet with the greatest living Tibetan masters of Great Completion, receiving very pure transmissions of the ultimate levels of this teaching directly in Tibetan and practising them there in retreat. In that way, I have studied and practised extensively not in one Tibetan tradition as is usually done, but in three of the four Tibetan traditions—Gelug, Kagyu, and Nyingma—and also in the Theravada tradition, too.

With that as a basis, I have taken a comprehensive and long term approach to the work of translation. For any language, one first must have the lettering needed to write the language. Therefore, as a member of the Nalanda Translation Committee, I spent some years in the 1980's making Tibetan word-processing software and high-quality Tibetan fonts. After that, reliable lexical works are needed. Therefore, during the 1990's I spent some years writing the *Illuminator Tibetan-English Dictionary* and a set of treatises on Tibetan grammar, preparing a variety of key Tibetan reference works needed for the study and translation of Tibetan Buddhist texts, and giving our Tibetan software the tools needed to translate and research Tibetan texts. During this time, I also translated full-time for various Tibetan gurus and ran the Drukpa Kagyu Heritage Project—at the time the largest project in Asia for the preservation of Tibetan Buddhist texts. With the dictionaries, grammar texts, and specialized software in place, and a wealth of knowledge, I turned my attention in the year 2000 to the translation and publication of important texts of Tibetan Buddhist literature.

Padma Karpo Translation Committee (PKTC) was set up to provide a home for the translation and publication work. The committee focusses on producing books containing the best of Tibetan literature, and, especially, books that meet the needs of practitioners. At the time of writing, PKTC has published a wide range of books that, collectively, make a complete program of study for those practising Tibetan Buddhism, and especially for those interested in the higher tantras. All in all, you will find many books both free and for sale on the PKTC web-site. Most are available both as paper editions and e-books.

It would take up too much space here to present an extensive guide to our books and how they can be used as the basis for a study program. However, a guide of that sort is available on the PKTC web-site, whose address is on the copyright page of this book and we recommend that you read it to see how this book fits into the overall scheme of PKTC publications. In short, the author of the texts presented in this book is one of the important figures in the transmission of the Quintessence Great Completion teachings in Tibet; the importance of his texts for those studying the Thorough Cut aspect of that teaching has been explained in the introduction. We have published many texts on the Thorough Cut teaching, each one carefully selected for its particular treatment of the subject.

When studying the Thorough Cut teaching, our books on the Three Lines teaching originally from Garab Dorje will be essential reading:

The Feature of the Expert, Glorious King by Dza Patrul
About the Three Lines by Dodrupchen III
Relics of the Dharmakaya by Ontrul Tenpa'i Wangchug

And the following books that deal with Thorough Cut will add further ornamentation:

Empowerment and AtiYoga by Tony Duff
Peak Doorways to Emancipation by Shakya Shri
Alchemy of Accomplishment by Dudjom Rinpoche
The Way of the Realized Old Dogs by Ju Mipham
The Method of Preserving the Face of Rigpa by Ju Mipham
Essential Points of Practice by Zhechen Gyaltshab
Words of the Old Dog Vijay by Zhechen Gyaltshab
Hinting at Dzogchen by Tony Duff

When studying Direct Crossing, these books will be helpful:

> *Key Points of Direct Crossing called Nectar of the Pure Part* by Khenchen Padma Namgyal
>
> Jigmey Lingpa's most important text *Guidebook called "Highest Wisdom" (Triyig Yeshe Lama)*

We make a point of including, where possible, the relevant Tibetan texts in Tibetan script in our books. We also make them available in digital editions that can be downloaded free from our web-site, as discussed below. The Tibetan texts for this book are included at the back of the book. Digital Tibetan texts of all the texts in this book are available for download from the PKTC web-site.

Electronic Resources

PKTC has developed a complete range of electronic tools to facilitate the study and translation of Tibetan texts. For many years now, this software has been a prime resource for Tibetan Buddhist centres throughout the world, including in Tibet itself. It is available through the PKTC web-site.

The wordprocessor TibetDoc has the only complete set of tools for creating, correcting, and formatting Tibetan text according to the norms of the Tibetan language. It can also be used to make texts with mixed Tibetan and English or other languages. Extremely high quality Tibetan fonts, based on the forms of Tibetan calligraphy learned from old masters from pre-Communist Chinese Tibet, are also available. Because of their excellence, these typefaces have achieved a legendary status amongst Tibetans.

TibetDoc is used to prepare electronic editions of Tibetan texts in the PKTC text input office in Asia. Tibetan texts are often corrupt so the input texts are carefully corrected prior to distribution. After that, they are made available through the PKTC web-site. These electronic texts are not careless productions like so many of the Tibetan texts found on the web, but are highly reliable editions useful to non-scholars and scholars alike. Some of the larger collections of these texts are for purchase, but most are available for free download.

The electronic texts can be read, searched, and even made into an electronic library using either TibetDoc or our other software, TibetD Reader. Like TibetDoc, TibetD Reader is advanced software with many capabilities made specifically to meet the needs of reading and researching Tibetan texts. PKTC software is for purchase but we make a free version of TibetD Reader available for free download on the PKTC web-site.

A key feature of TibetDoc and Tibet Reader is that Tibetan terms in texts can be looked up on the spot using PKTC's electronic dictionaries. PKTC also has several electronic dictionaries—some Tibetan-Tibetan and some Tibetan-English—and a number of other reference works. The *Illuminator Tibetan-English Dictionary* is renowned for its completeness and accuracy.

This combination of software, texts, reference works, and dictionaries that work together seamlessly has become famous over the years. It has been the basis of many, large publishing projects within the Tibetan Buddhist community around the world for over thirty years and is popular amongst all those needing to work with Tibetan language or deepen their understanding of Buddhism through Tibetan texts.

TIBETAN TEXTS

༄༅། །ཐེག་མཆོག་ཨ་ཏིའི་མན་ངག་གནས་ལུགས་གསལ་སྟོན་བཞུགས་སོ།།

༄༅། །བླ་མ་དམ་པ་རྣམས་ལ་ཕྱག་འཚལ་ལོ། །གང་ཟག་དབང་པོ་རབ་འབྲིང་ཐ་མའི་རིམ་པ་གསུམ་སོ་སོ་བས་རང་བཞིན་རྫོགས་པ་ཆེན་པོའི་གནས་ལུགས་སྐྱོང་ཚུལ་ནི། དང་པོ་སེམས་འཚོལ་གྱི་རིམ་པས་གདར་ཤ་ལེགས་པར་བཅད་ཅིང་བརྗོད་མེད་ཀྱི་དོན་དོ་ལེགས་པར་འཕྲོད་པ་གཞིར་བཞག་ནས། སྐྱོང་ཚུལ་དངོས་ནི། དབང་པོ་རབ་ཀྱིས་སེམས་ཁོ་རང་གནས་རུང་སེམས་ཡིན། འགྱུ་རུང་སེམས་ཡིན། སེམས་སྟོང་པར་ཐག་ཆོད་ཕྱིན་ཆད་ནས། གནས་འགྱུ་གཉིས་ལ་ཁྱད་པར་ཅི་ཡང་མེད་པས། རྣམ་རྟོག་གང་ཤར་གང་སྣང་ཐམས་ཅད་ཡེ་ཤེས་ཀྱི་རོལ་པ་རྒྱལ་བའི་དགོངས་པ་ཟབ་མོ་སྟོང་པ་ཉིད་ཡིན། དེ་ལ་བཅོས་སླད་གང་ཡང་མ་བྱེད་པར་དེ་ཁའི་ངང་ལ་ཞོག །གནས་སྐབས་སུ་རྣམ་རྟོག་རང་གཱ་མར་འདུག་ནའང་། ངང་རམ་ཤུགས་ཀྱིས་གྲོལ་ཡོད་ལས་ཏིང་འཛིན་པོ་ན་ཡིན། ཆོས་སྐུ་ཡིན། རང་བྱུང་གི་ཡེ་ཤེས་ཡིན། ཕྱག་རྒྱ་ཆེན་པོ་ཡིན། ཤེས་རབ་ཀྱི་ཕ་རོལ་ཏུ་ཕྱིན་པ་ཡིན། དཔེ་ཐག་པ་མེས་ཀྱིག་པ་དར་འདྲ། དེས་འཆིང་མི་ནུས། ཁོ་རང་གི་ངོ་བོ་སྟོང་པ་ཡིན། རྣམ་རྟོག་ལྟར་སྣང་བ་དེ་སྟོང་པའི་གདངས་ཤར་བ་ཡིན། རྣམ་རྟོག་དང་

སྟོང་པ་ལ་ཁྱད་པར་མི་འདུག་པས། ཨོ་རྒྱན་ཆེན་པོས། རྣམ་རྟོག་ངོ་བོ་སྟོང་པས་
ཆོས་སྐུར་གོ །ཞེས་གསུངས། སྒོམ་ན་བློ་ཡིན་པས་བསྒོམ་རྒྱུ་ཅི་ཡང་མེད།
རྣམ་རྟོག་རང་གམར་ཞོག །དེ་ལ་བཅས་བཅོས་བྱས་ན། རྣམ་རྟོག་རང་རྒྱུད་པ་
འཁྲུལ་པ་ལུ་གུ་རྒྱུད་ཡིན་པས་བཅས་བཅོས་གང་ཡང་མི་བྱ། རང་ཐོག་ཏུ་འཛོག་དེ་
ལས་ཡེངས་ན་འཁྲུལ་པ་དངོས་ཡིན་པས་མ་ཡེངས་པ་དགོས་ཏེ་དེ་གཅིག་པུས་
ཆོག །དམིགས་པ་གང་ལ་ཡང་མ་གཏད་ཅིང་མ་ཡེངས་པ་གཅིག་གོ །རྫོགས་
ཆེན་གུ་རུ་ཞི་བ་ལས། སྒོམ་མ་སྒོམ་དང་འབྲལ་མ་སྒོམ་། མི་སྒོམ་དོན་དང་མི་
འབྲལ་བ། །ཞེས་པ་གང་ཤར་སྒོམ་ཡིན་པས་ན་བློས་བཅོས་པའི་སྒོམ་རྒྱུ་མེད་པས་
སྒོམ་མ་སྒོམ་། ཡེ་ནས་དོན་མེད་འཆལ་བ་མིན་པས་རང་ཐོག་ཏུ་འཛོག་པ་དེ་དང་
འབྲལ་མ་སྒོམ་། མི་སྒོམ་དོན་དེ་ལྟ་བུ་དང་རྒྱུན་དུ་མི་འབྲལ་བར་གྱིས་ཞེས་པའི་དོན་
ནོ། འདི་ལ་དབང་པོའི་ཁྱད་པར་གྱིས་ཞག་བདུན་ནམ་བཅུ་བཞིའམ་ཟླ་བ་གཅིག་ལས་
ཆེད་འཛིན་གྱིས་མ་ཡེངས་པ་དེ་ལ་བརྩོན་མི་དགོས་པར་གང་ཤར་རྩོལ་མེད་དུ་འཛོག
ཐུབ་པ་གཅིག་འོང་། འདི་ལ་རྫོགས་ཆེན་པོ་ཡེ་གྲོལ་གློང་ཡངས་ཀྱི་དགོངས་པ་ཟེར།
ཕྱག་ཆེན་པ་རང་གསལ་གྱི་དྲན་པ་ཟེར་བར་གདའ། དེའི་རྒྱུན་མ་ཆད་པར་བསྐྱངས་
པས་རྣམ་པ་ཐ་མལ་གྱི་ཤེས་པ་འཇིག་རྟེན་པའི་རྣམ་རྟོག་རང་ག་དང་ཁྱད་པར་སྤྱུ་ཙམ་
ཡང་མེད་ལ། ངོ་བོ་དེར་འཛིན་མེད་པའི་ས་ལེ་ཧྲིག་གེ་བ། མཉམ་བཞག་ཡུལ་
ཕུད། རྗེས་ཐོབ་ཆང་སྟོང་། བག་ཆགས་གཡའ་དག་པའི་ཤེས་པ་ངོས་བཟུང་དང་
བྲལ་ཀྱང་རྣམ་རྟོག་ལྟར་སྣང་བ་ཅིག་འོང་། དེ་ཆོས་སྐུ་དངོས་ཡིན། རྫོགས་ཆེན་
སེམས་ཕྱོགས་པས། རྣམ་རྟོག་མི་མངའ་ཅིར་ཡང་སལ་ལེར་མཁྱེན་བྱ་བའང་འདི་ལ་
ཟེར་ཏེ། གྲུབ་ཆེན་མི་ཏྲ་ཛོ་ཀིས། ཅིར་སྣང་དྲང་པོ་བཞག་ན་བྱ་བྲལ་ལྷུན་གྱིས་
གྲུབ། །ཅེས་གསུངས། དེ་ལྟར་འཛིན་པའི་རྣམ་རྟོག་རང་གིས་རང་གྲོལ་བ་ན།
ཕྱི་གཟུང་བའི་ཡུལ་གཟུགས་སྒྲ་ལ་སོགས་པའང་རང་གྲོལ་དུ་ཤུགས་ཀྱིས་འགྲོ་སྙེ་མིག
གི་ཡུལ་དུ་གཟུགས་བཟང་ངན། རྣ་བར་སྒྲ་སྙན་མི་སྙན་དེ་བཞིན་དུ་དྲི་རོ་རེག་བྱ་

རྣམས་ཀྱི་བཟང་ངན་དང་། སེམས་བདེ་སྡུག་ཆགས་སྡང་། དགྲ་གཉེན་ས་ཆུ་མེ་རླུང་ལ་སོགས་པ་མདོར་ན་གང་ཤར་གང་སྣང་དེ་ག་ལ་བཟོ་བཅོས་མེད་པར་འཇོག་པ་ཡིན་ཏེ། རྫོགས་ཆེན་ལས། སྒོ་ལྔའི་རྣམ་ཤེས་གསལ་བ་ལ། ཡིད་ཀྱི་ཞེན་རྟོག་མ་ཞུགས་ན། རྒྱལ་བའི་དགོངས་པ་དེ་ཀ་རང་། །ཞེས་དང་། ཞི་བྱེད་ལས། དོན་གྱི་རྟོག་པའི་མཚང་རིག་ན། རྣམ་རྟོག་ཤར་ཚེ་གནས་པ་ཆེ། །ཉོན་མོངས་རགས་ཚེ་ཡེ་ཤེས་གསལ། །ཅེས་བཞེད་དོ། དེ་བས་ན་རྫོགས་པ་ཆེན་པོའི་དགོངས་པ་ནི། གང་ཤར་དེ་སྤྱོངས་ཡང་མི་སྤྱོངས། དེའི་རྗེས་སུ་ཡང་མི་འབྲང་། དེ་ཀ་ལ་བཅས་བཅོས་མི་བྱེད་པར་འཇོག་པ་འདི་ཀ་ཡིན་ནོ། དེ་ཡིན་པས་དེ་ལ་སྤང་བྱ་མེད། གཉེན་པོ་མེད། དགག་སྒྲུབ་བླང་དོར་ལ་སོགས་པ་བློ་བྱས་ཀྱི་ཆོས་གང་ཡང་མེད་པས་ན། བློ་འདས་ཆོས་སྐུ་དེ་བཞིན་ཉིད། །ཅེས་པའང་དེ་ཡིན། དེ་དག་ནི་དབང་པོ་རབ་ཀྱི་དབང་དུ་བྱས་པ་ཡིན་པས། རབ་ཀྱི་རབ་འབྲིང་ཐ་མ་གསུམ་ལ་སོ་སོའི་བློ་ནུས་དང་སྦྱར་ཏེ་འཁྲིད་ཤེས་པར་བྱའོ། དབང་པོ་འབྲིང་གསུམ་ནི་ཞི་ལྷག་ཟུང་འབྲེལ་གྱི་སྒོ་ནས་འཁྲིད་པར་བྱ་སྟེ། དེ་ཡང་རྒྱལ་བ་ཡང་དགོན་པས། ཡེ་བསྒོམ་ལ་བློ་ཡིས་མ་བསྒོམ་མཛོད། །རང་བབས་ལ་བཟོ་ཡིས་མ་བཅོས་མཛོད། །བློ་རྟོག་ལ་སྐྱོན་དུ་མ་ལྟ་བར། མི་རྟོག་པ་ཆེད་དུ་མ་སྒོམ་པར། །སེམས་རང་ལུགས་སུ་ཞོག་ལ་རྒྱངས་སོ་ཚུག །སྒོམ་ཞི་གནས་ཀྱི་མཐིལ་དུ་ཕེབས་པ་གཅིག་འོང་གི །ཞེས་དེ་ཀ་ལྟར་གོམས་འདྲིས་བྱེད་པ་ལ། གཙུགས་བསྲིངས་པས་འཁྲུ་བ་རྗེ་ཉུང་ལ་སོང་། སེམས་ཀྱི་གནས་པ་རྗེ་བརྟན་ལ་འགྲོ། །འདི་ལ་དྲན་པ་སླེབ་ན་ཞི་ལྷག་ཟུང་འབྲེལ་ཡིན། དེའི་རྒྱུན་བསྐྱངས་ནས་སྒོམ་པས་རྣམ་རྟོག་ཕྲ་རགས་ཀུན་འགགས་ཏེ་ཏིང་ངེ་འཛིན་གྱི་ངོ་བོ་གང་དུའང་མ་གྲུབ་པའི་སྟོང་པ། གསལ་ལ་རྟོག་པ་མེད་པ་ལུས་སེམས་ཡོད་དུ་མི་ཚོར་ལ། ཏིང་ངེ་འཛིན་དེ་དང་འབྲལ་མི་ཕོད་པའི་བདེ་ཉམས་ཅན་གཅིག་འཆར། དེ་སུ་མཐུད་ནས་བསྒོམ་པས་སྤྱན་ལྔ་དང་། མངོན་ཤེས་ཀྱི་ཡོན་ཏན་ཀྱང་འབྱུང་སྐྱེ་བསམ་གཏན་ཟེར། ཞི་གནས་འཐུག་པོ་དེ་

བསྒོམ་ནས་བསམ་གཏན་བཞི་དང་སྐྱེ་མཆེད་མུ་བཞིའི་ཏིང་འཛིན་རྩེ་གཅིག་པ་སྐྱེ། མཐར་གྱིས་གནས་པའི་སྙོམས་པར་འཇུག་པ་དགུ་ཟེར། དགུ་པོ་འདི་མུ་སྟེགས་པ་ལ་འང་ཡོད་པས་ཕྱི་ནང་ཐུན་མོང་གི་ལམ་ཡིན་ཀྱང་། རྣམ་རྟོག་འཕྲོ་མང་ནས་ཁ་བྲི་མ་ཐུབ་པ་དེ་ལ་ཐོག་མར་ཞི་གནས་བཙལ་དགོས་པ་ཡིན། དེ་ལ་ཡང་ལྷག་མཐོང་མེད་ན་ས་ལམ་མི་བགྲོད་པས་སེམས་ཀྱི་གནས་ཆ་ཙམ་རྙེད་ནས་རྣམ་རྟོག་འདི་མ་འཕྲོས་ན་དགའ་བ་ལ་སླམ་པའི་དུས་དེར་རྣམ་རྟོག་དེ་རང་ངོ་ཤེས་ཙམ་བྱས་ལ་ཁོ་རང་གི་ངོ་ལ་བལྟས་པས་ཡལ་ཏེ་གནས་པ་དང་གཅིག་ཏུ་སོང་པ་ནི་ཞི་ལྷག་ཟུང་འཇུག་གམ་ཟུང་འབྲེལ་བྱ་བ་ཡིན། དྭགས་པོ་བཀའ་བརྒྱུད་པས་གནས་འགྱུའི་བར་ལག་འཁྱོལ་བ་ཟེར། ངོ་བོ་བློས་བྱས་པའི་བསྒོམ་ཡིན། འདི་ལ་ངོ་ཤེས་ཀྱི་དྲན་པ་དང་མ་བྲལ་བར་དགོས་པས་བཀའ་བརྒྱུད་པས་སྐྱོང་ཉིད་གཟུང་དྲན་ཟེར། འདི་ཀ་རྒྱུན་བསྐྱངས་ནས་བསྒོམ་པས་གཟུང་དྲན་དེ་རང་གསལ་གྱི་དྲན་པར་འགྲོ། མ་ཡེངས་པ་རང་བྱས་ན་འདི་ཡང་ཁ་གཟྲ་མོ་གཅིག་ཡིན་ཏེ། ཟླ་བ་གཅིག་ཙམ་ནས་ཉིན་སྣང་འདྲེས་ཐུབ། རྒྱལ་བ་རྐྱོད་ཚངས་པས། སྣང་བ་ཐམས་ཅད་སྟོང་པར་མི་བསྒོམ། མི་སྟོང་པར་ཡང་མི་བསྒོམ་གང་ཤར་དེ་ལ་དྲན་པས་བཟུང་ན་ཟླ་བ་གཅིག་རང་གིས་ཆོག་སྐྱེ། སྤྲོས་བྲལ་དང་པོའི་རང་གནས་འོང་། །ཞེས་གསུངས་པར། ཧྲིལ་གྱིས་དྲིལ་ན། སྔར་གྱི་ཞི་གནས་ཀྱི་ཏིང་ངེ་འཛིན་དེ་རང་ངོ་ཤེས་པས་ཞི་ལྷག་ཟུང་འབྲེལ་ལ། ཕྱག་རྒྱ་ཆེན་པོ་རྫོགས་པ་ཆེན་པོ་ཞེས་ཟེར་ཏེ། ཡང་དགོན་པས། བློ་རྟོག་པ་འགྱུ་བ་གནས་ལུགས་ཀྱི་སྒོ། རང་ངོ་ཤེས་པ་ཉམས་ལེན་གྱི་གནད། །ཅེས་གསུངས་པ་ལ་འདུའོ། འདི་ལ་འཁྲིད་གི་འཁྲིད་དང་ཐ་མ་གཉིས་ཀྱིས་རྣམ་རྟོག་རང་ག་མ་དེ་སྒོམ་ཡིན་པར་ཡིད་ལ་མི་བྱེད་ན། རྣམ་རྟོག་གང་ཤར་དེ་ལ་བལྟས་པས་ཐམས་ཅད་སྟོང་པར་ཡལ། ཡལ་བ་དེའི་ངང་ནས་གཅིག་རྟེང་ལ་གཅིག་འཆར། དེ་ལ་ཡང་བལྟས་པས་ཤར་ལྷར་ཡལ་དེ་ཁའི་རྒྱུད་སྐྱོང་བ་ཡིན་ཏེ། མགུར་ལས། སེམས་ངོས་བཟུང་མེད་པ་སྟོང་པའི་དབྱིངས། སྣ་ཚོགས་སུ་འཆར་བ་རིག་པའི་སྒོ། བློ

བྲལ་གྱི་གསལ་སྟོང་རྗེན་པ་འདིའི། ངང་ལ་བཞག་བཞིན་དབྱིངས་ལ་ལྟོས་དང་། བསྒོམ་ལྷག་མཐོང་གི་མཐིལ་དུ་ཕེབས་པ་གཅིག་འོང་གི །ཞེས་གསུངས་པ་བཞིན་ཉམས་སུ་ལེན། འདི་ལ་མི་ཏྲ་ཛཱོ་གིས། གང་ཤར་ངོ་ཡིན་བཟུང་བ་རིག་པར་རང་སར་གྲོལ། །ཞེས་པས། ལས་སླ་ལ་ཆུན་ཆེ་བ་གཅིག་ཡིན་ནོ། །རབ་འབྲིང་གསུམ་ཀའི་ཐུན་མོང་དུ་སྒོམ་ལུགས་ནི། མགུར་ལས། མ་ཡེངས་དྲན་པ་སོ་མ་ཤོར། མ་བསྒོམ་པའི་གནས་ལུགས་བཟོ་མ་བྱས། བསམ་མེད་ཀྱི་རིག་པ་སླ་མ་འདོད། ཧྲག་ཆད་ཀྱི་མ་བསླད་ཡུན་དུ་སྐྱོངས་དང་། བསྒོམ་ཞི་ལྷག་ཟུང་དུ་ཆུད་པ་གཅིག་འོང་གི །ཞེས་གསུངས་པ་གོ་སླ་ཡང་། དྲན་པ་མ་ཡེངས་པས་གང་ཤར་ལ་བཟོ་བཅོས་མི་བྱེད། ཤར་ཡང་ཡོད་པར་མི་བལྟ། ཡལ་ཡང་མེད་པར་མི་འཛིན། རྣམ་རྟོག་གི་སྣ་སྐྱིལ་བར་འགྲོ་བཙུག་ནས་ངོ་ཤེས་ཙམ་བྱེད་པའོ། ། རྫོགས་ཆེན་སེམས་སྡེ་ལས། གདོད་ནས་དག་པ་དབྱིངས་ཀྱི་ངང་ཉིད་ནས། རིག་པ་ཐད་སྐྱེས་སྐད་ཅིག་དྲན་པ་དེ། རྒྱ་མཚོའི་གཏིང་ནས་ནོར་བུ་རྙེད་པ་འདྲ། སུས་ཀྱང་མ་བཅོས་མ་བྱས་ཆོས་ཀྱི་སྐུ། །ཞེས་གསུངས་པ་ལྟར་ངོ་སྤྲོད་དོ། །དབང་པོ་ཐ་མ་གསུམ་ནི། ཕལ་ཆེར་ལྷག་མཐོང་ཡིད་མི་ཆེས། ཞི་གནས་གཤའ་མ་ཡང་སྐྱེ་མི་ཐུབ་སྟེ། རེས་འབྲིངས། རེས་རྒོད་ནས་སྒོམ་མི་འཆར་བས། སྔོན་འགྲོ་མཐར་ཕྱིན་རྫོགས་པ་དང་། སྟན་བདེ་བར་རྐང་པ་སྐྱིལ་ཀྲུང་། ལག་པ་མཉམ་བཞག་ལྕེ་ཡར་རྐན་ལ་སྦྱར། མིག་སྣ་རྩེར་ཕབ་པ་སོགས་ཆོས་བདུན་ཚང་བར་བྱས་ཤིང་། རླུང་རོ་དགུ་སྦྱུགས་སུ་བུས་ལ། སྤྱི་བོའམ་སྙིང་ཁར་བླ་མ་བསྒོམ་ཞིང་གསོལ་བ་བཏབ། ལུས་སེམས་ལྷོད་ཀྱིས་གློད་པའི་ངང་ནས་རྣམ་རྟོག་གང་ཤར་དེ་ག་ལ་བལྟས་ནས་དེ་རང་གི་ཐོག་ཏུ་ལྷོད་ཀྱིས་གློད། ཡང་ཤར་ན་དེའི་ཐོག་ཏུ་སྔར་ལྟར་གློད། ཡལ་ནས་སྟོང་པར་སོང་བ་དེའི་དགའ་བྲོད་མི་བྱ། རྣམ་རྟོག་མང་པོར་སོང་བ་ལ་སྐྱོན་དུ་མི་བལྟ། སྒོམ་ཡོང་དུ་རེ་བ་དང་མ་བྱུང་བའི་དོགས་པ་གཉིས་ཀ་མི་བྱ། གང་ཤར་གྱི་སྟེང་དུ་ལྷོད་དེ་འཇོག །ལྷོད་ཆེན་རྣམ་རྟོག་མེད་པའི་མི་རྟོག་པ་འདྲ་མོ་

འགྱུ་དྲན་གང་ཡང་མེད་པ་གཅིག་འོང་བས། དེ་དྲན་པས་གྲིམ་གྱིས་སྒྲིམ་ཏེ་ངོ་ཤེས་པ་མ་བྱུས་ན་རང་གིས་མི་ཚོར་བར་རྟོག་པ་འོག་འགྱུ་ཞུབ་མའི་འོག་གི་ཆུ་དོང་ལྟ་བུ་གཅིག་ཡོད། དེས་འཕྲལ་དུ་མི་གནོད་པ་ལྟར་ལ་ཞུགས་སུ་ཁོ་རྒྱལ་ནས་སྒོམ་ཡོངས་སུ་མི་སྟེར་བས་སྒྲིམ་དགོས། རྟོག་པ་ཁ་གྱུ་ནི་ངོས་ཟིན་པའི་འགྱུ་དྲན་ཚོ་ཡིན་པ་དེ་ཐོག་ཏུ་གློད་ནས་འཇོག །ཇེ་ཞིག་ནས་རྣམ་རྟོག་མང་དུ་སོང་ནས་རང་ཚིག་པ་ཟ། ང་ལ་སྒོམ་མི་ཡོང་བར་འདུག་སྙམ་པ་འོང་སྟེ་སྐྱོན་མེད། ཉམས་དང་པོ་རི་གཟར་གྱི་ཆུ་ལྟ་བུ་བྱུ་བ་དེ་བཀའ་བརྒྱུད་པས་རྩེ་གཅིག་རྟོག་པའི་ཟླ་ལ་གཡེང་ཟེར་ཏེ་རྩེ་གཅིག་ཆུང་ངུའི་སྐབས་ཡིན། དེ་ཀ་ལ་སྲན་བསྐྱེད་དེ་སྒོམ་པས། སྐབས་རེ་སྡོད། སྐབས་རེ་འཕྲོ་བ་ཆུ་ནང་གི་ཉིའུ་ཆུ་ལ་རེས་འཛུལ་རེས་འཐོན། སྐབས་རེ་རྡོ་སྟེང་དུ་བག་རེ་སྡོད་པ་དང་འདྲ། ཉམས་གཉིས་པའི་སྐྱེ་ལུགས་ཡིན། ཡང་སྨུ་མཐུད་དེ་སྒོམ་ན་རེ་ཞིག་ནས་སྐབས་རེ་འཕྲོ་ཡང་། ཤས་ཆེར་གནས་པ་འདྲ་བ་གཅིག་འོང་། དཔེ་མི་རྒན་དང་འདྲ་སྟེ་སྡོད་པ་ཤས་ཆེ། ཉམས་གསུམ་པའི་སྐྱེ་ལུགས་ཡིན། ཡང་རྒྱུན་མཐུད་བས་རེ་ཞིག་ན་སྦུབ་ནང་གི་ཡུར་བའི་ཆུ་ལྟར་འཕྲོ་བ་མི་མངོན་པའོ། །འདི་དུས་ཀྱང་དྲན་པ་ཙུང་ཟད་སྒྲིམ་དགོས། ཉམས་བཞི་པའི་སྐྱེས་ལུགས་ཡིན། དེ་རྒྱུན་མཐུད་པས་ཇི་ཞིག་ན་སེམས་གང་དུ་མི་འཕྲོ་བར་ཉིན་མཚན་ཀུན་ཏུ་གནས་པས་སྒོམ་དང་གོས་ཀྱི་སྲེད་པ་ཡང་མི་འབྱུང་ཞིང་། གཡོ་འགུལ་མེད་པ་ཞག་དང་ཟླ་བ་སྒྲོལ་བར་གནས་པས་དཔེ་རི་བོ་ལྟ་བུ་སྟེ། འདི་ཉེས་ན་ཁ་ཐལ་ནས་ཉན་ཐོས་འགོག་པར་འགྲོ། ལེགས་ན་ལུས་ཤིན་སྦྱངས་ཐོབ་ནས་ཞི་གནས་ཞུལ་དུ་ཕྱིན་པ་ཡིན། ཉམས་ལྔ་བའི་སྐྱེ་ལུགས་ཡིན། །འདི་དག་ཀྱང་གཙོ་ཆེ་བའི་དབང་དུ་བྱས་ཀྱི། གང་ཟག་སོ་སོའི་རྩ་ཁམས་དང་དབང་པོའི་རིམ་པ་ལ་གཅིག་ཏུ་མ་ངེས་པ་ཡང་སྲིད་དོ། །དེ་ཚེ་དབང་པོ་ཐ་མའི་རབ་ལ་རིམ་ལས་ཡོད་མེད་ཀྱིས་འབྲིང་ཐ་གཉིས་ལ་གནས་པ་སྐྱེ་དཀའ་བས། ལུས་གནད་སྟར་ལྟར་ལ། མདུན་དུ་སྨིན་མཚམས་ཀྱི་ཐད་འདོམས་གང་ཙམ་གྱི་སར་ཤིང་བུ་གཅིག་བཙུགས་ནས། དེ་ལ་ཡིད་དམིགས་

རླུང་གསུམ་དྲིལ་ལ་གཏད་དེ། །སེམས་མི་འགྲོ་བའི་རྟེན་ཙམ་དུ་བྱས་ལ། སྒྲིམ་ཆེ་ན་སུན་སྐྱེན། ལྷོད་ཆེ་ན་སྒོམ་འཆོར་བས་རན་པར་ཐུན་ཆུང་ལ་གྲངས་མང་བར་བྱ། དེ་ནས་རིམ་པར་ཐུན་ཆེ་ལ་གྲངས་ཉུང་དུ་བཏང་། སེམས་གནས་པར་སོང་ན་ཤིང་བུ་དེའི་རྩེ་མོར་ཨ་དཀར་པོ་གཅིག་བསམ་ལ་སྟར་ལྷར་བསྒོམ། །དེ་ནས་ཐིག་ལེ་དཀར་པོ་དང་སེར་པོ་ལ་སོགས་རིམ་བས་སྦྱོ་ཞིང་དམིགས་རྟེན་རེ་ལ་ཞག་གཅིག་གམ་གསུམ་ལ་སོགས་པར་མ་སུན་པར་བྱས་ལ་ཅི་རིགས་སུ་བསྒོམ། ཡང་ཤིང་བུའི་ཤུལ་དུ་རྡེའུ་གཅིག་བཞག་ལ་སྟར་ལྷར་རིམ་པས་བསྒོམ། དེ་ནས་རང་ལུས་ཀྱི་གནས་གསུམ་དང་། ནང་གི་མགྲིན་པ་སྙིང་ཁ་རྣམས་སུ་ཡིག་འབྲུ་དང་ཐིག་ལེ་སོགས་གང་རིགས་ལ་དམིགས་རྟེན་བཅས་ཏེ་བསྒོམས་པས་རིམ་གྱིས་གནས་པ་བརྟན་པར་འགྱུར་རོ། །དེ་ཡང་དང་ཐུང་མི་བྱ་བར་རིམ་གྱིས་གོམས་བཙུག་ཅིང་མི་སུན་པ་བྱ་བ་གལ་ཆེའོ། །ཞི་གནས་ཀྱི་སྐབས་འདིར་སྟུག་བཅེར་དུ་མ་སོང་བར་སྟར་གྱི་འཇོག་ལུགས་ལ་མ་ཡེངས་པ་རལ་སྐོར་མཁན་གཡུལ་དུ་ཞུགས་པ་ལྟ་བུ་གསུངས། དེ་ཡང་རལ་བསྐོར་མཁན་སྐད་ཅིག་ཀྱང་མ་ཡེངས་ན་མདའ་མཁན་གྱི་མདའ་འཕང་ཚོད་རལ་གྲིས་བླངས་ཏེ་ཁོལ་མི་ཐོག་པ་ལ། བུ་མེད་མཛེས་མའི་སྤྱོད་ལམ་ལ་མིག་སྐད་ཅིག་ཡེངས་པས་ཁོ་ལ་མདའ་ཐོག་ཏེ་འཆི་ཁ། མདའ་ཡིས་མ་ལན་ཡེངས་པས་ལན། ཕྱིན་ཆད་རལ་བསྐོར་མཁན་པོ་ཀུན། སྐད་ཅིག་ཙམ་ཡང་མ་ཡེངས་ཅིག ། ཡེངས་ནང་བཞིན་སྲོག་དང་བྲལ། ཟེར་ནས་ཤིའོ། དཔེ་དེ་བཞིན་དུ་མ་ཡེངས་པ་གལ་ཆེའོ། །ད་ནི་ལྷག་མཐོང་སྟོན་ཏེ། ལྷག་མཐོང་ནི་ཤེས་རབ་ཀྱི་ཕ་རོལ་ཏུ་ཕྱིན་པ་ཞེས་བྱ་བ་ཡིན་ཏེ། འདི་མེད་ན་ས་ལམ་མི་བགྲོད་པས་ཕར་ཕྱིན་གཞན་རྣམས་མིག་མེད་པ་དང་འདྲ་བར་བཤད་ཅིང་། རྗེ་སྒམ་པོ་པས། མཉམ་བཞག་གཅིག་གིས་ཞག་བདུན་ཐུབ་པ་བྱུང་གསུངས་པ་ལ་རྗེ་མི་ལས་བསམ་གཏན་བཞིའི་ལྷའི་ཏིང་ངེ་འཛིན་དུ་རྡོ་སྦྲིད་པ་ལྟ་བུའོ། །ལྷག་མཐོང་ལ་གསུམ་སྟེ། ཆོས་རབ་ཏུ་རྣམ་པར་འབྱེད་པའི་ལྷག་མཐོང་ནི། མདོ་སྔགས་ཐམས་ཅད་ཀྱི་དགོངས་དོན་གང་ཡིན་པའི་ལྷག་

མཐོང་ཕྱིན་ཅི་མ་ལོག་པ་ཞེས་པ་ལ་ཟེར། སེམས་རང་བཞིན་གྱིས་རྣམ་པ་དག་པའི་གནས་ལུགས་ཇི་ལྟར་ཞེས་པའི་ལྷག་མཐོང་ནི། ད་ལྟ་ངོ་སྤྲོད་ཅིང་བསྒོམ་པ་འདི་ཡིན། འདི་གོམས་པས་གནས་ལུགས་ཕྱིན་ཅི་མ་ལོག་པ་མངོན་དུ་གྱུར་པའི་ལྷག་མཐོང་ནི། འབྲས་བུ་སངས་རྒྱས་ཐོབ་པའི་དུས་དེར་འབྱུང་ངོ་། །ད་ཞི་གནས་ཀྱི་སྐབས་ལྟར་རྣམ་རྟོག་མཉམ་བཞག་ཏུ་ཤར་འདུག་ཀྱང་དེ་ངོ་ཤེས་ཙམ་ལ་བཞག་པས་ཆོག །རྣམ་རྟོག་སྣ་ཚོགས་སུ་འགྱུ་ན་ཡང་དེ་ངོ་ཤེས་ཙམ་གྱི་ངང་དུ་འཇོག མདོར་ན་གང་ཤར་གང་བྱུང་ངོ་ཤེས་ཙམ་གྱི་ངང་དུ་འཇོག་པ་འདི་ག་ཡིན། བསྒོམ་ནས་བསྒོམ་རྒྱུ་ཅི་ཡང་མེད་དོ། །སྤང་གཉེན་དུ་བལྟས་ན་རྩོལ་སྒྲུབ་གང་བྱས་འཁོར་བའི་རྒྱུ་འབྲས་ལས་མ་འདས་སོ། །དེ་ཡང་ཏིང་ངེ་འཛིན་གྱི་མི་མཐུན་པའི་ཕྱོགས་ནི་རྣམ་རྟོག་ཡིན་ལ་དེ་སྤངས་མི་དགོས་ཁོ་བའི་སྟེང་དུ་ཁོ་རང་བཞག་བཞག་པས་རང་དག་ལ་འགྲོ་བ་ཡིན། འཁྲུལ་སྣང་འཛིན་པ་བཟློག་སྤངས་མིན། མི་མཐུན་པ་ཉིད་གཉེན་པོར་རྫོགས། །ཞེས་སོ། དབང་པོ་ཐ་མའི་ཐ་མས་དེ་ལྟར་བྱས་ཀྱང་སེམས་ལས་སུ་མ་རུང་ན་རྣམ་རྟོག་གང་སྐྱེས་དེ་ངོས་བཟུང་ནས་དེ་ཇི་ལྟར་འདུག་དང་། གར་འགྲོ་བ་ལྟས་བས་རང་དག་ཏུ་འགྲོ་ཞིང་། དེའི་རྒྱུན་བསྐྱངས་པས་ཕྱིས་ཆེད་དུ་རྩད་གཅོད་མི་དགོས་པར་རྣམ་རྟོག་ཁོས་ཁོ་རང་གྲོལ་བར་བྱེད་དེ་རང་བྱུང་གི་ཡེ་ཤེས་ཞེས་བྱའོ། འགྱུ་བའི་རྩད་གདར་བཅད་ན་དེ་གཅིག་པོས་དྲན་རྟོག་དབྱིངས་སུ་ཡལ། །ཞེས་པའི་དོན་ཏོ། སྤྱིར་ན་ཐ་མལ་གྱི་ཤེས་པ་ཞེས་བྱ་བ་རྣམ་རྟོག་གང་ཤར་ཀྱི་ངོ་བོ་ལ་བཟོ་བཅོས་མི་བྱེད་པ་འདི་ལས་མ་ཡེངས་ན་དེ་གཅིག་པུས་ཆོག་སྟེ། དབང་པོ་ཐ་མས་དེ་ལྟར་མི་འོང་བས་རྩོལ་བཅས་ཀྱི་མཉམ་བཞག་སྐྱོང་བ་ཡིན། རྣམ་རྟོག་གང་ཤར་ལ་བལྟས་ཀྱང་ཞི་མ་ནུས་པར་འཕྲོ་ཆེ་ན། ལུས་གནད་བཤིག ། འཕྲོ་མཁན་ཁོ་རང་འཕྲོ་བཙུག་ནས་ཁོའི་དད་དེ་ལ་བལྟས་པས་ཞི་མལ་གྱིས་འགྲོ། འཕྲོ་བ་དང་གནས་པ་གཉིས་ཀ་སེམས་ཡིན་པས་རང་མལ་དུ་གཅིག་ཏུ་འགྱུར་ཏེ། སྒོམ་སྲན་བསྐྱེད་པས་གཏིང་ཚུགས་པར་འགྱུར་རོ། དེ་ཡང་། ཇི་ལྟར་གཟིང་

ལས་འཕུར་བའི་བྱ་རོག་ནི། །བསྐོར་ཞིང་བསྐོསྐྱུ་ཞིང་སླར་ཡང་དེ་རུ་འབབ། ། ཅེས་པའི་དཔེས་སྟོན་ཏེ། རྒྱ་མཚོའི་ཟུར་ནས་བྱ་རོག་གི་རྐང་པར་ལྕུགས་ཐག་ཕྲ་མོས་བཏང་དགོས་ལ། མཚོ་དཀྱིལ་དུ་སླེབ་ནས་ཡར་འཕུར་ན་ནམ་མཁའ་སྟོང་པ་པར་ཚུར་ནི་བར་སྣང་སྟོང་པ། འོག་ཏུ་ནི་ཆུ་ལས་མ་འདས་པས་ཡར་མར་ཕྱོགས་མཚམས་གང་དུ་འཕུར་ཀྱང་འཁྲོས་དང་སླེབ་ས་མ་རྙེད་པས། ཕྱིར་གྱི་ཞུལ་གཟིང་ཐོག་ཏུ་འབབ་པ་བཞིན་དུ། རྣམ་རྟོག་ཁོ་རང་འཕྲོ་རུང་སྟོང་པ། མི་འཕྲོ་རུང་སྟོང་པ། གནས་རུང་འགྱུ་རུང་སྟོང་པ་ལས་མ་འདས་པས། ཁོ་རང་གང་ཤར་དེ་ཁའི་ངང་དུ་བབས་པས་དབང་པོ་ཐ་མས་ཀྱང་རབ་ཀྱིས་སོར་འཇོག་ཏུ་འགྱུར་བས་ནན་ལྟར་གཟབ་པས་དཔྱད་ནས་འདི་ལ་བསླབ་ན་ལེགས་སོ། དེ་ལྟར་དབང་པོ་རབ་འབྲིང་ཐ་གསུམ་དགུ་ཕྲུགས་སུ་ཕྱེ་ནས་ཉམས་སུ་ལེན་ཚུལ་བསྟན་པ་སྟེ་རྫོགས་ཆེན་སྙན་བརྒྱུད་ལས། དབང་པོ་རབ་ལྟ་ཐོག་ནས་བསྒོམ་ནུས། འབྲིང་བསྒོམ་ཐོག་ནས་བསྒོམ་ནུས་ལ། ཐ་མ་སྤྱོད་ཐོག་ནས་སྒྲུབ་ནུས་པའོ། །ཞེས་གསུངས་པའི་དགོངས་པའོ། དེ་ཡང་བསྒོམ་ལ་སྙིང་རུས་བསྐྱེད་དགོས་སྟེ། ཆོས་ཟབ་ཀྱང་མ་སྒོམ་ན་གདམས་ངག་ཟབ་མོ་དཔེ་ཆའི་ལོགས་ལ་ལུས་ཟེར་བ་དེ་ཡིན་མོད། ད་རེས་སྒོམ་རྒྱུད་ལ་ཐེབས་ཀྱང་། དུས་རྒྱུན་དུ་མ་བསྒོམ་ན་བློ་བྲེད་ཆོས་བྲེད་ཉམས་ལེན་བྲེད་ནས་འཆི་དུས་མི་ཕན་པས་གཟབ་དགོས། རྒྱལ་བ་རྒོད་ཚང་པས། ཕྱི་འཚམས་རི་ཁྲོད་དུ་སྡོད་ཚུགས་པ། ནང་འཚམས་སྤྱིལ་པོར་སྡོད་ཚུགས་པ། གསང་འཚམས་མལ་དུ་སྡོད་ཚུགས་པ། གཉིས་མེད་ལྟ་བའི་སྟེང་དུ་སྡོད་ཚུགས་པ། ཡེངས་མེད་བསྒོམ་པའི་སྟེང་དུ་སྡོད་ཚུགས་པ། ཆགས་མེད་སྤྱོད་པའི་སྟེང་དུ་སྡོད་ཚུགས་པ་དང་དྲུག་ཚང་དགོས་གསུངས། སྤྱིར་སྒོམ་ལ་ཕར་འཛུས་དང་ཚུར་འཛུས་གཉིས་ཡིན། སེམས་ལས་སུ་མ་རུང་བར་འཕར་འཛུས་བྱེད་དགོས་པས་དྲན་པ་དང་མི་བྲལ། དེ་ནས་རྣམ་རྟོག་ཁོ་རང་གིས་ཚུར་འཛུས་ནས་གང་ཤར་ཐམས་ཅད་སྒོམ་དུ་འགྲོ་པ་ཡིན། དེ་ཡང་ཐ་མལ་གྱི་ཤེས་པ་ཁོ་རང་ལ་འཛིན་པ་མེད་པའི་ངང་དུ་འགྲོ་བ་ཡིན་ནོ། །

བསྒོམ་ཆེན་པས་བསྒོམ་བཏང་ཀྱང་། བསྒོམ་གྱིས་བསྒོམ་ཆེན་པ་མི་གཏོང་བའི་དུས་ཟེར། དེ་འོང་བ་ལ་བར་མ་ཆད་དུ་བསྒོམ་དགོས། མ་བསྒོམ་ན་ད་ལྟ་ཉམས་མྱོང་ཁྲན་བུ་རེ་སྐྱེས་ཀྱང་ཡལ་འགྲོ་བས་བསྒོམ་འདང་འཚོན་མ་བྱ་བ་ཡིན། ལྷུགས་ཀྱུ་མ་བྱ་བ་དྲན་པས་ཟིན་དུས་ཡོད་ལ། མ་ཟིན་ན་མེད་པ་ཡིན་དེ་ལ་མ་ཡེངས་པ་བྱུར་བསྒྲིམ་དགོས། ཡ་བྲལ་མ་བྱ་བ། དྲན་པ་ཡོད་ལ་སྙིང་རྗེ་དང་མ་འབྲེལ་བ་ཡིན། དེ་ལ་ཐུན་འགོར་སེམས་ཅན་ཐམས་ཅད་ཀྱི་དོན་དུ་བསྒོམ་མོ་སྙམ་པ་དང་། ཐུན་མཐར་དགེ་བས་སེམས་ཅན་ཐམས་ཅད་སངས་རྒྱས་ཐོབ་པར་གྱུར་ཅིག་བར་བསྔོ། ཨོ་རྒྱན་ཆེན་པོས། སྙིང་རྗེ་མེད་ན་ཆོས་ཀྱི་རྩ་བ་རུལ། །ཞེས་གསུངས་པས་གལ་ཤིན་ཏུ་ཆེ། བདག་མེད་མ་བྱ་བ་སྒོམ་སྐྱེས་ནས་མ་བསྐྱངས་པར་བོར་བ་ལ་ཟེར། བློ་ནང་དུ་བཀུག་ནས་སྒོམ་དུ་བཅུག །རེས་འཇོག་མ་བྱ་བ་རེས་སྒོམ་འོང་། རེས་མི་འོང་བ་དེ་ཡིན། དེ་ལ་བྱུང་མ་བྱུང་ཁྱད་མེད་པའི་ཐོག་ཏུ་འཇོག་ཅིང་ཉམས་སུ་བླངས། །འཁོར་ཡུག་མ་བྱ་བ་ཉིན་མོའི་དྲན་པ་མཚན་མོ་ཡང་འོང་བ་དེ་ཡིན། འདི་སྒོམ་གྱིས་ཚུར་འཛུས་པའི་དུས་དེ་ཡིན། རྣལ་འབྱོར་མཆོག་ཅེས་པ་རྫོགས་པ་ཆེན་པོ་བྱ་རྩོལ་དང་བྲལ་བའི་དུས་ཞེས་བྱ་བ་དེ་ཡིན། ཕྱག་རྒྱ་ཆེན་པོ་བསྒོམ་མེད་ཟེར་བ་ཡིན་ནོ། ཡང་གང་ཟག་རིགས་ཆད་ཅེས་པ་ཁྲིགས་ཆོད་ཐོད་རྒལ་གྱི་སྣོད་དུ་མ་གྱུར་བ་དག་ཀྱང་ཡོད་པས། དེ་འདྲའི་རིགས་ལ་དབང་བསྐུར་རྩ་རླུང་སྦྱངས་ནས་ལས་ཀྱི་ཕྱག་རྒྱ་གཏད། དབང་པོ་གཉིས་སྦྱོར་གྱིས་དགའ་བཞི་འབྲོས་འདེད་ཀྱིས་བདེ་བའི་ངོ་བོ་སྟོང་པར་ངོ་སྤྲོད་དེ་གོང་བཞིན་སེམས་ཁྲིད་ལ་འཇུག་པར་གསུངས་ལ། དེའང་མི་ནུས་པ་ལ་ནི་བཏགས་གྲོལ་མཐོང་གྲོལ་མྱོང་གྲོལ་སོགས་པའི་ཐབས་ཀྱིས་རིམ་གྱིས་གྲོལ་བར་འགྱུར་བའི་ཚུལ་ལ་འཇུག་པར་བྱའོ། །སྦྱོར་སེམས་ཕྱོགས་དང་། ཕྱག་རྒྱ་ཆེན་པོ་ནི། ཡེ་ཤེས་སྦྱོར་གསལ་ཞེས་བྱ་སྟེ། བརྟན་པ་མ་ཐོབ་བར་དུ་ཡིད་དཔྱོད་འཛིན་པའི་ལྟ་བ་ཞེས་བཤད། འོན་ཀྱང་རྫོགས་ཆེན་པ་དེ་ངོ་སྤྲོད་ནས་བསྒོམ་ན་ཕྱི་སྣང་བའི་ཡུལ་དང་། ནང་འཛིན་པའི་སེམས་ཀྱི་འགྲོ་གནས་ཐམས་ཅད་ཡེ་ཤེས་སུ་

འཆར་བས།   རྫོགས་ཆེན་རང་སྣང་རིས་མེད་ཀྱི་དགོངས་པ་ཟེར་གཡེར་པོ་ཆེ་བྱེད།
གང་ལྷར་རུང་སྟེ།   སེམས་ངོ་འཕྲོད་ཕྱིན་ཆད་སྣང་ཐོག་ཏུ་ཉམས་ལེན་སྐྱོང་བ་ལ།
ཐོད་རྒལ་ཞུགས་ཏེ་མུན་ཁྲིད་དམ།   སྣང་ཁྲིད་བྱས་ནས་འོད་གསལ་སྟོང་གཟུགས་ཀྱི་
ཐོག་ཏུ་ཉམས་ལེན་བསྐྱངས་ན་རང་བྱུང་གི་ཡེ་ཤེས་མངོན་སུམ་དུ་འགྱུར་ཏེ།   ཆོས་
ཉིད་ཀྱི་བར་དོ་ལ་གྲོལ་བར་ཐེ་ཚོམ་མེད་དོ།   །བདག་ལྷ་བུའི་བསྒོམ་པའི་ཉམས་མྱོང་
མེད་ཅིང་།   ཐོས་པ་ཕལ་ཆེར་ཀྱང་བརྗེད་པའི་མན་ངག་ལ་མྱོང་བ་མེད་པ་འདི་འདྲ་བ།
རྗེ་འབའ་ར་བས།   བསྒོམ་པའི་ཉམས་མྱོང་མེད་པའི།   །ཡིག་ནག་དཔེ་ཆའི་སྟེང་
ནས།   བསྒོམ་ཁྲིད་འདེབས་བློ་བྱས་ཀྱང་།   །ལམ་ལོག་གོམ་པར་སྤྱུར་ཏོ།   །
ཞེས་གསུངས་པ་བཞིན་དང་།   ཡང་དེས་ས་ཐོབ་ཡོན་ཏན་མེད་ཀྱང་།   །བཟོད་ཐོབ་
ལས་བཞི་འགྲུབ་ཅིང་།   །སྙིང་རྗེའི་རྩ་བ་བརྟན་པས།   །འགྲོ་དོན་བྱས་ཀྱང་ཆོག་གོ
།ཞེས་གསུངས་པས།   བཟོད་པ་མ་ཐོབ་ཀྱང་རུང་རྒྱུད་ལ་སྙིང་རྗེ་ཅུང་ཟད་ཅིག་ཡོད་པ་
དང་།   ཁྱད་པར་དུ་སེམས་དང་ཆོས་སུ་འདྲེས་ཤིང་།   ཏིང་འཛིན་ལས་སུ་རུང་བ་
དང་།   སངས་རྒྱས་ལྷ་བུའི་བླ་མ་དམ་པ་རྣམས་ཀྱི་གསུང་རྒྱུན་གང་དྲན་བཀོད་པ་
ཡིན་ནོ།   །སློབ་དཔོན་ཤྲཱི་སེང་ཧས།   དང་པོ་ཐུག་གར་གཏུག   །བར་དུ་འཇོག་
སར་ཞོག   །ཐ་མ་འགྲོ་སར་ཐོང་གསུངས།   དེ་ལ་དང་པོ་ནི་ཁྲིད་སྟོན་ཤེས་པའི་བླ་
མ་ལ་གཏུགས་ནས་སེམས་ཀྱི་རྩད་གདར་བཅད་དེ་ཞུན་གཏུག་བྱེད་པའོ།   །བར་དུ་
གང་ཤར་བ་བཟོ་བཅོས་མེད་པར་འཇོག་པའོ།   །ཐ་མཉམ་མྱོང་ཏིང་ངེ་འཛིན་གྱི་རོལ་
ཞེན་པ་མེད་པར་འཛིན་མེད་དུ་གཏོང་བའོ།   །རྫོགས་ཆེན་སེམས་སྡེའི་ཁྲིད་ཡིག་ལས་
བཏུས་པའོ།   །ཀུན་ལ་ཕན་པར་ཤོག   ༄   གཞན་ཡང་ཞལ་ཤེས་འཁོར་བུ་ནི།
ཉམས་རྟོགས་སྣ་ཚོགས་སུ་ཤར་བ་བསྒོམས་པའི་ལག་རྗེས་བཟང་རྟོག་གི་མཐུ་བརྟས་པ་
ཡིན་ཀྱང་རྟག་པ་མེད་པས་བདེན་འཛིན་མ་ཞུགས་པས་གནད་དུ་ཆེ།   ད་ལྟ་གཟུང་དྲན་
ལ་མ་ལྟོས་པར་གང་ཤར་རང་གྲོལ་རྗེན་པར་འགྲོ་བ་དེ་དག་རྣམ་དག་ལེགས་པའི་ལམ་དུ་
གོ   །བླ་མའི་སྐུའི་སྣང་བ་དང་ཡི་དམ་གྱི་བསྐྱེད་རིམ་སོགས་ཀྱང་སྣང་མེད་དུ་ཧྲ་ལེ་

རྗེན་ནེ་བའི་ངང་ནས་བཟླས་པ་སོགས་བྱེད་པ་ལས། སྐུའི་སྣང་བ་དེ་དག་སྣང་ལ་རང་
བཞིན་མེད་པ་གསལ་ལ་རྟོག་པ་མེད་པ། བདེ་ལ་ཞེན་པ་མེད་པ་སྟེ་མཚན་ཉིད་གསུམ་
ལྡན་སྟོང་པ་ཉིད་ཀྱི་རང་གདངས་སུ་མ་འགགས་པར་ས་ལེར་སྣང་བའི་ངང་ནས་བཟླས་
བརྗོད་སོགས་གནང་ན་རྩལ་ཆེ་ཞིང་ཆེད་དུ་བླ་མ་སྤྱི་བོར་བསྒོམ་པ་སོགས་མི་དགོས།
ལམ་དུས་ཀྱི་གཞི་ལམ་འབྲས་བུའི་བཞག་མཚམས་ནི། ལམ་གྱི་དུས་སུ་འང་སེམས་
ཉིད་རྩ་བྲལ་རིས་མེད་ཁྱབ་གདལ་དེ་གཞི། དེའི་ངང་ལ་བསལ་བཞག་མེད་པར་ཡུལ་
མེད་རང་གསལ་དུ་སྐྱོང་བ་དེ་ལམ། དེས་འབྲས་བུའི་རྫོགས་རིམ་གྱི་ལྷ་སྐུ་ཞུ་བདེ་
དང་མཚུངས་ལྡན་དུ་རང་ཤར་བ་ནས་ལམ་གྱི་འབྲས་བུའི་གྲངས་སུ་འགྲོ་བ་ཡིན་
ནོ། །དེའང་རྫོགས་ཆེན་གྱི་གཞུང་ནས་ངོ་རང་ཐོག་ཏུ་སྤྲོད་པ་ཞེས་པ་ནི། དུས་
གསུམ་རྟོག་པ་དང་བྲལ་པའི་ད་ལྟའི་ཤེས་པ་ལ་བཅོས་སླད་མ་བྱས་པར་གཉུག་མའི་ངང་
དུ་ཨ་ལེ་སང་ངེ་། ཆམ་བརྡལ་བ་ཉིད་བཙན་ཐབས་སུ་ངོས་བཟུང་ནས་རང་བྱུང་གི་ཡེ་
ཤེས་ངོ་སྤྲོད་པ་དག་ཐག་གཅིག་ཐོག་ཏུ་བཅད་པ་ཞེས་པ་ནི་དྲན་བསམ་སྤྲ་མ་འགགས།
ཕྱི་མ་མ་སྐྱེས། ད་ལྟའི་ཤེས་པ་རྟོག་བཅས་དྲན་བསམ་གྱི་བློ་འགགས་ནས་བཞི་ཆ་
གསུམ་འབྲལ་གྱི་རིག་པས་སོ་མ་རྣམ་པར་མི་རྟོག་པའི་ཡེ་ཤེས་རིག་གེ །སང་ངེ་།
ཡེར་རེ། ཨ་ལེ་བར་གནས་པ་འདི་ཉིད་དོ། །བཞི་ཆ་གསུམ་བྲལ་ཞེས་པ་ནི།
འདས་མ་འོངས་ད་ལྟ་བ་སྟེ་རྟོག་བཅས་ཀྱི་དུས་གསུམ་དང་། རྟོག་མེད་ད་ལྟར་བའི་
དུས་གསུམ་དྲན་བསམ་གྱིས་བཅོས་སླད་མེད་པའི་སོ་མ་སྟེ་ཆ་བཞི་ལས་རྟོག་བཅས་ཀྱི་
དུས་གསུམ་དང་བྲལ་བའི་རྣམ་པར་མི་རྟོག་པའི་དུས་དེ་བཞི་ཆ་གསུམ་བྲལ་ཆོས་སྐུ་བློ་
འདས་ཀྱི་དགོངས་པའོ། །གདེངས་གྲོལ་ཐོག་ཏུ་བཅའ་ཞེས་པ་ནི། གང་ཤར་གྱི་
རང་ངོ་ལ་བཅོས་བསླད་མེད་པར་ཅེར་རེ་བལྟས་ཏེ་དེའི་ངང་ལ་གློད་པས། དྲན་རྟོག་
རྗེས་མེད་དུ་ཡལ་བས་ཐ་རླབས་ཆུར་ཐིམ་པ་ལྟར་གང་ཤར་རང་གྲོལ་སྤང་གཉེན་དང་
བྲལ་བའི་ངང་ལ་གདེངས་འཆོས་པའོ།། ༄ །།རྫོགས་ཆེན་སེམས་ཀློང་གཉིས་ཀྱི་
གནད་མན་ངག་གི་སྡེར་འདུས་སྟེ། ཀ་དག་གི་ངང་ལ་མཉམ་པར་བཞག་པས།

སྣོད་བཅུད་ཀྱི་སྣང་བ་ཐམས་ཅད་སེམས་ཉིད་རང་བྱུང་གི་ཡེ་ཤེས་བརྗོད་བྲལ་ཆོས་སྐུར་ཐག་ཆོད་པས་སེམས་སྡེའི་གནད་འདུས། དེ་ཉིད་གང་ལའང་བྱ་རྩོལ་བྲལ་བའི་ཆོས་ཉིད་ཀྱི་ཀློང་དུ་ཐག་ཆོད་པས་ཀློང་སྡེ་འདུ། དེའི་ཕྱིར་སེམས་ཀློང་གཉིས་ཀྱི་ཉམས་ལེན་ཐམས་ཅད་མན་ངག་གི་སྡེའི་ཁྲེགས་གཅོད་ཀྱི་ཉམས་ལེན་གྱི་ཁོངས་སུ་འདུས་པས་རྫོགས་པ་ཆེན་པོའི་ལམ་གྱི་མཆོག་རྩེ་མོ་ནི་མན་ངག་གི་སྡེ་སྟེ། འཁོར་འདས་སྤང་བླང་དང་བྲལ་བའི་ཡིན་ལུགས་གནད་ཐོག་ཏུ་འབེབས་པའི་ཐབས་ཀྱིས་བློ་འདས་རང་བྱུང་གི་ཡེ་ཤེས་སྐད་ཅིག་ལ་འཆར་བ་བྱེད་པས། དོན་ལ་ཆོས་ཐམས་ཅད་ཀྱི་ཆོས་ཉིད་རང་གསལ་གྱི་གནས་ལུགས་མངོན་སུམ་དུ་གཏན་ལ་ཕབ་ནས་ཡེ་ཤེས་འོད་གསལ་ལྷུན་གྲུབ་གཞི་གནས་སུ་ངོ་སྤྲོད་པའི་ཐབས་མཆོག་བླ་ན་མེད་པའོ། །ཚོགས་དྲུག་གི་སྣང་བ་གང་ཤར་རང་གྲོལ་དུ་ལམ་དུ་འཁྱེར་བ་དང་ལྷ་སྔགས་སུ་རྒྱས་བཏབ་པ་གཉིས་སྔ་མ་ནུས་པ་ཆེ་མོད། འོན་ཀྱང་རང་གྲོལ་གཅུག་མིའི་རྩལ་སྣང་ལྷ་སྔགས་ཀྱི་རང་གདངས་སུ་བྱ་རྩོལ་མེད་པར་ལམ་དུ་ཁྱེར་ཤེས་པ་ཟུང་འབྲེལ་གྱི་ལམ་ཁྱད་པར་ཅན་དུ་འགྲོ་བ་ལགས། ༄ །རིག་པ་རྗེན་པར་འཆར་སྒོ་སྣ་ཚོགས་སུ་འཆར་ཡང་གང་ཤར་ཐམས་ཅད་དྲན་པ་ཁོ་རང་ལས་མ་གཡོས་པ་གཟུང་དྲན་ལ་མ་ལྟོས་པར་སྐྱེད་ཐུབ་པ་དེ། རྫོགས་ཆེན་པའི་ལུགས་ལ་ཉམས་ཀྱི་སྐྱེ་རིམ་བཞི་ལས་གནས་པའི་ཉམས་དང་། ཕྱག་ཆེན་པའི་ལུགས་ཀྱི་རྩེ་གཅིག་ཏུ་གནས་པ་ཕྱོགས་འདྲ་བས་སེམས་ཀྱི་ངོ་བོའི་ཕྱོགས་མཐོང་ཙམ་ལོས་ཡིན། འོན་ཀྱང་བརྟན་པ་ཐོབ་མ་ཐོབ་ཙམ་ལས་འདི་བས་ལྷག་པ་ཞིག་མཐོང་རྒྱུའམ་རྟོགས་རྒྱུ་མེད་དམ་སྙམས་པ་དེ། ཡིན་ལུགས་དང་མཐུན་པའི་གོ་མྱོང་གི་ཆ་ནས་བློ་མ་འབྲེལ་པའི་ཡེ་ཤེས་འདྲ་ཡང་། འདི་ལས་ལྷག་པ་མེད་དམ་སྙམ་པའི་ཆོས་ཀྱི་བདག་འཛིན་གྱི་བློ་དང་བཅས་པའི་རྣམ་རྟོག་ཅན་དུ་འགྱུར་བས། རང་གི་རིག་པ་ལ་རྗེན་ཅེར་བལྟས་པའི་དུས་ཀྱི་གཤིས་སྤྲོས་བྲལ་ལ་བློས་གང་དུ་ཡང་གཟུང་དུ་མེད་པ་དེ་དང་། གོ་བའི་སྟོང་ཉིད་གཉིས་ལ་མྱོང་ལུགས་མི་འདྲ་པ་མཁྱེན་དགོས། འོན་ཀྱང་སེམས་ཀྱི་ངོ་བོ་མཐོང་བ་ཞེས་པ་ཡང་དོན་སྤྱི་ཙམ་མཐོང་པའི་

དཔེའི་ཡེ་ཤེས་ལ་རང་ངོ་སྤྲོད་པའི་ཐབས་མཁས་ལས། རང་རིག་པའི་ཡེ་ཤེས་རྣམ་པར་མི་རྟོག་པའི་ངོ་བོ་རང་མཚན་པ་ནི་འཕགས་པའི་ས་ཐོབ་ནས་མ་གཏོགས་སྒོམ་བྱུང་ལ་རང་དབང་འབྱོར་པའི་སྦྱོར་ལམ་ངེས་འབྱེད་ཀྱི་དུས་སུ་འང་མེད་ན་ཚོགས་ལམ་པ་དང་མ་ཞུགས་ཀྱི་བསམ་གཏན་པའི་རྒྱུད་ལ་ལྟ་ཅི་སྨོས། དེས་ན་ཤན་ཕྱེད་དགོས། རྨི་ལམ་རང་ངོ་ཤེས་པའི་དྲན་པའི་ངང་ནས་རྩལ་སྦྱོང་དང་རྨི་ལམ་མོ་སླམ་པའི་དྲན་ཤེས་མེད་པར་རྩལ་སྦྱོང་ཉིན་མོ་ལས་གསལ་དྭངས་ཆེ་བ་ཡོང་བ་དེ་རྨི་ལམ་ཟིན་སྦྱོང་སྤྲུལ་སྒྱུར་གྱི་ངོས་ནས་སྔ་མ་མི་འགྱུར་ཞིང་བརྟན་ལ་ཕྱིས་བོགས་ཆེ། ཕྱི་མ་དེ་ཉིན་མོའི་དགེ་སྦྱོར་གྱི་ཤུགས་ཀྱིས་སླེབ་པའི་ཉམས་སྣང་ཙམ་དུ་ཟད་པས་རྨི་ལམ་ཟིན་སྦྱོང་བརྟན་ཆགས་ཀྱི་གནད་དུ་འགྲོ་བ་ཉུང་། ཕལ་ནས་གཉིད་འཐུག་གི་སྐབས་སུ་གསལ་སྟོང་གི་རིག་པ་རྣམ་རྟོག་གི་གཡའ་དང་བྲལ་ཞིང་རང་ངོ་སྐྱོང་ཐུབ་པ། དེའི་རྩལ་སྣང་རྨི་ལམ་གྱི་སྤྲུལ་བསྒྱུར་དུ་ལྡང་ཐུབ་པ་ཞིག་ཀྱང་འབྱུང་སྟེ། གཉིད་ཀྱི་འོད་གསལ་ཟིན་པའི་གྲངས་སུ་འགྲོ་ཞིང་། དེ་འདྲ་དེ་རྨི་ལམ་དུ་ལངས་ནས་ཀྱང་རྨི་ལམ་དུས་ཀྱི་དྲན་ཤེས་ཀྱིས་མ་ཟིན་ནའང་གནད་དུ་འགྲོ། ཐོད་རྒལ་གྱི་དུས་སྐོང་གཟུགས་ཀྱི་རྟགས་སྣང་ལ་ལྟ་སྣང་གྱི་ལམ་ནས་དྭངས་ཏེ་རྣམ་པར་རྟོག་མེད་ཀྱི་ངང་དུ་འཛོག་པ་དེ་ལ་གོམས་པས་ཞི་གནས་ཙམ་ལས་སོ་སོར་རྟོག་པའི་ཤེས་རབ་ཀྱི་དཔྱད་པ་མེད་པས་ལྷག་མཐོང་མི་འགྲོ་བར་སླམས་མཁན་མང་ནའང་། རྣམ་པར་མི་རྟོག་པའི་ཏིང་ངེ་འཛིན་གོམས་པ་ལས་མི་རྟོག་པའི་ཡེ་ཤེས་སྐྱེས་པ་གྱུར་པ་དེ་ཀ་སོ་སོར་རྟོག་པའི་ཤེས་རབ་ཀྱི་ལྷག་མཐོང་སྐྱེས་པ་ཡིན་པར་དུས་འཁོར་སོགས་ལས་ཀྱང་བཤད་ཅིང་། ཁྱད་པར་རྫོགས་པ་ཆེན་པོ་རང་གི་ལུགས་ལ། ལུས་བཞུགས་སྟངས། མིག་ལྟ་སྟངས། རླུང་མི་འགྱུལ་བ་གསུམ་ལ་གཞི་བཅས་པས་རིམ་པར་རྩ་རླུང་ལ་གནད་དུ་བསྣུན་པས་རྣམ་རྟོག་འགགས། མངོན་སུམ་ཡུལ་ལ་གསལ་པས་ཡིད་དཔྱོད་ཚིག་གི་སྒྲོ་འདོགས་དང་བྲལ། ཆོས་ཉིད་རང་ངོར་གནས་པས་མ་བུ་འདྲེས་ཏེ་གདོད་མའི་དབྱིངས་སུ་ལ་ཟློ་བ་ཡིན་པས་ཐིག་ལེ་ལུ་གུ་རྒྱུད་བཅས་པའི་རྟགས་སྣང་ལ་ལྟ་སྟངས་

ཀྱིས་ཅེར་རེ་གཏད་དེ། ཧྲགས་སྣང་དེ་ཁའི་རང་བཞིན་ཧྲིག་གེ་བའི་ངང་ལ་བཟོ་མེད་ཡེངས་མེད་དུ་འཛོག་པ་ཁོ་ནས་གནད་དུ་འགྲོ་བ་ལགས། ཆོས་ཉིད་བར་དོའི་སྐབས་ཀྱི་བསམ་གཏན་གྱི་ཞག་གི་ཚད་མཉམ་རྗེས་འདྲེས་ནས་ཏིང་ངེ་འཛིན་ཐུན་ཚོད་ལས་འདས་པ་ཡེ་ཤེས་ལྷུན་གྲུབ་ཀྱི་ཉམས་སྐྱེས་པ་ལ་མཐའ་འདི་ཙམ་ཞེས་ཚོད་འཛིན་དཀའ་མོད། སྤྱི་ཙམ་དུ་བསམ་གཏན་ལ་མཉམ་པར་བཞག་པས་རྣམ་རྟོག་གིས་བར་མ་ཆོད་པར་ཧེ་ཙམ་གནས་པའི་ཡུན་དེ་ཙམ་དུ་འཛོག །ཆོས་ཉིད་བར་དོར་དེ་གྲོལ་ནུས་ཀྱི་ཚད་འོད་གསལ་སྣང་བ་བཞི་ལ་ད་ལྟ་ནས་རང་བྱན་ཆུད་པ་ཞིག་གལ་ཆེ་བས་རྨི་ལམ་གྱི་ཉམས་ལེན་ཚད་དུ་སོང་མ་སོང་གིས་འཛིན་པ་ལགས། ༔ །མཉམ་བཞག་གི་ངོར་འཕྲོ་བར་སྣང་ཡང་དྲན་པ་ཁོ་རེ་འཁྱོངས་ཙམ་བདེ་གསལ་གྱི་ཉམས་དང་བཅས་ཤར་བ་དེ་ལ་སྒྱོང་བྱ་སྒྱོང་འདོད་ཀྱི་འཛིན་པ་མ་ཞུགས་ན་གནས་དུ་འགྲོ། གང་ཤར་རང་སེམས་སུ་ཐག་ཆོད་ཅིང་སེམས་ཉིད་རྩ་བྲལ་གསལ་སྟོང་འཛིན་མེད་དུ་ཤར་བས་མཉམ་བཞག་གི་ངོ་ནས་ལུས་སྣང་སེམས་སོགས་ཐ་དད་དུ་འཛིན་པ་རང་དག་ནས་ཕྱི་ནང་བར་མེད་སང་ཧྲེན་པར་གནས་པས་རྣམ་རྟོག་རང་ག་མ་མི་འཆར་ལ། ཤར་ཡང་ངོ་ཤེས་ཙམ་གྱིས་ཆོག་པར་སྣང་བ་དེ། སྣང་སེམས་འདྲེས་ཏེ་སྣང་བསྒོམ་དུ་ཤར་ཤར་འདྲ་ཡང་ད་དུང་སྟོང་ཉིད་གཟུང་དྲན་མ་ལ་ལྟོས་དགོས་མི་དགོས་ཤན་འབྱེད་དགོས་པས། སྣང་རིག་སོ་མ་འདི་རང་རིག་རང་གསལ་ལ་རྩོལ་སྒྲུབ་དང་དགག་སྒྲུབ་བྲལ་བ་ཞིག་བྱུང་ན་སྣང་བ་སྒོམ་དུ་ཤར་བས་གཟུང་དྲན་ལ་རག་མ་ལུས་ལགས། དེས་ན་རྩོལ་བཅས་ཀྱང་འཛིན་པ་མ་ཞུགས་གང་ཤར་རང་གྲོལ་དུ་ཡངས་སུ་འཆར་ན་གནད་དུ་འགྲོ་ཞིང་། ལར་ནི་ཅོག་བཞག་གསུམ་གྱིས་རང་གི་དགེ་སྦྱོར་རྒྱུན་བསྐྱངས་ཏེ་དེ་རྟོགས་པའི་ངོ་བོ་ལ་ཅེར་གྲོལ་གྱིས་བལྟས་ནས། ཕྱི་ཆོས་ཅན་ལ་བལྟས་པས་འཁྲུལ་སྣང་བདེན་མེད་དུ་སྣང་བ་སྒྱུ་མ་ལྟ་བུ་རྟོགས་པའི་ངང་ལ་ཞེན་འཛིན་མེད་པར་སློད། ནང་ཆོས་ཉིད་ལ་བལྟས་པས་ཡུལ་མེད་ནམ་མཁའ་ལྟ་བུར་རྟོགས་པའི་ངང་ལ་འཛིན་མེད་དུ་སློད། གསང་བ་རིག་པའི་ངོ་བོ་ལ་བལྟས་པས་སྟོང་གསལ་འགགས་མེད་དུ་རྟོགས་

ནས་དེའི་ངང་རྩོལ་སྒྲུབ་མེད་པར་སློད་དེ་མཉམ་པར་བཞག་པས་གནས་སྐབས་སུ་སྨིན་དང་མངོན་ཤེས་སོགས་ཡོན་ཏན་དཔག་ཏུ་མེད་པ་ལ་རང་དབང་བསྒྱུར་ནུས་ཤིང་ཉོན་མོངས་པ་རང་སར་གྲོལ་བ་ལ་དཀའ་ཚེགས་མེད། དེའང་ལས་དང་པོ་དང་ཡོངས་སུ་སྦྱང་བ་བྱས་པ་དང་། གོམས་པ་གློང་དུ་གྱུར་པའི་ཡོན་ཏན་རྣམས་སྐྱེ་རིམ་གྱིས་འཕེལ་ནས་སངས་རྒྱས་ཀྱི་ཡེ་ཤེས་འགྲུབ་པའི་ཐབས་ཟབ་མོར་འགྲོ་ཞེས་རྗེ་བླ་མ་དམ་པའི་ཞལ་ནས་མང་དུ་ཐོས་ཤིང་གསུང་དེ་ལ་ཡིད་ཆེས་ཀྱིས་ཚོད་མར་བཟུང་ནས་གཞན་ལའང་འདོམས་པ་ལགས་པས་ཐུགས་ལ་བཅུག་འཚལ། ལྟ་བའི་ངོ་བོ་གཉིས་ཆོས་སུ་སྣང་བ་ཐམས་ཅད་སོ་སོར་མ་དམིགས་པར་རང་རིག་ཡེ་གྲོལ་ལྷུན་གྲུབ་སྟོང་གསལ་སྤྲོས་བྲལ་རྒྱ་ཆད་ཕྱོགས་ལྷུང་བྲལ་བ་དུ་མ་རོ་གཅིག་ཏུ་རྟོགས་པས་ཅི་ལའང་ཡ་ང་བག་ཚ་མེད་པར་སྣང་ཡང་། ཡུལ་ལ་བརྟེན་ནས་ཆགས་སྡང་སོགས་འཆར་འཆར་འདྲ་བ་བྱུང་བ་བདག་འཛིན་གྱི་བློ་མ་ནུབ་གྱི་བར་ལྟ་བའི་གོ་ཡུལ་བཟང་ཡང་སྤྱོད་ཐོག་ཏུ་དེ་དང་འགལ་བ་ལྟར་སྣང་བའང་ཆོས་ཉིད་པས། དེ་ཚེ་གང་ཤར་རང་གྲོལ་རྗེན་པར་ལམ་དུ་ཁྱེར་བས་གནད་དུ་འགྲོ། དེས་ན་གྲུབ་མཐའི་རྟོག་དཔྱོད་དང་། ཞེན་པའི་སྣང་ཡུལ་དང་། ཡིད་ཀྱི་སྤྱོད་ཡུལ་ལས་འདས་པའི་རང་བཞིན་མཐའ་གྲོལ་གློང་ཡངས་ཆེན་པོར་ཡེ་ནས་གནས་པ་ལྟར་དེའི་ངང་བསྐྱངས་པ་གནད་དུ་ཡིན། གང་ལྟར་ཡང་དབྱར་དུས་ཀྱི་ས་གཞི་ལ་སྨྱུ་གུ་གང་ཡང་སྐྱེ་བ་ལྟར་རྣལ་འབྱོར་པའི་ཉམས་ལ་མཐོ་དམན་མཐའ་གཅིག་ཏུ་མ་ངེས་པའི་བཟང་རྟོག་ངན་རྟོག་གིས་བསྡུས་པའི་རྟོག་པའི་རི་མོ་ལྟ་ཅི་སྨོས། མི་རྟོག་པའི་རང་གདངས་ཀྱི་རྩལ་ལ་མཐའ་དང་བྲལ་བའི་ལྟ་བ། གཉེན་པོས་མ་བཅིངས་པའི་སྒོམ་པ། གང་ཤར་རང་གྲོལ་དུ་གཏོང་བའི་སྤྱོད་པ། རེ་དོགས་གཉིས་འཛིན་དང་བྲལ་བའི་འབྲས་བུའི་སྣང་བ་གང་ཤར་ཡང་སྤྱོད་འདོད་ཀྱི་བློ་ཞུགས་ན་སྨན་མ་ཞུ་བ་དུག་ཏུ་སོང་བ་དང་འདྲ་བས། དེའི་ཚེ་ཐག་ཆོད་པའི་དོན་དེ་ཁོའི་ངང་ལ་འཛིན་ཞེན་གྱིས་མ་བཅིངས་པར་མ་ཡེངས་མི་སྒོམ་པའི་རང་འགྲོས་ཀྱིས་རྟག་ཏུ་འཚོ་བར་མཛད་ན་འཚེངས་པ་ལགས། རྨི་ལམ་རགས་པ་རྟག་ཏུ་ཟིན་པ་འདྲ་

བ་དེའང་ཟིན་པ་ཙམ་གྱིས་མི་ཆོག་པས། ད་དུང་ཉིན་སྣང་ཚོགས་དྲུག་གི་སྣང་བ་ལ་འཛིན་པ་མ་ཞུགས་པར་འབད་རྩོལ་གྱིས་འཆུན་པར་མཛད་ནས་གཉིད་དུ་འགྲོ་དུས་ཉིན་པར་གྱི་དྲན་ཤུགས་མ་ཤོར་བར་གཉིད་ལོག་པས་ཉམས་དང་རྟོགས་པ་འོད་གསལ་རྣམས་རིམ་པར་འཆར་བ་ཡིན་ནོ། ༈ །ཉམས་གང་ལྟར་སྐྱེས་ཀྱང་དགག་སྒྲུབ་དང་བླང་དོར་གྱི་རྟོག་བསམ་བསླད་པར་གང་ཤར་གྱི་རང་ངོ་བསྐྱངས་པས་གཟུང་འཛིན་གྱི་རྟོག་ཚོགས་ནམ་མཁའ་ལ་སྤྲིན་དེངས་པ་ལྟར་སངས་ཤིང་འཁོར་བའི་ས་བོན་ཟད་དེ། དབྱིངས་རང་བཞིན་གྱི་རྣམ་པར་དག་པའི་ཀློང་དུ་རིག་པ་རང་བཞིན་གྱིས་རྣམ་པར་དག་པ་ཐིམ་པས་མ་བུ་འདྲེས་ནས་གཟུང་འཛིན་གཉིས་མེད་ཀྱི་ཡེ་ཤེས་འགྱུར་མེད་ཀྱི་དབྱིངས་སུ་གཏན་ལ་ཕེབས་ཏེ། ཆ་རླབས་ཆུར་ཐིམ་པ་བཞིན་དུ་རྣམ་རྟོག་དབྱིངས་སུ་དག་པས་འཁོར་འདས་ཀྱི་བར་ལག་འགྲེལ། ལམ་ལྔ་ས་བཅུ་རིམ་གྱིས་ལམ་ཅིག་ཅར་དུ་འགྲོ་དེ་གྲོལ་བར་འགྱུར་རོ།། །།

༄༅། །རྫོགས་ཆེན་གསང་བ་སྙིང་ཐིག་གི་རྒྱུད་ཀྱི་གནད་དོན་རྣམ་པར་དབྱེ་བའི་འཕྲུལ་མུན་ཁྱུང་གི་སྒྲོན་མེ་ཞེས་བྱ་བ་བཞུགས་སོ།།

༄༅། །ཀུན་མཁྱེན་ཡབ་སྲས་ཆོས་ཀྱི་རྒྱལ་པོ་ལ་སྒོ་གསུམ་གུས་པས་ཕྱག་འཚལ་ཞིང་སྐྱབས་སུ་མཆིའོ། འདིར་རང་བཞིན་རྫོགས་པ་ཆེན་པོ་གསང་བ་སྙིང་ཐིག་གི་རྒྱུད་ཆེན་པོ་དག་གི་དོན་འཆད་པ་ན་རྟོགས་ཏེ་སངས་རྒྱས་མ་བྱུང་། མ་རྟོགས་ཏེ་འཁོར་བ་མ་བྱུང་བ་རིག་ནས་སྐབས་ན་གདོད་མ་གཞིའི་གནས་ལུགས་ཇི་ལྟར་ཡིན་ཞེས་པ་ཚིག་གི་དོན་བཅུ་གཅིག་གི་དང་པོར་འཆད་པ་འདི་ལ་ལྷ་བ་བོན་ལུགས་ཀྱི་ཤན་ཤོར་བར་སྒྲོ་སྐུར་སྣ་ཚོགས་སུ་སྨྲ་བ་དེང་སང་ཆེས་མང་བས་འདི་ལ་གནད་དོན་རྣམ་པར་དབྱེ་བའི་འཕྲུལ་མུན་ཁྱུང་གི་སྒྲོན་མེ་ལྷ་བུ་འདེགས་པ་ལ་དོན་གསུམ་སྟེ། གཞི་ངོས་འཛིན་པ། དེ་མཁས་པའི་བཞེད་པ་སྒྲུབ་པ། དེ་ལ་རྩོད་པ་སྤང་བའོ། དང་པོ་ནི། སྔོན་པ་བདེ་བར་གཤེགས་པའི་གསུང་གི་གསང་བ་ཟབ་མོ་ཐེག་པ་ཆེན་པོ་ཤིན་ཏུ་རྒྱས་པའི་མདོ་སྡེ་དག་ལས་ཁམས་བདེ་བར་གཤེགས་པའི་སྙིང་པོ་རྒྱ་ཆེར་བཤད་པ་དེ་ཉིད་གསང་སྔགས་རྡོ་རྗེ་ཐེག་པའི་གཞུང་ལ་རང་བཞིན་གཞི་རྒྱུད་ཅེས་བཞག་པ་དེ་ལ་གསང་སྔགས་ཐུན་མོང་མ་ཡིན་པ་འདིར་གདོད་མའི་ཡེ་གཞི་ཞེས་བཞག་པ་ཡིན་ཏེ་མཚན་གཞི་ལ་མི་མཐུན་པ་ཅུང་ཟད་མེད་དོ། དེ་སྐད་དུ་ཆོས་མངོན་པའི་མཛོད་ལས། ཐོག་མ་མེད་དུས་ཅན་གྱི་དབྱིངས། །ཆོས་རྣམས་ཀུན་གྱི་གནས་ཡིན་ཏེ། །འདི་ཡོད་པས་ན་འགྲོ་ཀུན་དང་། །མྱ་ངན་འདས་པ་འབྱུང་བར་འགྱུར། །ཞེས་དང་། དོ་ཧ་ལས། སེམས་ཉིད་གཅིག་པུ་ཀུན་གྱི་ས་བོན་ཏེ། །གང་ལ་སྲིད་དང་མྱ་ངན་འདས་འཕྲོ་བ། །འདོད་པའི་འབྲས་བུ་ཐམས་ཅད་རབ་སྟེར་པའི། །ཡིད་བཞིན་ནོར་འདྲའི་སེམས་ལ་ཕྱག་འཚལ་ལོ། །ཞེས་དང་། གསང་སྙིང་ལས། ཨེ་མ་ཧོ་བདེ་གཤེགས་སྙིང་པོ་ལས། །རང་གི་རྣམ་རྟོག་ལས་ཀྱིས་སྤྲུལ། །སྣ་ཚོགས་ལུས་དང་ལོངས་སྤྱོད་དང་། །བདག་དང་བདག་གིས་སོ་སོར་འཛིན། །ཞེས་དང་།

དགོངས་འདུས་ལས། གདོད་ནས་བདེ་གཤེགས་སྙིང་པོ་ལ། །རྣམ་རྟོག་གློ་བུར་ལས་ཀྱིས་བསྒྲིབ། །ཅེས་དང་། ཡང་། དཔག་ཏུ་མེད་པའི་རྒྱལ་བ་རྣམས། །འཁོར་བའི་སེམས་ཅན་རྒྱུ་ལས་བྱུང་། །ཞེས་དང་། མགོན་པོ་ཀླུས། གང་ཞིག་ཀུན་ཏུ་མ་ཤེས་ན། །སྲིད་པ་གསུམ་དུ་རྣམ་འཁོར་བ། །སེམས་ཅན་ཀུན་ལ་ངེས་གནས་པའི། །ཆོས་ཀྱི་དབྱིངས་ལ་ཕྱག་འཚལ་འདུད། །ཞེས་དང་། ཡང་། གང་ཞིག་འཁོར་བའི་རྒྱུར་གྱུར་བ། །དེ་ཉིད་སྦྱང་བ་བྱས་པ་ལས། །དག་པ་ཉིད་དེ་མྱ་ངན་འདས། །ཆོས་ཀྱི་སྐུ་ཡང་དེ་ཉིད་དོ། །ཞེས་དང་། ཀུན་བྱེད་ལས། ང་ནི་སྟོན་པ་ཀུན་བྱེད་བྱང་ཆུབ་སེམས། །བྱང་ཆུབ་སེམས་ནི་ཀུན་བྱེད་རྒྱལ་པོ་སྟེ། །དུས་གསུམ་སངས་རྒྱས་བྱང་ཆུབ་སེམས་ཀྱིས་བྱས། །ཁམས་གསུམ་སེམས་ཅན་བྱང་ཆུབ་སེམས་ཀྱིས་བྱས། །ཞེས་པ་ལ་སོགས་རྒྱ་ཆེར་བསྟན་པ་ཡིན་ཏེ། མདོ་སྔགས་དགོངས་པ་གཅིག་ཏུ་བབས་པ་ཡིན་ནོ། འོ་ན་རྣལ་འབྱོར་སྤྱོད་པ་སེམས་ཙམ་པ་ཀུན་གཞིའི་རྣམ་ཤེས་བདེན་པར་གྲུབ་པ། བདེ་གཤེགས་སྙིང་པོར་འདོད་པ་ཡོད་ན་འདི་དེ་དང་གཅིག་གམ་ཞེ་ན། དེ་ནི་མི་གཅིག་མོད་ཀྱི་བདེན་གྲུབ་བདེ་གཤེགས་སྙིང་པོར་འདོད་པ་ནི་གྲུབ་མཐའི་བློ་སྐྱོན་ཡིན་གྱི། དེ་དང་མཚུངས་མི་དགོས་ཀྱང་དབུ་མ་ཡན་ཆད་གཞིའི་འཇོག་ལུགས་མཐུན་པ་ཡིན་ནོ། འདིར་དེའི་མཚན་ཉིད་རྣམ་པར་བཞག་པའི་སྐབས་སུ་རང་བཞིན་རྫོགས་པ་ཆེན་པོའི་རྒྱུད་སྡེ་དག་ལས། ངོ་བོ་རང་བཞིན་ཐུགས་རྗེ་གསུམ་གྱི་བདག་ཉིད་དུ་བཤད་དེ། ཐལ་འགྱུར་ལས། ཐོག་མའི་ངོ་བོ་རང་བཞིན་དང་། །ཐུགས་རྗེ་རྣམ་པ་གསུམ་དུ་གནས། །ཞེས་སོ། །དེ་དང་མཐུན་པར་རྒྱུད་བླ་མ་ལས་ཀྱང་གསུམ་དུ་བཞག་སྟེ། ངོ་བོ་དེ་བཞིན་ཉིད་དང་། རང་བཞིན་ཆོས་སྐུ་དང་། ཐུགས་རྗེ་ཁམས་དང་རིགས་ཞེས་བཞག་པ་ཡིན་ལ། དང་པོ་ངོ་བོ་སྟོང་པའི་ངོས་ནས་གཞལ་ན་ཡོད་མེད་པའི་ཡིན་མིན་སྤྲོས་པའི་མཐའ་ཐམས་ཅད་དང་བྲལ་བ་ནམ་མཁའི་དཀྱིལ་ལྟར་གནས་ཏེ། རྒྱུད་བླ་མའི་འགྲེལ་པ་ལས། དེ་བཞིན་ཉིད་ནི་གཞན་དུ་འགྱུར་བ་མ་ཡིན་པ་ཉིད་ཀྱིས་

རང་གི་ངོ་བོའི་མཚན་ཉིད་ལས་བརྩམས་ནས། ནམ་མཁའ་དང་ཆོས་མཐུན་པ་ཉིད་དུ་རིག་པར་བྱའོ། །ཞེས་དང་། རིན་ཆེན་ཕྲེང་བ་ལས། ངོ་བོ་རབ་ཏུ་མི་གནས་ན། ཡོད་མིན་མེད་མིན་གཉིས་ཀ་མིན། །སྟོང་པ་མ་ཡིན་མི་སྟོང་མིན། །རྒྱུ་མེད་མ་ཡིན་ཡང་དག་མིན། །བདེན་པ་མ་ཡིན་རྫུན་པ་མིན། །དག་པ་མ་ཡིན་མ་དག་མིན། །བླང་མེད་དོར་མེད་དེ་ཁོ་ན། །ཞེས་དང་། སྐྱེ་མེད་རིན་པོ་ཆེའི་མཛོད་ལས། །སྟོང་ཉིད་འཁོར་འདས་སྙིང་པོ་ཅན། །གཞི་ལམ་འབྲས་བུ་སྐྱེ་མེད་ཀྱི། །གཞི་རྩ་དྲན་མེད་བློ་ལས་འདས། །སེམས་མེད་སེམས་ལས་བྱུང་བའང་མེད། །བྱ་བྲལ་རེ་དོགས་རྒྱུན་འཆིང་ཆད། །ཅེས་དང་། དབུ་མ་སྤྱོད་པ་འཕོ་བ་ལས། རང་བཞིན་ཐམས་ཅད་མཁའ་དང་མཉམ། །རྒྱུ་མེད་འབྲས་བུ་མེད་པ་དང་། །ལས་ཀྱི་དངོས་པོ་མེད་པ་དང་། །དངོས་པོ་ཐམས་ཅད་འདི་ལྟར་མེད། །འཇིག་རྟེན་འདི་དང་ཕ་རོལ་དང་། །སྐྱེ་བ་མེད་པའི་ངོ་བོ་ཉིད། །ཅེས་དང་། མུ་ཏིག་ཕྲེང་བ་ལས། ཐོག་མ་ཉིད་ཀྱི་ཀ་དག་ལ། །འཁྲུལ་ཞེས་ཚམ་དུ་བརྗོད་དུ་མེད། །དེ་བཞིན་མ་འཁྲུལ་པའང་ཅི། །ཞེས་སོགས་རྒྱ་ཆེར་བཤད་ཅིང་རང་བཞིན་ཆོས་སྐུའི་ངོས་ནས་ཡོན་ཏན་ལྷུན་གྱིས་གྲུབ་པར་བསྟན་ཏེ། རྒྱུད་བླ་མའི་འགྲེལ་པ་ལས། དེ་ལ་རེ་ཞིག་དེ་བཞིན་གཤེགས་པའི་ཆོས་ཀྱི་སྐུ་ལ་ནི་བསམ་པའི་དོན་འགྲུབ་པ་ལ་སོགས་པའི་མཐར་ཐུག་གི་ངོ་བོ་ཉིད་ཀྱི་མཚན་ཉིད་ལས་བརྩམས་ནས། ཡིད་བཞིན་གྱི་ནོར་བུ་དང་ཆོས་མཐུན་པ་ཉིད་དུ་རིག་པར་བྱའོ་ཞེས་དང་། དོ་ཧ་ལས། སེམས་ཉིད་གཅིག་པུ་ཀུན་གྱི་ས་བོན་ཏེ་སོགས་སྤར་དྲངས་བ་ལྟར་དང་། ཏིང་འཛིན་རྒྱལ་པོའི་མདོ་ལས། དག་པ་དང་བ་འོད་གསལ་བ། །མི་འཁྲུགས་འདུས་མ་བྱས་པ་ཉིད། །བདེ་བར་གཤེགས་པའི་སྙིང་པོ་སྟེ། །ཡེ་ནས་གནས་པའི་ཆོས་ཉིད་དོ། །ཞེས་དང་། འཇམ་དཔལ་ཞལ་ལུང་ལས། རྫོགས་པ་ཆེན་པོ་ཡེ་ཤེས་སྒྱི་ཡི་གཟུགས། །ཡོངས་སུ་དག་སྐུ་རྡོ་རྗེ་འཆང་ཆེན་པོ། །ཞེས་དང་། སྒྱུ་འཕྲུལ་ལས། རང་བྱུང་ཡེ་ཤེས་བྱང་ཆུབ་སེམས། །བྱང་ཆུབ་སྙིང་པོ་འདུས་མ་

བྱས། །ལྷུན་རྫོགས་ཡོན་ཏན་འབར་བས་བརྒྱན། །ལྷུན་གྲུབ་དཀྱིལ་འཁོར་བླ་མེད་པའོ། །ཞེས་དང་། ཆོས་དབྱིངས་བསྟོད་པ་ལས། ཇི་ལྟར་བུམ་ནང་མར་མེ་ཡིས། །ཕྱི་རོལ་ཀུན་ཏུ་མི་སྣང་ལྟར། །དེ་བཞིན་ཆོས་ཀྱི་དབྱིངས་འདི་ཡང་། །འཁོར་བར་འོད་ནི་གསལ་མ་ཡིན། །བུམ་པ་དེ་ཉིད་བཅག་གྱུར་ན། །ཐམས་ཅད་ཀུན་ཏུ་སྣང་བ་ལྟར། །གང་ཚེ་ཏིང་འཛིན་རྡོ་རྗེ་ཡིས། །སྒྲིབ་པ་ཀུན་ཏུ་བཅོམ་གྱུར་བ། །དེ་ཚེ་ནམ་མཁའི་མཐར་ཐུག་གསལ། །ཞེས་དང་། ཀུན་བྱེད་ལས། ཀུན་གྱི་སྙིང་པོ་བྱང་ཆུབ་སེམས་འདིར་ནི། །ཡེ་ནས་རང་གི་རང་བཞིན་ལྷུན་གྲུབ་པས། །རང་བཞིན་བཙུ་ཡིས་བཙལ་ཞིང་བསྒྲུབ་མི་དགོས། །ཞེས་སོགས་རྒྱ་ཆེར་བཤད་ཅིང་། ཐུགས་རྗེ་རིག་པའི་ཡེ་ཤེས་དེ་བཞིན་གཤེགས་པའི་རིགས་སུ་བཞག་པ་ཡིན་ཏེ། རྒྱུད་བླའི་འགྲེལ་བ་ལས། དེ་བཞིན་གཤེགས་པའི་རིགས་ལ་ནི་སེམས་ཅན་ལ་སྙིང་བརྩེ་བས་བརླན་པའི་རང་གི་ངོ་བོ་ཉིད་ཀྱི་མཚན་ཉིད་ལས་བརྩམས་ནས་ཆུ་དང་ཆོས་མཐུན་པ་ཉིད་དུ་རིག་པ་བྱའོ། །ཞེས་དང་། སྡུད་པ་ལས། ཡེ་ཤེས་མེད་ན་ཡོན་ཏན་འཕེལ་མེད་བྱང་ཆུབ་མེད། །རྒྱ་མཚོ་འདྲ་བའི་སངས་རྒྱས་ཆོས་ཀྱང་མེད་པར་འགྱུར། །ཞེས་དང་། །འཇམ་དཔལ་ཞལ་ལུང་ལས། དངོས་ཀུན་གཙོ་བོ་རང་སེམས་ཀྱི། །ངོ་བོ་ཉིད་དེ་དེ་རྟོགས་ན། །སངས་རྒྱས་བྱང་ཆུབ་དེ་ཉིད་དེ། །འཇིག་རྟེན་གསུམ་ཡང་དེ་ཉིད་དོ། །ཅེས་དང་། ཡང་། སངས་རྒྱས་མྱ་ངན་མེད་པའི་ཁམས། །སྐྱེ་མེད་རྡོ་རྗེ་མངོན་བྱང་ཆུབ། །བདེ་གཤེགས་སྙིང་པོ་ཀུན་གྱི་མཆོག །གཉིས་མེད་རྟོག་བྲལ་དོན་ཆེའོ། །ཞེས་དང་། ཀྱེ་རྡོར་ལས། སེམས་ཅན་རྣམས་ནི་སངས་རྒྱས་ཉིད། །འོན་ཀྱང་གློ་བུར་དྲི་མས་བསྒྲིབ། །དེ་བསལ་ན་ནི་སངས་རྒྱས་ཉིད། །ཅེས་དང་། ཐལ་འགྱུར་ལས། ཐུགས་རྗེ་ཀུན་ཁྱབ་ཡེ་ཤེས་ལས། །མི་མཛད་སྣ་ཚོགས་འཆར་བའི་སྒོ། །མཛད་པ་ལྟར་སྣང་ངོ་བོར་རྫོགས། །ཆོས་སྐུ་སྟོང་པའི་རང་བཞིན་ལས། །ཡེ་ཤེས་མཁྱེན་པ་རྫོགས་པའི་ཆ། །ཤུགས་ཀྱིས་སེམས་

ཅན་རྣམས་ལ་འཆར། །དེ་མེད་འཁོར་འདས་ལྷེ་ཆད་པས། །མཁྱེན་པས་རིག་ཅིང་གསལ་བའོ། །རང་རིག་གསལ་བའི་བདག་ཉིད་ལས། །རང་བཞིན་ཤུགས་ཀྱི་ཐུགས་རྗེ་ཉིད། །མ་འགག་འགག་པ་མེད་པའོ། །ཞེས་སོགས་རྒྱ་ཆེར་བསྟན་ཅིང་དོན་འདི་དག་འཁོར་ལོ་བར་པའི་མདོ་རྣམས་སུ་ནི་ངོ་བོ་སྟོང་པ་ཉིད་དང་། རང་བཞིན་མཚན་ཉིད་མེད་པ། ཐུགས་རྗེ་སྨོན་པ་མེད་པའི་རང་བཞིན་བདེ་གཤེགས་སྙིང་པོ་རྣམ་ཐར་སྒོ་གསུམ་དུ་བསྟན་པ་ཡིན་ཏེ། ཚངས་པ་ཁྱད་པར་སེམས་ཀྱིས་ཞུས་པའི་མདོ་ལས། ཆོས་ཐམས་ཅད་ཀྱི་རང་བཞིན་དེ་གང་ཞེ་ན་ཆོས་ཐམས་ཅད་ནི་སྟོང་པ་ཉིད་ཀྱི་རང་བཞིན་ཅན་ཏེ་དམིགས་པ་དང་བྲལ་བའོ། ཆོས་ཐམས་ཅད་ནི་མཚན་མ་མེད་པའི་རང་བཞིན་ཏེ་རྟོག་པ་དང་བྲལ་བའོ། ཆོས་ཐམས་ཅད་ནི་སྨོན་པ་མེད་པའི་རང་བཞིན་ཅན་ཏེ་བླང་བ་མེད་པ་དོར་བ་མེད་པའི་རང་བཞིན་ཏེ་རྣམ་པ་རྟོག་པ་དང་ནུས་པ་མེད་པ། ཤིན་ཏུ་ངོ་བོ་ཉིད་དང་བྲལ་བ་ཡིན་ཏེ། དེ་ནི་རང་བཞིན་གྱི་འོད་གསལ་བའོ། འཁོར་བའི་རང་བཞིན་གང་ཡིན་པ་དེ་མྱ་ངན་ལས་འདས་པའི་རང་བཞིན་ཡིན་ནོ། མྱ་ངན་ལས་འདས་པའི་རང་བཞིན་གང་ཡིན་པ་དེ་ཆོས་ཐམས་ཅད་ཀྱི་རང་བཞིན་ཡིན་ཏེ། དེའི་ཕྱིར་སེམས་རང་བཞིན་གྱི་འོད་གསལ་བའོ། །ཞེས་དང་། ཡང་ཀར་གཤེགས་པ་ལས། བློ་གྲོས་ཆེན་པོ་དེ་བཞིན་གཤེགས་པའི་སྙིང་པོ་བསྟན་པ་ནི་མུ་སྟེགས་ཅན་གྱི་བདག་ཏུ་སྨྲ་བ་དང་མཚུངས་པ་མ་ཡིན་ཏེ། བློ་གྲོས་ཆེན་པོ་དེ་བཞིན་གཤེགས་པ་དགྲ་བཅོམ་པ་ཡང་དག་པར་རྫོགས་པའི་སངས་རྒྱས་རྣམས་ནི་སྟོང་པ་ཉིད་དང་། ཡང་དག་པའི་མཐའ་དང་། མྱ་ངན་ལས་འདས་པ་དང་། མ་སྐྱེས་པ་དང་། མཚན་མ་མེད་པ་དང་། སྨོན་པ་མེད་པ་ལ་སོགས་པའི་ཚིག་གི་དོན་རྣམས་ལ་དེ་བཞིན་གཤེགས་པའི་སྙིང་པོར་བསྟན་པར་བྱས་ནས་ཞེས་སོགས་བཤད་པ་ཡིན་ཏེ། ཐེག་ཆེན་མདོ་སྔགས་གཉིས་ཀ་གཞིའི་མཚན་ཉིད་ལའང་མི་མཐུན་པ་ཙུང་ཟད་ཀྱང་མེད་དེ་ངོ་བོ་རང་བཞིན་ཐུགས་རྗེ་གསུམ་དུ་གནད་གཅིག་པ་ཡིན་ནོ། །དོན་གཉིས་པ་དེ་ཉིད་མཁས་པའི་བཞེད་པར་བསྒྲུབ་པ་ནི། དེ་ལ་འདི་སྐད་ཅེས་རྫོགས་པ་

ཆེན་པོའི་རྒྱུད་ལས་བཤད་པའི་ཡེ་གཞི་ནི་འཁོར་འདས་སྤྱི་མཚན་ལ་ལྟོས་པའི་སྔོན་རོལ་གྱི་གཞི་ཡིན་གྱི་གཞུང་གཞན་ནས་བཤད་པའི་བདེ་གཤེགས་སྙིང་པོ་དང་གཅིག་པའི་སྐབས་མེད་དེ། འདི་ནི་ཁྱོད་ཀྱི་རང་བཟོ་ཞིག་གོ་ཞེ་ན། དོན་འདི་ཀུན་མཁྱེན་ཆོས་ཀྱི་རྒྱལ་པོའི་བཞེད་པ་མ་ནོར་བ་ཉིད་ཡིན་ཏེ། རེ་ཞིག་དེའི་ཚུལ་ཙུང་ཟད་ཅིག་བརྗོད་ན། ཐོག་མ་ཁོ་ནར་ཡིད་བཞིན་མཛོད་དུ་འདི་སྐད་ཅེས་བཤད་དེ། ཐོག་མའི་འོད་གསལ་བདེ་གཤེགས་སྙིང་པོ་ཉིད། །དོན་གྱི་ཀུན་གཞི་རང་བཞིན་འདུས་མ་བྱས། །ཡེ་ནས་རྣམ་དག་ཉི་མཁའ་ལྟ་བུ་ལ། །མ་རིག་པ་ཡི་བག་ཆགས་གོས་པ་ན། །སེམས་ཅན་རྣམས་ལ་འཁྲུལ་པ་འདི་ཉིད་དོ། །ཞེས་དང་། གྲུབ་མཐའ་མཛོད་ལས། འོད་གསལ་རྡོ་རྗེ་སྙིང་པོའི་ཐེག་པ་འཆད་པའི་སྐབས་སུ་རང་བཞིན་གཞིའི་གནས་ལུགས་དེ་ལས་སེམས་ཅན་འཁྲུལ་ལུགས་སོགས་རྒྱ་བའི་ས་བཅད་ལྔ་བཞག་སྟེ། དང་པོའི་སྐབས་སུ་འདི་སྐད་ཅེས། དང་པོ་ནི་གདོད་མའི་གཞི་རང་བྱུང་གི་ཡེ་ཤེས་རྒྱ་ཆད་དང་ཕྱོགས་ལྷུང་མེད་པ་དེ་ཉིད་ངོ་བོ་སྟོང་པ་ནམ་མཁའ་ལྟ་བུ། རང་བཞིན་གསལ་བ་ཉི་མ་ལྟ་བུ། ཐུགས་རྗེ་ཁྱབ་པ་འོད་ཟེར་ལྟ་བུ་དེ་གསུམ་ངོ་བོ་དབྱེར་མེད་པ་སྐུ་གསུམ་ཡེ་ཤེས་ཀྱི་རང་བཞིན་དུ་ཡེ་ནས་རྟག་པར་འཕོ་བ་དང་འགྱུར་བ་མེད་པའི་དབྱིངས་སུ་གནས་ཏེ། ངོ་བོ་སྟོང་པ་ཆོས་སྐུ། རང་བཞིན་གསལ་བ་ལོངས་སྐུ། ཐུགས་རྗེ་ཁྱབ་པ་སྤྲུལ་པའི་སྐུའི་སྙིང་པོ་ཅན། འཁོར་འདས་གང་ཡང་མ་ཡིན་ལ། གོ་འབྱེད་པའི་ཆ་ནས་དབྱིངས་རང་བཞིན་རྣམ་དག་ཅེས་བཏགས་པའོ། ཚུལ་འདི་མདོ་སྡེ་ལས་ཀྱང་། ཐོག་མ་མེད་པའི་དུས་ཀྱི་དབྱིངས། །ཆོས་རྣམས་ཀུན་གྱི་གནས་ཡིན་ཏེ། །འདི་ཡོད་པས་ན་འགྲོ་ཀུན་དང་། །མྱ་ངན་འདས་པ་ཐོབ་པ་ཡིན། །ཞེས་གསུངས་སོ། དེའང་འཁོར་འདས་གཉིས་འགྲོ་གཞིར་བྱུང་སྟེ། དོ་ཧ་ལས་ཀྱང་། སེམས་ཉིད་གཅིག་པུ་སོགས་དྲངས་ནས་གསལ་བར་བཤད་ལ། ཆོས་དབྱིངས་མཛོད་ཀྱི་འགྲེལ་པར། ཐོག་མའི་དབྱིངས་བདེ་བར་གཤེགས་པའི་སྙིང་པོ་རང་བཞིན་ལྷུན་གྱིས་གྲུབ་པའི་སངས་རྒྱས་སུ་བརྗོད་ཅིང་

འདི་ཉིད་རྟོགས་མ་རྟོགས་ལས་གཞན་པའི་འཁོར་འདས་མེད་ལ། འདིའི་སྟོན་རོལ་དུ་སངས་རྒྱས་དང་སེམས་ཅན་ཞེས་ཐ་སྙད་གང་དུའང་གྲུབ་པ་མེད་དེ། རིག་པ་མེད་ན་འཁོར་འདས་སུ་གང་གིས་ངེས་པ་དང་། གྲོལ་འཁྲུལ་གྱི་སྤྱི་གཞི་གང་ཡང་མེད་པའི་ཕྱིར་རོ། དེས་ན་རིག་པ་རང་བྱུང་གི་ཡེ་ཤེས་ནི་ཆོས་ཀྱི་དབྱིངས་ཏེ། འཁོར་འདས་ཀྱི་ཆོས་མ་ལུས་པ་དེའི་དབྱིངས་ལས་འབྱུང་བས་ན་མཛོད་ཁང་སྦྲུས་ཉེ་བར་བརྗོད་པ་ཉིད་དོ། །ཞེས་རང་ཤར་གྱི་ལུང་དང་བཅས་ཏེ་མཚན་དོན་འཆད་པའི་སྐབས་སུ་བཤད་ཅིང་། གནས་ལུགས་རིན་པོ་ཆེའི་མཛོད་ལས་ཀྱང་། ཡེ་ནས་ལྷུན་གྱིས་གྲུབ་པའི་རང་བཞིན་ནི། །སུས་ཀྱང་མ་བྱས་ཡེ་ནས་གནས་པ་སྟེ། །ཀུན་འབྱུང་ནོར་བུ་དང་འདྲ་བྱང་ཆུབ་སེམས། །འཁོར་འདས་ཆོས་ཀུན་འབྱུང་བའི་གཞི་མར་གྲུབ། །ནམ་མཁའི་ངང་ལས་སྣང་སྲིད་སྣང་བ་ལྟར། །བྱང་ཆུབ་སེམས་ལས་འཁོར་འདས་མ་འགགས་ཤར། །སྣ་ཚོགས་རྨི་ལམ་གཉིད་ལས་བྱུང་བ་ལྟར། །འགྲོ་དྲུག་ཁམས་གསུམ་སེམས་ཀྱི་ངང་ལས་ཤར། །ཤར་བའི་དུས་ནས་ཆོས་ཀུན་རིག་པའི་ངང་། །སྟོང་པ་ལྷུན་གྲུབ་གཞི་སྣང་ཆེན་པོ་ཡིན། །ཞེས་རིག་པ་བྱང་ཆུབ་ཀྱི་སེམས་ཆོས་ཉིད་བདེ་གཤེགས་སྙིང་པོ་གདོད་མའི་ཡེ་གཞིར་ལེགས་པར་བཤད་ཅིང་། དེར་མ་ཟད་ཐེག་མཆོག་རིན་པོ་ཆེའི་མཛོད་དུ་གཞི་དང་གཞི་སྣང་གི་རྣམ་གྲངས་རྒྱ་ཆེ་བཤད་ནས་དེའི་མཇུག་ཏུ། དེས་ན་འཁྲུལ་གཞི་དང་། གྲོལ་གཞི་གཉིས་ཀ་ལྷུན་གྲུབ་ཀྱི་སྒོ་ལ་ཐུག་པས་ལེགས་པར་རྟོགས་པར་བྱའོ། །ཞེས་དང་། གསུམ་པ་འཆར་ནུབ་སྣང་ཚུལ་གྱི་འཐད་པ་དགོད་པ་ལ་གཉིས་ཏེ། འདི་དང་བར་དོའམ་ཚེ་འདིར་གང་ཟག་བརྩོན་འགྲུས་ཅན་གྱིས་ཉམས་སུ་བླངས་པའི་དུས་ན། གཞི་དེ་སྙིང་ག་ན་གནས་པའི་རང་གདངས་གཞི་སྣང་གི་ཁ་འོད་རྩ་དང་ཕྱིའི་ནམ་མཁའ་ལ་སྣང་སྟེ་ཞེས་སོགས་ལྷུན་གྲུབ་སྒོ་བརྒྱད་ཀྱི་འཆར་ཚུལ་རྒྱས་པ་བཤད་ཅིང་། ཡང་། སངས་རྒྱས་དང་སེམས་ཅན་ཡང་སྣང་བ་རང་ངོ་ཤེས་མ་ཤེས་ཙམ་སྟེ། འཁོར་འདས་རིག་པར་རྒྱ་གཅིག་པ་ལག་པའི་ལྟོ་རྒྱབ་བཞིན་ནོ། ད་ལྟའི་སྣང་བ་འདི་ཡང་མ་

དག་པའི་སྒོ་ལ་སྣང་བ་སྒྱུ་མའི་དཔེ་བརྒྱད་ཙམ་ལས། ཕྱི་ནང་ཡུལ་མེད་གཞི་བྲལ་མཉམ་པ་ཕྱལ་ཕྱལ་བ་གཅིག་ལས་སྤྱངས་མི་དགོས་བླང་མི་དགོས་སྣང་བ་གཞན་ཤར་དུས་གཞི་མེད་རང་ལོག་ཆེན་པོ་གཉིད་ཡལ་ན་རྨི་ལམ་ལོག་པ་ལྟར་གཞི་གྲོལ་ལ་རང་ལོག་སྟེ། ཡེ་སྟོང་ལ་ཡང་སྟོང་གཅིག་ཏུ་གྲོལ་བས་གནད་གཅིག་ལེགས་པར་རྟོགས་ན་ཚོགས་མེད་པར་རྒྱ་གྲོལ་ལ་འགྲོ་བ་ཡིན་ནོ། །ཞེས་རིག་པ་བྱང་ཆུབ་ཀྱི་སེམས་གདོད་མའི་ཡེ་གཞིར་བཞད་ཅིང་ད་ལྟའི་སྣང་བ་འདི་ཡང་གཞི་སྣང་གི་རོལ་བར་བསྟན་པ་ཡིན་ལ། ཚིག་དོན་མཛོད་ཀྱིས་བཅད་འཆད་པའི་སྐབས་སུ། རྟོགས་ཏེ་སངས་རྒྱས་མ་བྱུང་མ་རྟོགས་ཏེ་འཁོར་བ་མ་བྱུང་བའི་སྔོན་རོལ་ན་གདོད་མའི་གཞིའི་གནས་ལུགས་བསྟན་པ་དང་གཅིག །དེ་ལས་སེམས་ཅན་འཁྲུལ་ལུགས་དང་གཉིས། འཁྲུལ་དུས་གཞི་དེས་ཁྲུབ་ཚུལ་དང་གསུམ་ཞེས་བཤད་པ་འདིས་ཀྱང་གོ་ཞིང་། ཁྲིད་པར་ཡང་ཧྲིག་ཡིད་བཞིན་ནོར་བུའི་ཐོད་རྒལ་གྱི་རྒྱབ་ཡིག་ཉི་ཟླ་གཟའ་སྐར་ལས། །རང་བཞིན་གཞིའི་གནས་ལུགས་དེ་ལས་སེམས་ཅན་གྱི་འཁྲུལ་ལུགས་སེམས་དང་ཡེ་ཤེས་ཀྱི་དབྱེ་བ་སྟེ་ས་བཅད་གསུམ་དུ་བཞག་ནས་དང་པོ་འཆད་པའི་སྐབས་སུ། རང་བཞིན་གདོད་མའི་སྤྱི་གཞིའི་ཁམས་རང་བཞིན་གྱིས་རྣམ་པར་དག་པ་བདེ་བར་གཤེགས་པའི་སྙིང་པོ་འོད་གསལ་བའི་དབྱིངས། ངོ་བོ་རང་བཞིན་ཐུགས་རྗེ་གསུམ་དུ་གནས་སོ། །ཞེས་དང་། ཡང་ཡིག་ནམ་མཁའ་ཀློང་གསལ་ལས། དང་པོ་གདོད་མའི་སྤྱི་གཞི་ནི། ངོ་བོ་རང་བཞིན་ཐུགས་རྗེ་གསུམ། །སྟོང་གསལ་འཆར་གཞི་མ་འགག་བས། །ནམ་མཁའ་ཉི་ཟླ་མེ་ལོང་བཞིན། །ཡེ་ནས་ལྷུན་གྲུབ་ཆེན་པོར་གནས། །འཁོར་འདས་གཉིས་སུ་མ་ཆད་པའི། །འཆར་གཞི་འཆར་གནས་ལུང་མ་བསྟན། །ཆོས་ཀུན་འབྱུང་བའི་གཞི་ཞེས་བྱ། །རང་རིག་ཉིད་དང་འདུ་འབྲལ་མེད། །ཡོན་ཏན་ལྷུན་གྱིས་གྲུབ་པའི་ཕྱིར། །བདེ་གཤེགས་སྙིང་པོ་ཞེས་སུ་བཤད། །ངོ་བོ་སྟོང་བས་རྟག་མ་མྱོང་། །རང་བཞིན་གསལ་བས་ཆད་མ་མྱོང་། །ཐུགས་རྗེ་རིག་པས་བེམ་སྟོང་མིན། །གཅིག་དང་ཐ་དད་ལས་གྲོལ་

བས། །དབྱེར་མེད་སྐུ་གསུམ་འདུ་འབྲལ་མེད། །རང་བཞིན་གཞི་ཡི་སངས་རྒྱས་སོ། །སངས་རྒྱས་མར་མེ་མཛད་པ་དང་། །གདོད་མའི་མགོན་པོ་འོད་མི་འགྱུར། །འོད་དཔག་མེད་ཅེས་བྱ་བར་བཏགས། །དེ་ནི་གདོད་མའི་གནས་ལུགས་ཆོས། །དེ་ལས་གཞི་སྣང་ཤར་ཚུལ་ནི། །དཔེར་ན་ཤེལ་ལས་འོད་ལྟར་ཤར། །ཞེས་དང་། ནམ་མཁའ་ཀློང་ཆེན་ལས། གཞི་དབྱིངས་ལམ་དང་རྣམ་གྲོལ་འབྲས་བུ་ལས། །དབྱིངས་ནི་འོད་གསལ་རང་བཞིན་ལྷུན་གྱིས་གྲུབ། །སྟོང་དང་གསལ་དང་རིག་པའི་སྙིང་པོ་ཅན། །རྣམ་པར་དབྱེར་མེད་ཡོན་ཏན་ཚོགས་མང་ལྡན། །ཉི་བཞིན་ལྷུན་གྲུབ་པ་རང་བཞིན་རྣམ་པར་དག །རྣམ་དབྱེར་བཅས་པའི་དྲི་མས་ཡེ་སྟོང་ཞིང་། །གདོད་ནས་རྣམ་དག་འོད་གསལ་ཆོས་ཉིད་དོན། །འདི་ཡོད་པས་ན་རིག་དང་མ་རིག་ལས། །མྱ་ངན་འདས་དང་འགྲོ་དྲུག་སྣང་བཤད། །ཤར་ཙམ་ཉིད་ནས་སྙིང་པོའི་དབྱིངས་དེ་ལ། །བཟང་ངན་འཕོ་འགྱུར་དག་དང་མ་དག་མེད། །ཇི་ལྟར་ནམ་མཁའི་དབྱིངས་ནས་འབྱུང་བཞི་ཡི། །འཕོ་འགྱུར་སྣང་བས་གོས་བ་མེད་པ་བཞིན། །ཀུན་གྱི་གོ་འབྱེད་འབྱུང་གནས་དབྱིངས་ཞེས་བྱ། །དྲི་བཅས་སེམས་རྟེན་རང་བཞིན་ལྷུན་གྲུབ་བས། །སེམས་ཅན་དུ་འཛིན་པས་ན་དེ་ལ་སྲིད་ཡོད། དེ་ལྟར་སྲིད་པ་བདེན་པར་བཟུང་ནས་སྤྱང་བྱར་བྱེད་པ་དེས་ནི་སྲིད་པ་སྤྱངས་མི་ནུས་ཏེ་དཔེར་ན་ལུས་མ་སྤྱང་བར་གྲིབ་མ་སྤྱང་མི་ནུས་པ་ལྟར། འཁོར་བའི་རྩ་བ་བདེན་ཞེན་མ་སྤྱང་བར་འཁོར་བའི་སྡུག་བསྔལ་སྤྱངས་མི་ནུས་པས་ན་འཁོར་བའི་སྡུག་བསྔལ་ཡོད། དེ་བཞིན་དུ་གཉིས་འཛིན་ཕྱོགས་རེ་ལ་ཞེན་པ་རྣམས་ཆོས་དང་ཐེག་པའི་ཞེ་འདོད་སྣ་ཚོགས་ཀྱིས་བཅིངས་ཏེ་འདི་ནི་བཟང་པའོ། །འདི་ནི་ངན་པའོ། །འདི་ནི་རང་ལུགས་སོ། །འདི་ནི་གཞན་ལུགས་སོ། །ངེད་ནི་མཆོག་གོ །གཞན་ནི་དམན་ནོ། །ཞེས་ཆགས་སྡང་དང་རྩོད་པ་མངོན་པར་འཕེལ་བས་ན། གང་ལ་ཆོས་ཡོད་ཐེག་པའི་ཞེ་འདོད་ཡོད། །དེ་ལྟ་བུ་དེ་ནི་རང་གཞན་གཉིས་འཛིན་གྱི་རྗེས་སུ་འབྲང་ནས་ཉོན་མོངས་པའི་གཟེབ་ཏུ་ཆུད་ཅིང་འཁོར་བའི་འཆིང་བ་ཐམས་ཅད་ཀྱིས་བཅིང་པ

ཡིན་བས་ན། དེ་ལ་ཉོན་མོངས་གཟེབ་ཡོད་འཆིང་བ་ཡོད། །འདི་ལྟ་བུ་འདི་ནི་
མགོན་པོ་ཀླུ་སྒྲུབ་ཀྱིས་དབུ་མ་རིན་ཆེན་ཕྲེང་བ་ལས་གསུངས་ཏེ། ཇི་སྲིད་ཕུང་པོར་
འཛིན་ཡོད་པ། །དེ་སྲིད་དེ་ལ་ངར་འཛིན་ཡོད། །ངར་འཛིན་ཡོད་ན་ཡང་ལས་
ཏེ། །ཞེས་སོགས་གསུངས་པ་ལྟར་རོ། །གཤིས་ཀ་དག་གི་ངང་དུ་ཡེ་སྟོང་རྩབ་
བྲལ་བས་གཞི་འཛིན་པ་དང་པ་ལ། རང་རིག་ཟང་ཐལ་རྗེན་པར་རྩོལ་སྒྲུབ་ཀྱི་སྒྲོག
ལས་གྲོལ་བས་ལམ་གྱི་གོ་རིམ་འགག །ཐམས་ཅད་ཡེ་གྲོལ་དུ་ཤེས་པས་བསྒྲུབ་བྱའི་
འདོད་པ་མེད་པས་འབྲས་བུ་ཞི་འདོད་ཟད་པས་ན། གཞི་བྲལ་ལམ་འགག་འབྲས་བུ་
ཞི་འདོད་ཟད། །ཆོས་ཟད་ཀྱི་རིག་པ་མཚོན་བརྗོད་ལས་འདས་ཏེ་ཐེག་པའི་ཚིག་གིས་
ཇི་བཞིན་མཚོན་མི་ནུས་ཤིང་ཕྱོགས་རེ་ནས་གཞལ་ན་ཐེག་པ་ཐམས་ཅད་ཀྱང་འཐད་པས་
ཐེག་པ་དང་གྲུབ་མཐའི་ལྟ་གྲུབ་ལ་མཆོག་དམན་གྱི་འདོད་ཞེན་དང་བྲལ་བས་ན།
ཐེག་པར་འདོད་ཞེན་རྡུལ་ཙམ་མི་གནས་པ། །དེ་ལྟ་བུའི་རྣལ་འབྱོར་པ་དེ་རང་རིག་
ཟང་ཐལ་དུ་རྟོགས་པས་རྣམ་རྟོག་ཐམས་ཅད་ཤར་གྲོལ་དུས་མཉམ་དུ་དག་སྟེ་ཆུ་ལ་རི་མོ་
བྲིས་པ་ལྟར་སྐད་ཅིག་གིས་ཞིག་པས་ལས་མི་གསོག་པས་ན་དེ་ལ་ལས་མེད། ལས་
མི་གསོག་པའི་ལྟ་སྣང་གི་རྟོག་པ་ཆགས་སྡང་ལྟར་སྣང་ཡང་དེའི་ཕན་གནོད་གང་ཡང་
མེད་པས་ན་རྣམ་སྨིན་གོས་པ་མེད། འཁོར་བ་མེད་སྣང་དུ་ཤེས་པས་སྲིད་པའི་མཐའ་
ལ་མི་གནས་ཤིང་སྐུ་གསུམ་ལམ་སྣང་དུ་རྫོགས་པས་ཞི་བ་ཕྱོགས་གཅིག་ཏུ་མི་ལྟུང་བས་
ན་སྲིད་ཞིར་མི་གནས། ཆོས་ཉིད་ནམ་མཁའ་ལྟ་བུའི་ངང་དུ་གཉུག་མ་རྒྱུན་ཆད་མེད་
པས་ནམ་མཁའི་ངང་དུ་གྲོལ། ཕྱི་ཡུལ་འཁྲུལ་པའི་སྣོད་བཅུད་ལྟར་སྣང་བ་ཐམས་
ཅད་ཀྱང་སྟོང་གཟུགས་སྒྱུ་མའི་རྣམ་པར་ཤར་བས་ན་ཡུལ་གྱི་མཁའ་ལ་རིག་རྩལ་
སེམས་ཀྱི་རྣམ་རྟོག་ཡད་ཡུད་དུ་འཕྱོ་བ་ཡང་ཤར་གྲོལ་རྒྱུན་མི་འཆད་བས་ན་རིག་པའི་
རྩལ་འབྱོང་། འདི་ཡིན་གྱི་གཏད་སོ་དང་བྲལ་བའི་རིག་པའི་རྒྱལ་པོ······ཀློང་དུ་དེ་
ལྟར་ཤར་ཡང་རྩལ་ཡི་འཛིན་མེད་གཅུག་པར་ནག་བས་ན། གཏད་མེད་རྒྱལ་པོ་
འཛིན་མེད་ཤར་བའི་མི། །དེ་ལྟར་ཡུལ་གཏད་མེད་ལ་བློ་འཛིན་མེད་དུ་ཤར་བས་

ཡུལ་གཟུང་བ་དང་ཡུལ་ཅན་འཛིན་པའི་རྣམ་རྟོག་གཟུང་འཛིན་སྲིད་པའི་འཁྲུལ་སྣང་
ཐམས་ཅད་ལས་རྣམ་པར་གྲོལ་བས་ན། ཡུལ་དང་ཡུལ་ཅན་སྲིད་ལས་རང་གྲོལ་
ནས། །དེ་ལྟར་རང་གྲོལ་གྱི་གནས་ལུགས་མངོན་དུ་གྱུར་བ་དེ་ཉིད་དུས་དང་རྣམ་པ་
ཐམས་ཅད་དུ་འབྲལ་མི་ཤེས་ཤིང་གཅིག་མ་རྒྱུན་ཆད་མེད་པར་འཆར་བས་ན། དུས་
གསུམ་འདུ་འབྲལ་མེད་པའི་ངང་དུ་གནས། །དེ་ལྟར་གཅིག་མ་མ་བཅོས་པའི་ཆོས་
སྐུ་ཟང་ཐལ་རྗེན་པའི་ཀློང་དུ་ངང་གནས་སུ་འཛོག་པ་ནི་སྒོམ་པ་དང་། རང་གྲོལ་དུ་
སྤྱོད་པ་ནི་འབྲས་བུ་ཡིན་པས་དེ་ཡན་གྱིས་ས་བཅད་གཉིས་པ་སོང་། གསུམ་པ་ནི།
དེ་ལྟར་ཀ་དག་རིག་པའི་ཡེ་ཤེས་སྟོང་གསལ་ཆོས་སྐུའི་དགོངས་པ་མ་བཅོས་པར་
གནས་པའི་སྟོང་གདངས་རིག་རྩལ་ཡེ་ཤེས་ཀྱི་རྣམ་རོལ་སྤྲུལ་པའི་སྐུ་རུ་འབར་བས་ན།
རིག་པའི་རྒྱལ་པོ་སྟོང་གསལ་ཆོས་སྐུའི་གདངས། །ལྷུན་གྲུབ་སྣང་ཆའི་འཆར་གཞི་
མི་འགྱུར་གཞི་རྩ་བྲལ་བས་འོད་གདངས་ལོངས་སྤྱོད་རྫོགས་སྐུའི་སྣང་བ་འཆར་བས་ན།
མི་འགྱུར་ལྷུན་གྲུབ་གཞི་རྩ་བྲལ་བའི་གདངས། །གདངས་ཐམས་ཅད་ཀྱི་འཆར་གཞི་
གདོད་མའི་ཆོས་ཉིད་སྤྲོས་བྲལ་བརྗོད་ལས་འདས་པ་ཆོས་སྐུའི་དགོངས་པ་འགྱུར་བ་
མེད་པ་སྐྱེ་མེད་གཅིག་མའི་གཏན་སྲིད་ཟིན་བས་ན། གདངས་དང་ལྡན་པ་གདོད་མའི་
ཀློང་དུ་ཨཿ །ཞེས་སོ། །ཆོས་ཟད་ཆོས་སྐུའི་དགོངས་འཕོ་འགྱུར་མེད། །འོད་
གསལ་ལོངས་སྐུའི་ཞིང་སྣང་རྟག་པར་གཟིགས། །ཐུགས་རྗེ་སྤྲུལ་པས་སྲིད་ན་འགྲོ་
དོན་མཛད། །དྲིན་ཆེན་བླ་མའི་ཞབས་ལ་གུས་ཕྱག་འཚལ། །སྙིང་ནས་གུས་པས་
གསོལ་བ་འདེབས་པ་བདག །ཚེ་རབས་ཀུན་ཏུ་མཚུངས་མེད་བླ་མ་དང་། །
མཇལ་ནས་ཅི་གསུང་བསྒྲུབ་ཤིང་གུས་པས་བརྟེན། །ཕྲིན་ལས་འགྲོ་བ་འདྲེན་པའི་
ཁོལ་པོར་ཤོག །ཟབ་མོའི་ཚིག་དོན་རྟོགས་པར་དཀའ་བའི་གནས། །བཀྲལ་བར་
དབང་བ་ཁོ་བོ་མ་ཡིན་ཡང་། །ཀུན་མཁྱེན་བརྒྱུད་པའི་གཞུང་ལ་ཐོས་བསམ་
གྱིས། །ཆུང་ཟད་འབྲིས་པའི་དབང་བྱས་འདི་བཀོད་དོ། །དགེ་བ་དེ་ཡང་འགྲོ་བ་
མ་ལུས་པ། །ཟབ་མོའི་ལམ་འདིར་བརྟེན་ནས་འབད་མེད་དུ། །རྣམ་གྲོལ་རྒྱལ་

བའི་འཁྲོར་བ་ཐོབ་པ་དང་། །གནས་སྐབས་ཆགས་སྡང་སྣང་བ་ཞི་ཕྱིར་བསྔོ། །
དགེ་འོ།། །།

༄༅། །རྫོགས་པ་ཆེན་པོའི་ཉམས་ལེན་གྱི་གནད་མཐར་ཐུག་པའི་རྩ་འགྲེལ་འོད་གསལ་གྱི་སྣང་ཆ་ཞེས་བྱ་བ་བཞུགས་སོ།།

༄༅། །དུས་གསུམ་སངས་རྒྱས་ཐམས་ཅད་ཀྱི་ངོ་བོ་རིགས་ཀྱི་བདག་པོ་དྲིན་ཆེན་འཇིགས་མེད་རྒྱལ་བའི་མྱུ་གུའི་ཞབས་ལ་སྒོ་གསུམ་གུས་པ་ཆེན་པོས་ཕྱག་འཚལ་ལོ། །ཀུ་ཡོས་ཟླ་བ་དང་པོའི་ཚེས་ཉེར་ལྔ་ལ། བདག་སྤྲུལ་མིང་ཚོགས་དྲུག་རང་གྲོལ་ས་སྐྱོད་རྒྱལ་པོའི་ཚེ་སྒྲུབ་བསྙེན་སྐབས། ནངས་པར་ཐོ་རེང་གི་ཆ་ཐུན་གྱི་འོད་གསལ་གྱི་ངང་ནས། བདག་མཆོད་རྟེན་བདེ་བྱེད་བརྩེགས་པར་སླེབས་འདུག །ཁོ་བོ་བུམ་པའི་ནང་དུ་འདུག་སྐབས། མདུན་གྱི་ནམ་མཁའ་ནས་དཔའ་བོ་མཁའ་འགྲོ་རྣམས་ཀྱིས་རོལ་མོའི་སྒྲ་མང་དུ་བསྒྲགས་ཤིང་། དྲི་བཟང་གི་དུད་པས་ཕྱོགས་ཀུན་ཏུ་ཁྱབ་པར་རྒྱས་ཤིང་། བདག་ལ་མཁའ་འགྲོ་ཞིག་གིས་ཕ་ཀི་རིག་འཛིན་ཆེན་པོ་འཇིགས་མེད་རྒྱལ་བའི་མྱུ་གུ་འཇིག་རྟེན་མི་ཡུལ་ནས་ཨོ་རྒྱན་མཁའ་འགྲོའི་ཚོགས་དཔོན་ལ་གཤེགས་སོ་ཟེར་བས་དཔའ་བོ་མཁའ་འགྲོའི་ཚོགས་ཀྱི་དབུས་སུ་མཁའ་འགྲོ་མ་བཞིས་དར་དཀར་གྱི་འདོ་ལི་ཕྱོགས་བཞིར་རྡོ་རྗེ་ཕྱེད་པས་མཚན་བས་བཏེགས་པའི་སྟེང་དུ་སེང་གེའི་ཁྲི་པདྨ་ཉི་ཟླའི་གདན་གྱི་སྟེང་དུ་དྲིན་ཆེན་རྩ་བའི་བླ་མ་དེ་ཉིད་རྣལ་འབྱོར་གྱི་ཆ་བྱད་ཅན་གཟི་བརྗིད་སྔོན་ལས་ཆེས་ཆེར་ལྷག་པ། ཕྱག་གཉིས་རྡོ་རྗེ་དང་དྲིལ་བུ་འཛིན་པ་ཐུགས་ཀར་བསྣོལ་ཏེ་བཞུགས་པ། དར་གྱི་གྲ་བཞིར་ཤར་ལྷོ་ནུབ་བྱང་གི་མཁའ་འགྲོ་མ་དཀར་སེར་དམར་ལྗང་བཞིའི་ཕྱག་གཡས་རང་རྟགས་དང་གཡོན་དར་གྱི་གྲ་བཞིའི་རྡོ་རྗེ་བཟུང་བཏེག་པ། མཁའ་འགྲོ་བཞི་གླང་ཆེན་རྟ་མཆོག་རྨ་བྱ་ཤང་ཤང་རྣམས་ལ་ཞོན་པ་འཇའ་སྤྲིན་འོད་ལྔའི་ཀློང་ན་དཔའ་བོ་མཁའ་འགྲོ་རྣམས་གདུགས་རྒྱལ་མཚན་གླུ་གར་རོལ་མོའི་བྱེ་བྲག་སྣ་ཚོགས་བྱེད་པར་འདུག་པའི་མོད་ལ་ཁོ་བོས་མི་ཡུལ་དུ་འགྲོ་དོན་མཛད་པར་ཞུས་པའི་ལན་དུ། རྗེ་སྒྲོན་བཙུན་ནས་ད་ལྟའི་བར་དག་ཏུ། །འགྲོ་དྲུག་གི་གདུལ་བྱ་བྱུས་ཟིན་ཏེ། །ཁྱེད་པར་དུ་མི་ཡུལ་འདི་ཉིད་

དུ། །ཁམས་གསུམ་གྱི་སེམས་ཅན་ཐམས་ཅད་ལ། །དཀར་ནག་གི་ལས་འབྲས་
སྣང་དོར་དང་། །རྫོགས་ཆེན་གྱི་ཁྱད་ཆོས་ཨ་ཧྲི་ཡིས། །ཐམས་ཅད་ལ་འགྲོ་དོན་
བྱས་ཟིན་ཏེ། །རྗེས་འཇུག་གི་བུ་སློབ་ཐམས་ཅད་ཀྱིས། །རང་ལུགས་ལས་གཞན་
ན་མེད་པའི་ཆོས། །ཁོ་བོ་ཡི་རིག་འཛིན་ཆེན་པོའི་གསུངས། །དོན་མ་ནོར་བར་
ཁྱོད་ལ་གདམས་པར་བྱ། །གདོད་ནས་རྣམ་དག་བསམ་ཡུལ་འདས་པའི་ཀློང་། །
སེམས་ཉིད་རྒྱལ་པོ་རང་བཞིན་རྫོགས་པ་ཆེ། །གང་ཡང་མ་སྤྱངས་ཀུན་ལས་འདས་
པའི་དོན། །གང་ཤར་ཞེན་མེད་ལྷུན་འབྱམས་རིག་པའི་ཀློང་། །ཅོག་བཞག་རང་
གྲོལ་གཅེར་མཐོང་བསམ་ཡུལ་མེད། །རང་བཞིན་བབས་ཡིན་བཅོས་བསླད་མ་བྱེད་
ཅིག །སྨྱོངས་པ་གང་གིས་ངོ་བོ་དེ་བོར་ནས། །གཅུག་མའི་སེམས་ལ་སྤྲིན་པོའི་
གཟེབ་བསྐུར་ནས། །བཅོས་ཤིང་བཅོས་ཤིང་སྙིང་པོའི་དོན་ལ་སྒྲིབ། །གྲོལ་བ་
མེད་པ་དེ་ཡིས་སྣར་བཙིང་བྱེད། །གང་ལ་བློ་ཡི་ཁོངས་ན་ལྷོད་ཡོད་ན། །རང་
བཞིན་ཉིད་དེ་དེ་ལ་བཅོས་མི་དགོས། །འཁྲུ་མཐོང་རང་དག་གཉེན་པོས་མ་བསླད་
ཅིང་། །སྤྱངས་བྱས་མ་བསྒྱུར་གཞིས་དེ་རྫོགས་པ་ཆེ། །ཡོད་ཉིད་མེད་ལ་མེད་པ་
ཡོད་པའི་མཐའ། །དངོས་ཀུན་ཞིག་པའི་སྟོང་པ་རྫོགས་པ་ཆེ། །བཅོས་ཤིང་
བཅོས་ཤིང་གྲོལ་བར་འདོད་པའི་མི། །རྟག་ཆད་གཉིས་ལས་ཐར་བར་ཡོད་དམ་
ཅི། །གཞི་མེད་རྩ་བྲལ་ཡེ་ནས་རྫོགས་པ་ཆེ། །སྟོང་དང་སྣང་དང་ཡོད་དང་མེད་
པའི་སྒོམ། །གང་ལ་བསྒོམ་ཡོད་ལྟ་དང་སྤྱོད་པ་ཡོད། །དེ་ལ་སྲིད་ཡོད་འཁོར་
པའི་སྡུག་བསྔལ་ཡོད། །གང་ལ་ཆོས་ཡོད་ཐེག་པའི་ཞེན་འདོད་ཡོད། །དེ་ལ་ཉོན་
མོངས་གཉེན་ཡོད་འཆིང་བ་ཡོད། །གཞི་བྲལ་ལམ་འགགས་འབྲས་བུ་ཞེན་པ་དང་།
ཐོག་མའི་འདོད་ཞེན་རྡུལ་ཙམ་མི་གནས་པ། །དེ་ལ་ལས་མེད་རྣམ་སྨིན་གོས་པ་
མེད། །སྲིད་ཞིར་མི་གནས་ནམ་མཁའི་ངང་དུ་འགྲོ། །ཡུལ་གྱི་མཁའ་ལ་རིག
པའི་རྩལ་འཕྱོ་བར། གཏད་མེད་རྒྱལ་པོ་འཛིན་མེད་ཤར་བའི་མི། །ཡུལ་དང་
ཡུལ་ཅན་སྲིད་ལས་རང་གྲོལ་ཆོས། །དུས་གསུམ་འཕོ་འགྱུར་མེད་པའི་ངང་དུ་

གནས། །རིག་པའི་རྒྱལ་པོ་སྟོང་གསལ་ཆོས་སྐུའི་གདངས། །མི་འགྱུར་ལྷུན་གྲུབ་གཞི་རྩ་བྲལ་བའི་གདེངས། །གདེངས་དང་ལྡན་པ་གདོད་མའི་ཀློང་དུ་ཨཿ ཞེས་གསུངས་ཤིང་སྐད་ཅིག་ཉིད་ལ་ཛ་ཡབ་དཔལ་རིའི་གྲོང་ཆེན་པོའི་དབུས་སུ་རིག་འཛིན་བླ་མ་དེ་གནས་འགྱུར་ནས་ཆེ་མཆོག་ཧེ་རུ་ཀ་སྐུ་མདོག་མཐིང་ནག་ཞལ་གསུམ་ཕྱག་དྲུག་ཞབས་བཞི་བསྣམས་པ་གར་གྱི་ཉམས་དགུ་དུར་ཁྲོད་ཀྱི་ཆས་བརྒྱད་དང་ལྡན་པ་འཁོར་བདུན་རྒྱ་ཉེར་ལྔའི་ལྷ་ཚོགས་ཐམས་ཅད་ཡམ་གྱིས་ཤར་བྱུང་། ཁོ་བོའི་དབང་བསྐུར་བའི་གསོལ་བ་བཏབ་པའི་ཉམས་བྱུང་། ཡང་བདུན་བརྒྱ་ཉེར་ལྔའི་ལྷ་ཚོགས་ཐམས་ཅད་གཙོ་བོ་ལ་ཐིམ། དཔལ་ཆེན་པོ་ཡང་འོད་སྔོན་པོའི་རྣམ་པར་གྱུར་ཏེ་གུ་རུ་རིན་པོ་ཆེའི་ཐུགས་ཀར་ཐིམ། དེ་མ་ཐག་ཏུ་དཔའ་བོ་མཁའ་འགྲོ་རྣམས་ཀྱིས་བཛྲ་གུ་རུའི་སྒྲ་འབའ་ཞིག་བསྒྲགས་པའི་རྐྱེན་གྱིས་སད་མུས་ཁོ་བོར་རང་མལ་དུ་ཡོད་འདུག །ཉེར་ལྔའི་ཉིན་རེ་རིག་འཛིན་ཆེན་པོ་བླ་མ་དུས་དྲན་གྱི་ཚུལ་དུ་བླ་སྒྲུབ་རིག་འཛིན་འདུས་པའི་ཚོགས་པ་རྒྱ་ཞིག་ཕུལ་ལོ།། དགེའོ། །། ༄༅། །སངས་རྒྱས་ཀུན་འདུས་ཀྱི་ངོ་བོ་དྲིན་ཆེན་རྩ་བའི་བླ་མ་ལ་ཕྱག་འཚལ་ལོ། །འདིར་རང་བཞིན་རྫོགས་པ་ཆེན་པོའི་ལམ་ནས་གྲུབ་པ་བརྙེས་པའི་སྔོན་གྱི་སློབ་དཔོན་ཆེན་པོ་དགའ་རབ་རྡོ་རྗེ་ལ་སོགས་པ་རྣམས་ཀྱིས་རྟོགས་དོན་ཉམས་ལེན་གྱི་གནད་མཐར་ཐུག་པ་སྲས་ཀྱི་ཐུ་བོ་རྣམས་ལ་འདས་རྗེས། ཞལ་ཆེམས་ཀྱི་ཚུལ་དུ་གདམས་པས་རྟོགས་གྲོལ་དུས་མཉམ་ཞིང་སློབ་དཔོན་དང་དགོངས་པ་མཉམ་པར་གྱུར་པ་ཤ་སྟག་ཡིན་ལ། དེ་བཞིན་དུ་དེང་གི་སྐབས་སུ་ཡང་མཚུངས་མེད་ཆོས་ཀྱི་ཁྱབ་བདག་འཁོར་ལོའི་མགོན་པོའི་འཇིགས་མེད་རྒྱལ་བའི་མྱུ་གུ་ཞེས་ཡོངས་སུ་གྲགས་པ་དེ་ཉིད་དགོངས་པ་ཆོས་དབྱིངས་སུ་ཐིམ་པའི་སྐབས་སུ་ཐུགས་ཀྱི་སྲས་མཚུངས་པ་མེད་པ་སྤྲུལ་པའི་སྐུ་རིན་པོ་ཆེ་མི་འགྱུར་ནམ་མཁའི་རྡོ་རྗེ་ལ་འོད་གསལ་གྱི་སྣང་ཆར་རྫོགས་པ་ཆེན་པོའི་ཉམས་ལེན་གྱི་གནད་མཐར་ཐུག་པ། ཞལ་ཆེམས་འདས་རྗེས་ཀྱི་ཚུལ་དུ་གསུངས་པ་འདིའི་དོན་ཅུང་ཟད་འབྲལ་ནས་འཆད་པ་ལ་གསུམ། གཞི་མ་འཁྲུལ་བའི་ཆོས་ཉིད་གཉུག་མ་རང་གི་ངོ་བོ

བསྟན་པ། ལམ་མ་བཅོས་པའི་སེམས་ཉིད་རིག་སྟོང་རྗེན་པར་ཉམས་སུ་བླངས་ཚུལ། འབྲས་བུ་བླང་དོར་དང་བྲལ་བའི་ངང་དུ་འཁྲུལ་རྟོག་གི་གྲོལ་ས་བསྟན་པའོ། །དང་པོ་ནི། འདི་ལྟར་གདོད་མ་གཞིས་ཀྱི་གནས་ལུགས་སྤྲོས་པ་ཐམས་ཅད་དང་བྲལ་བའི་ཡེ་ཤེས་བདེ་གཤེགས་སྙིང་པོ་རང་གི་ངོ་བོ་གང་ཡིན་པ་དེ་རྟོགས་ཏེ་སངས་རྒྱས་མ་བྱུང་། མ་རྟོགས་ཏེ་སེམས་ཅན་མ་བྱུང་གི་དུས་ཙམ་འཁོར་འདས་ཀྱི་སྤྱི་གཞི་སྟེ་ཆོས་ཉིད་རང་གི་ངོ་བོ་སྒྲིབ་གཉིས་ཀྱི་དྲི་མས་བསླད་མ་མྱོང་བའི་གཞི་ཀ་དག་ཆེན་པོ་དེ་ལ་གདོད་ནས་ནམ་དག་ཅེས་བྱ་ལ། དེ་ལྟར་བུའི་ཆོས་ཉིད་དེ་བློས་རྟོག་དཔྱོད་དང་ཚིག་གིས་བརྗོད་བ་ལ་སོགས་པས་ཤེས་པར་མི་ནུས་ཤིང་བསམ་བའི་ཡུལ་ལས་འདས་པས་ན་ཀློང་དེ་ཡང་དོན་དུ་ནང་དབྱིངས་སྟོང་པ་ཉིད་སྤྲོས་པའི་མཐའ་ཐམས་ཅད་དང་བྲལ་བ་དེ་ནི་བསམ་བརྗོད་ཀྱི་ཡུལ་ལས་འདས་པ་ཡིན་ནོ། །ཞེས་བསྟན། དེ་ལྟ་བུའི་ཆོས་ཉིད་དེ་ཡང་གཞན་མེད་དེ་རང་གི་སེམས་ཀྱི་རང་བཞིན་འོད་གསལ་བ་དང་གཉིས་སུ་མེད་པས་ན་སེམས་ཉིད། སེམས་ཀྱི་གཅུག་མ་དེ་ནི་འཁོར་འདས་ཀྱི་ཆོས་ཐམས་ཅད་ཀྱི་བྱེད་པོ་ཡིན་ཞིང་ཆོས་ཐམས་ཅད་ལ་དབང་བསྒྱུར་བས་ན་རྒྱལ་པོ། དེ་ཡང་ཆོས་ཐམས་ཅད་ཀྱི་རང་བཞིན་སྟོང་པ་ཉིད་དང་དབྱེར་མེད་པས་ན་རང་བཞིན། ཆོས་ཉིད་དེའི་ཀློང་དབྱིངས་དོན་དམ་པའི་ངང་དུ་སྣང་སྲིད་གཞི་ལས་མ་གཡོས་པར་རྫོགས་པས་ན་རྫོགས་པ་ཆེན་པོ། དཔེར་ན་དངོས་པོ་ཐམས་ཅད་ལ་ནམ་མཁའ་ཁྱབ་ཅིང་ནམ་མཁས་དངོས་པོ་ཐམས་ཅད་མ་སྤངས་པ་ལྟར་ཆོས་ཐམས་ཅད་ལ་ཆོས་ཉིད་རྫོགས་པ་ཆེན་པོས་ཆོས་གང་ཡང་མ་སྤང་བས་ན་གང་ཡང་མ་སྤངས། །དངོས་པོའི་མཚན་ཉིད་དབྱིབས་དང་ཁ་དོག་ལ་སོགས་པ་ཐམས་ཅད་ནམ་མཁའ་ལ་མེད་ཅིང་ནམ་མཁའ་དེ་དག་གི་ཡུལ་ལས་འདས་པ་ལྟར། ཆོས་ཅན་ཐམས་ཅད་ལ་ཡོད་པའི་དངོས་པོ་དང་མཚན་མ་དང་སྒྲ་བརྗོད་ལ་སོགས་པ་ཐམས་ཅད་ཆོས་ཉིད་རྫོགས་པ་ཆེན་པོ་ལ་མེད་ཅིང་རྫོགས་པ་ཆེན་པོ་དེ་དག་གི་ཡུལ་ལས་འདས་པས་ན་ཀུན་ལས་འདས་པའི་དོན། དེ་ལྟར་དབྱིངས་ཆོས་ཉིད་རྫོགས་པ་ཆེན་པོའི་གཞིའི་གནས་ལུགས་གཅིག་མའི་ཡེ་ཤེས་

རང་གི་ངོ་བོ་བསྟན་ནས་དེ་ཉིད་ཤར་གྲོལ་གཉིས་མེད་ཀྱི་ཆོས་སྐུ་ཀ་དག་ཁྲེགས་ཆོད་ཀྱི་ལྟ་བར་ཐག་བཅད་པ་ནི། ཐོལ་སྐྱེས་ཀྱི་རྣམ་རྟོག་ཡུལ་ལ་ཤར་བའི་ཚེ། ཤར་བའི་ཡུལ་དང་ཤར་བའི་རྣམ་རྟོག་གཉིས་ཀ་ལ་ཞེན་འཛིན་གྱི་སྤྱོད་བླང་ཅུང་ཟད་ཀྱང་མི་བྱེད་པར་གང་ཤར་གྱི་ངོ་བོ་ལ་བལྟས་པས་རྣམ་རྟོག་རང་དག་སྟེ་རང་རིག་མ་བཅོས་པས་ཤར་བ་དེ་ལྷུན་གྲུབ་སྐུ་གསུམ་གྱི་ངང་དུ་འབྱམས་པའི་རིག་པ་ཡེ་ཤེས་ཀྱི་ཀློང་ཆེན་པོ་ཡིན་པས་ན། གང་ཤར་ཞེན་མེད་ལྷུན་འབྱམས་རིག་པའི་ཀློང་། །དེ་ལྟར་ལྟ་བའི་རང་ངོ་མཐོང་བ་དེའི་ངང་དུ་སེམས་མ་བཅོས་པར་ཅོག་གེ་བཞག་པས་རྣམ་རྟོག་རང་དག་སྟེ་རང་བཞིན་བབས་ཀྱི་བསམ་གཏན་ལ་གནས་པ་ནི་ཅོག་བཞག །དེའི་ཚེ་སྐྱེས་མེད་ཀྱི་ངང་ནས་འགགས་མེད་རིག་རྩལ་སྣ་ཚོགས་སུ་ཤར་ཡང་ཞེན་མེད་ཀྱི་ངང་དུ་གྲོལ་བས་ན་རང་གྲོལ། རྣམ་རྟོག་གང་སྐྱེས་ཀྱི་ངོ་བོ་ལ་གཅེར་གྱིས་བལྟས་པས་རྣམ་རྟོག་རང་ཡལ་བའི་ཚེ་གཉུག་མའི་ངོ་བོ་ལྷག་གིས་མཐོང་བ་ནི་གཅེར་མཐོང་། །དེ་ལྟ་བུའི་སྒོམ་དེ་ཡང་བདེ་གསལ་མི་རྟོག་ལ་སོགས་པའི་ཉམས་ཀྱི་ཞེན་པ་ཐམས་ཅད་དང་བྲལ་ཏེ་རང་བཞིན་འདི་ལྟ་བུ་ཞིག་གོ །ཞེས་བློས་བསམ་པའི་ཡུལ་ལས་འདས་པས་ན་བསམ་ཡུལ་མེད། སེམས་མ་བཅོས་པ་འདི་རང་ངོ་རང་ཤེས་དྲན་པས་སྐྱོང་བ་ཙམ་ཉམས་ལེན་གྱི་གནད་འགག་ཡིན་པས་ན་རང་བཞིན་རང་བབས་ཡིན་པའི་ཕྱིར་བློས་ནན་གྱིས་བཟུང་ནས་སེམས་ལ་བཟོ་བཅོས་ན་ཅི་ཙམ་བཅོས་པ་དེ་ཙམ་ལམ་གོལ་དུ་འགྲོ་བས་ན་བཅོས་བསླད་མ་བྱེད་ཅིག །དེ་ལྟར་མ་བཅོས་བའི་ཆོས་ཉིད་རང་ངོ་མ་ཤེས་པ་རྣམས་ནི་རང་བཞིན་རྫོགས་པ་ཆེན་པོའི་ལམ་ལ་སྒྲོངས་པ་ཡིན་པས་ན་སྒྲོངས་པ་གང་གིས། དེ་ལྟ་བུའི་སྒྲོངས་པ་རྣམས་ཀྱིས་སེམས་ཀྱི་ངོ་བོ་མ་བཅོས་པ་དེ་བོར་ཞིང་། བཅོས་མ་ལ་ལམ་དུ་བྱེད་པས་ན་ངོ་བོ་དེ་བོར་ཏེ། གཉུག་མའི་སེམས་ཡེ་གྲོལ་དུ་གནས་པ་ཉིད་ལ་རིག་པ་སྒྲིམ་པོའི་རྟོག་དཔྱོད་སྣ་ཚོགས་བཏང་ནས་རེ་དོགས་ཀྱི་གཟེབ་ཏུ་ཚུད་པས་ན། གཉུག་མའི་སེམས་ལ་སྒྲིམ་པོའི་གཟེབ་བསྐུར་ནས། །དེ་ལྟར་རེ་དོགས་ཀྱི་གཟེབས་སུ་ཚུད་པ་འདི་ནི་ཡིན་ནོ་འདི་ནི་མིན་ནོ་སྙམ་དུ་བློས་ཡང་དང་ཡང་དུ་

བཅོས་ཤིང་བཅོས་ཤིང་ཅི་ཙམ་བཅོས་པ་དེ་ཙམ་དུ་སྙིང་པོའི་དོན་མི་མཐོང་ཞིང་བློས་བྱས་
ཀྱི་ལྟ་སྒོམ་གྱིས་ས་མི་ཆོད་པས་ན་སྙིང་པོའི་དོན་ལ་སྒྲིབ། ནམ་མཁའ་ལ་ཡེ་ནས་
མདུད་པ་བྱུར་མེད་པས་ན་བཀྲོལ་རྒྱུ་ཡང་མེད་པ་ལྟར་སེམས་ཉིད་ཡེ་གྲོལ་དུ་གནས་པ་
ལ་གཟོད་འབད་པས་གྲོལ་བར་རློམ་པས་མི་གྲོལ་བས་ན་གྲོལ་བ་མེད། དེ་ལྟར་
འབད་ནས་བཅོས་པས་གྲོལ་པར་འདོད་པ་རྣམས་ནི་སྲིན་བུའི་ཁ་རྒྱུས་རང་ཉིད་བཅིང་བ་
ལྟར་ཞེ་འདོད་ཀྱི་སྒྲུབ་མཐས་སྣར་བཅིང་བས་ན་དེ་ཡིས་སྣར་འཆིང་བྱེད། དེ་དག་གི་
གནད་དོན་ཧྲིལ་དྲིལ་ན་ད་ལྟ་ཐ་མལ་གྱི་ཤེས་པ་བློའི་བཟོ་བཅོས་གང་ཡང་མ་སོང་པ་འདི་
ཀ་གཞི་གནས་ཀྱི་རིག་པ་ཡང་ཟེར། རྫོགས་པ་ཆེན་པོ་ཡང་ཟེར། དེ་བཞིན་དུ་
ཕྱག་རྒྱ་ཆེན་པོ། དབུ་མ་ཆེན་པོ། སྤྲོས་པ་དང་བྲལ་བ། སྐྱེ་བ་མེད་པ་ལ་
སོགས་མིང་ཅི་བཏགས་ཀྱང་དོན་དུ་ཐ་མལ་གྱི་ཤེས་པར་རིག་རྗེན་པ་འདི་ཀ་ཡིན་པས་དེ་
རང་ངོ་ཤེས་པ་ལ་ལྟ་བ་ཟེར་བ་ཡིན་ཏེ་དེ་ཡན་གྱིས་བཅད་དང་པོའོ། །གཉིས་པ་ནི།
དེ་ལྟར་རང་ངོ་ཤེས་པའི་ལྟ་བའི་གནས་ཚུལ་མ་བཅོས་པ་དེ་ཀའི་ངང་དུ་སེམས་བཅོས་མ་
དང་བྲལ་བར་ལྷོད་དེ་འཇོག་པ་ནི་བསྒོམ་པ་ཡིན་པས་ན། གང་ལ་བློ་ཡི་ཁོངས་ན་
ལྷོད་ཡོད་ན། །དེ་ལྟར་རང་བབས་ཀྱི་ངང་དུ་མ་ཡེངས་ཙམ་དུ་བཞག་ན་རིག་པ་ལ་
རང་གནས་ཀྱི་བསམ་གཏན་ཡོངས་པས་ན་རང་བཞིན་ཉིད་དེ་དེ་ལ་བཅོས་མི་དགོས།
དེ་ལྟར་རང་བབས་སུ་བཞག་པས་དེ་རྩལ་གྱི་རྣམ་རྟོག་སྣ་ཚོགས་ཡུལ་ལ་འཕྲོ་ཞིང་འགྱུ་
བའི་ཚེ། དང་པོ་རྣམ་རྟོག་འགྱུ་བ་དེ་ངོ་ཤེས། དེ་ནས་རང་ངོ་མཐོང་བའི་ངང་དུ་
བཞག་པས་རྣམ་རྟོག་རང་སར་དག་སྟེ་ཤར་གྲོལ་རྗེས་མེད་དུ་འགྲོ་བས་ན་འགྱུ་མཐོང་
རང་དག །དེ་ཡང་བཟང་རྟོག་དགེ་བའི་རྣམ་པ་ཅི་ཤར་ཡང་འདི་ནི་བཟང་པོ་ཡིན་ནོ་
སྙམ་དེ་ལ་ཞེན་འཛིན་གྱི་འཁྲིས་མི་གདགས་བར་ཞེན་མེད་དུ་བཞག་པས་རང་ཡལ་བས་
ན་གཉེན་པོས་མ་བསླད་ཅིང་། ངན་རྟོག་ཆགས་སྡང་དང་ཆོས་བརྒྱད་ཀྱི་རྟོག་པ་ཤར་
ཡང་འདི་ནི་ངན་པ་ཡིན་ནོ་སྙམ་ནས་འགྲོད་པ་དང་དགག་པ་སོགས་མི་བྱ་བར་རང་གྲོལ་
གྱི་གཞིས་ལ་བཞག་པས་ན་སྐྱང་བྱས་མ་བསྒྱུར། དེ་ལྟར་བཟང་རྟོག་དགེ་བའི་རྣམ་

པར་ཤར་ཡང་སེམས་ཀྱི་རང་ངོ་ལ་བཟང་པོར་བསྒྱུར་དུ་མེད་ཅིང་། ངན་རྟོག་མི་དགེ་བའི་རྣམ་པར་ཤར་ཡང་ངན་པར་བསྒྱུར་དུ་མེད་ལ་སེམས་ཅན་ནས་སངས་རྒྱས་ཀྱི་བར་དུ་སེམས་ཀྱི་གཤིས་ལ་ཁྱད་པར་མེད་པས་ན་གཤིས་དེ་རྫོགས་པ་ཆེ། དེ་ལྟ་བུའི་རང་བཞིན་རྫོགས་ན་གང་སྤྱང་བླང་མེད་པའི་ངང་དུ་རོ་མཉམ་སྟེ་ད་ལྟའི་བླང་དོར་དང་རེ་དོགས་དགག་སྒྲུབ་དང་ཆགས་སྡང་འདི་ནི་ཡིན་ནོ། །འདི་ནི་མིན་ནོ་སྙམ་དུ་བདེན་ཞེན་གྱིས་བཅིང་བའི་ཆོས་དང་ཚོགས་སྣ་ཚོགས་སུ་ཡོད་པ་དེ་ཐམས་ཅད་མེད་པར་རང་རིག་ཟང་ཐལ་ཡུག་འབྱམས་ཀྱི་ངང་དུ་ཐམས་ཅད་སྤྱང་བླང་མེད་པར་དག་པས་ན་ཡོད་ནི་མེད་ལ། དེའི་ཚེ་ཉམས་ལེན་རང་རིག་རྗེན་པ་དེ་ཡང་དེའི་རང་བཞིན་འདི་དང་འདི་ལྟ་བུ་ཡིན་ནོ་ཞེས། །བདེ་ལྷང་ངེ་བ་དང་། གསལ་སང་ངེ་བ་དང་། མི་རྟོག་པའི་ངང་དུ་ཆེམས་སེ་བ་ལ་སོགས་གང་ཡང་མིན་པས་ཚིག་གི་བརྗོད་པ་དང་བློས་བསམ་པའི་ཡུལ་དུ་མེད་ལ་རྣལ་འབྱོར་པ་ལ་དུས་ཐམས་ཅད་དུ་རང་རིག་ཟངས་མ་ཐལ་བྱུང་དུ་ལྷུག་གེར་ཤར་བ་ཉིད་སོ་སོར་རང་རིག་པའི་ཡེ་ཤེས་ཀྱི་སྤྱོད་ཡུལ་དུ་ཡོད་པས་ན་མེད་ལ་ཡོད་པའི་མཐའ། དེ་ལྟར་སེམས་ཉིད་མ་བཅོས་པའི་ངང་དུ་དངོས་པོ་བདེན་ཞེན་གྱི་ཆ་ཐམས་ཅད་རང་ཞིག་པས་ན་དངོས་ཀུན་བཞིགས་པས། །བདེན་ཞེན་གྱི་འཆིང་བ་དང་བྲལ་བའི་རང་བབས་དེ་ཀ་རིག་སྟོང་གཉིས་སུ་མེད་པའི་སྟོང་ཉིད་ཡིན་པས་བློའི་ཡུལ་དུ་བྱས་པའི་སྟོང་ཉིད་ལོག་ནས་ཆོལ་མི་དགོས་པས་ན་སྟོང་པ་རྫོགས་པ་ཆེ། དེ་ལྟར་མ་ཤེས་པར་ཡིད་དཔྱོད་ཀྱི་སྟོང་པ་ལ་རེ་བ་རྣམས་སྣང་ཐོག་ཏུ་སྟོང་པ་ལོག་ནས་བཙལ་ཏེ་སྟོང་འཛིན་གྱི་ཞེན་པས་བཅིངས་ནས་བཅོས་ཤིང་བཅོས་ཤིང་བརྟག་པའི་སྟོང་པ་ཡིན་ནོ་སྙམ་པའི་བློ་གྲོས་བར་འདོད་པས་ན། བཅོས་ཤིང་བཅོས་ཤིང་གྲོལ་བར་འདོད་པའི་མི། །དེ་ལྟ་བུ་དེ་ནི་སྣང་ཚོད་ལ་སྐུར་བ་བཏབ་ནས་སྟོང་པ་བཞིགས་པས་ཆད་པའི་མཐར་ལྷུང་ལ། སྟོང་པ་ལ་མཆོག་ཏུ་བཟུང་ནས་བདེན་པར་ཞེན་པས་རྟག་པའི་མཐར་ལྷུང་སྟེ། རྟག་ཆད་ཀྱི་གཡང་ས་ལས་མི་ཐར་བས་ན། རྟག་ཆད་གཉིས་ལས་ཐར་བ་ཡོད་དམ་ཅི། །དཔེར་ན། འབྱུང་བཞིས་བསྐུས་པའི་

སྣོད་བཅུད་ཐམས་ཅད་ནམ་མཁའ་ལ་བརྟེན་ནས་གནས་ཀྱང་ནམ་མཁའ་གང་ལའང་བརྟེན་ས་མེད་པ་ལྟར་ཆོས་ཐམས་ཅད་ཆོས་ཉིད་རྫོགས་པ་ཆེན་པོ་ལ་བརྟེན་ཀྱང་ཆོས་ཉིད་རྫོགས་པ་ཆེན་པོ་ནི་གང་ལ་ཡང་མི་བརྟེན་ཏེ། བརྟེན་པའི་གཞི་མེད་པས་ན་གཞི་མེད་འཁོར་འདས་ཀྱི་ཆོས་ཐམས་ཅད་རྒྱུ་དང་རྐྱེན་གྱིས་མ་བསྐྱེད་པ་མེད་ཀྱང་ཆོས་ཉིད་རྫོགས་པ་ཆེན་པོ་ནི་གང་གིས་ཀྱང་བསྐྱེད་པའི་རྩ་བ་མེད་པས་ན་རྩ་བྲལ། གཞི་རྩ་མེད་པའི་ཆོས་ཉིད་དེ་ནི་དུས་ཐམས་ཅད་དུ་བཅོས་བསླད་མེད་པར་ཡེ་ནས་གནས་པས་ན་ཡེ་གནས་རྫོགས་པ་ཆེ། དེ་ལྟར་ཡེ་གནས་གཉུག་མའི་ཆོས་ཉིད་རང་བབས་སུ་གནས་པ་མི་ཤེས་པ་རྣམས་ཁ་ཅིག་ནི་ཆོས་ཐམས་ཅད་སྟོང་པ་ཉིད་ཡིན་ནོ་སྙམ་དུ་སྟོང་འཛིན་ལ་ཆེད་དུ་གཉེར་ནས་བསྒོམ། ཁ་ཅིག་ནི་སྣང་ཆ་གཟུགས་ཀྱི་རྣམ་པ་ལ་དོན་དུ་འཛིན་ཞིང་ལྷ་དང་ཐིག་ལེ་ལ་སོགས་མཚན་བཅས་ཀྱི་སྒོམ་ལ་རེ། ཁ་ཅིག་ནི་ཆོས་ཉིད་དོན་དམ་པ་དེ་ནི་འདི་དང་འདི་ལྟ་བུ་ཡིན་ནོ་ཞེས། བདེན་བདེན་ཏག་ཏག་ཨ་འཐས་སུ་བཟུང་ནས་བློས་གཏད་སོ་ལ་སྒོམ་དུ་བཟུང་ནས་ཡོད་པར་སྒྲོ་འདོགས། ། ཁ་ཅིག་ཆོས་ཐམས་ཅད་སྟོང་པ་ཉིད་ཡིན་པས་འཁོར་བ་མེད་མྱང་འདས་མེད། ལས་འབྲས་མེད་ཅང་མེད་ཆད་པར་སྒོམ་ཞིང་མེད་པར་སྐུར་བ་འདེབས། དེ་ལྟར་མ་རྟོགས་པ་རྣམས་རང་རང་གི་ཞེ་འདོད་སྣ་ཚོགས་ལ་དམ་པའི་དོན་དུ་འཛིན་ཞིང་བསྒོམ་པས་ན། སྟོང་དང་སྣང་དང་ཡོད་དང་མེད་པའི་སྒོམ། །དེ་ལྟར་བློས་བྱས་གཉིས་འཛིན་གྱི་སྒོམ་པ་སུ་ལ་ཡོད་པ་དེ་ལ་ཞེ་འདོད་གྲུབ་མཐའི་ལྟ་བའང་ཡོད། བླང་དོར་ཕྱོགས་རིས་ཀྱི་སྤྱོད་པའང་ཡོད་པས་ན། གང་ལ་བསྒོམ་ཡོད་ལྟ་དང་སྤྱོད་པ་ཡོད། །དེ་ལྟར་བློས་བྱས་བཅོས་མའི་ལྟ་སྒོམ་ལ་རེ་བ་རྣམས་ལ་ཡེ་གྲོལ་སྤང་བླང་དང་བྲལ་བའི་གནད་མེད་པས་འཁོར་འདས་ལ་བཟབ་ཉིད་རང་བཞིན་འོད་གསལ་ཞེས་བྱ་ཞིང་། །ཉི་དང་སྤྲིན་བཞིན་གློ་བུར་དྲི་མ་ཡིས། །བསྒྲིབ་ཕྱིར་ཁམས་ཞེས་དུས་རིང་ཉིད་གནས་ཕྱིར། །ཐོག་མའི་ཆོས་ཁམས་དགེ་བ་ཞེས་བརྗོད་ཅིང་། །གནས་ལུགས་ཡིན་ཕྱིར་དོན་དམ་བདེན་པར་བཏགས། །བསམ་ཡུལ་འདས་ཕྱིར་ཤེས་རབ་

པ་རོལ་ཕྱིན། །འདུས་མ་བྱས་ཕྱིར་ལྷུན་གྲུབ་དཀྱིལ་འཁོར་ཉིད། །སྟོབས་སོགས་
ཡོན་ཏན་རྒྱ་མཚོའི་མཛོད་ཉིད་ཕྱིར། །བདེ་གཤེགས་སྙིང་པོས་འགྲོ་ཀུན་ཁྱབ་ཅེས་
གསུངས། །རང་ལ་ཡོད་ཀྱང་མི་མཐོང་སྒྲིབ་པའི་དཔེ། །ས་འོག་གཏེར་དང་བུམ་
ནང་མར་མེ་དང་། །སྦྲུན་པའི་འབྲས་དང་པད་ངན་བདེ་གཤེགས་དང་། །གོས་
ཧྲུལ་རིན་ཆེན་འདམ་རྫབ་ནོར་བུ་དང་། པད་ནང་སྦྲང་རྩི་རྡོ་ཁམས་རིན་ཆེན་
དང་། །ཁྲུད་ཀྱི་ནོར་བུ་རུལ་འདམ་གསེར་ཉིད་དང་། །ལྗོན་ཤིང་འབྲས་དང་འོ་
མའི་མར་ཉིད་དང་། །སྟོང་གསུམ་དར་ཡུག་ཆེན་པོ་ལ་སོགས་པས། །ཉེ་བར་
མཚོན་ཏེ་ལུང་ལས་གསུངས་དེ་བཞིན། །རིགས་ཁམས་སྙིང་པོས་འགྲོ་ཀུན་ཡོངས་
ལ་ཁྱབ། །འདི་ནི་ངེས་དོན་སྙིང་པོའི་གཞི་ཞེས་བྱ། །དེ་ལྟའི་དབྱིངས་ལས་རང་
རིག་རྣམ་གྲོལ་ཞིང་། །སྐད་ཅིག་བྱེ་བྲག་ཕྱེད་བས་སངས་རྒྱས་ཏེ། །གདོད་མའི་
མགོན་པོ་ཡོན་ཏན་པ་རོལ་ཕྱིན། །ནང་གི་ཇི་བཞིན་གཟིགས་པ་རྣམ་དག་བས། །
དང་པོའི་སངས་རྒྱས་ཆོས་ཚོགས་རྣམ་པར་བཞག །དུས་རིང་བརྟག་དཀའ་ཐོག་མ་
མེད་དབྱིངས་སུ། །མ་རིག་དབང་གིས་འགྲོ་དྲུག་འཁྲུལ་བ་ནི། །ཞེས་སོགས་
ལེགས་པར་བཤད་ཅིང་། མཁའ་འགྲོ་ཡང་ཐིག་གི་གནད་གསུམ་སྒྲོན་མར་ཡང་འདི་
དང་མཐུན་པར་ཞལ་ཤིན་ཏུ་གསལ་བར་བཤད་པས་ཁ་ཚོན་ལེགས་པར་ཆོད་པ་ཡིན་ལ།
དེས་ན་ཀུན་ཏུ་བཟང་པོ་གཞི་ཐོག་ནས་གྲོལ་བར་འཆད་པ་ལའང་བརྒལ་བརྟག་བྱེད་པ་
དང་གཞུང་གཞན་དང་མི་མཐུན་པ་འཛིན་པའང་གནད་མ་གོ་བའི་རྣམ་འགྱུར་ཡིན་ཏེ།
སངས་རྒྱས་ཡིན་ནས་གཞི་ཐོག་མ་གྲོལ་བ་མི་སྲིད་དེ་སྐུར་ཐེག་མཆོག་མཛོད་ཀྱི་ལུང་
དྲངས་པ་ལྟར། ཚེ་འདིར་འཆར་བའི་སྣང་བཞིའི་འོད་གསལ་དང་། བར་དོའི་
སྣང་ཆ་ཉིད་གཞི་སྣང་དུ་བཤད་ཅིང་། །འདིར་གདོད་མའི་བདེ་གཤེགས་སྙིང་པོར་ཁ་
ཚོན་ཆོད་པས་ན་བདེ་གཤེགས་སྙིང་པོའི་རང་བཞིན་རྟོགས་ཏེ་སངས་རྒྱས་པ་མ་ཡིན་
པའི་སངས་རྒྱས་ཀྱང་མི་སྲིད་ལ། དེར་མ་ཟད་ཐོད་རྒལ་གྱི་རྒྱབ་ཡིག་ཉི་ཟླ་གཟའ་
སྐར་དུ་ཀུན་ཏུ་བཟང་པོའི་གྲོལ་ལུགས་བཤད་པའི་རྗེས་སུ། དབྱིངས་སྣང་ལས་གྲོལ་

ཚད་ཐམས་ཅད་ཀྱང་འདི་ཡིན་ལ། ཁྱད་པར་བར་དོའི་གཞི་སྣང་ལས་གྲོལ་ཚད་
ལུགས་འདི་ཡིན་ནོ་ཞེས་དང་། ཐེག་མཆོག་མཛོད་དང་། ཚིག་དོན་མཛོད་གཉིས་
ཀར་གདོད་མའི་མགོན་པོའི་གྲོལ་ཚུལ་བཤད་པའི་རྗེས་སུ་རྒྱུད་བླའི་འགྲེལ་བའི་ལུང་དེ་
ལྟར་ཤིན་ཏུ་རྨད་དུ་བྱུང་ཞིང་བསམ་དུ་མེད་པའི་ཡུལ་ སངས་རྒྱས་ཉིད་དེ་གཞན་
ལས་མ་ཐོས་པར་རང་ཉིད་སློབ་དཔོན་མེད་པར་རང་བྱུང་གི་ཡེ་ཤེས་བརྗོད་དུ་མེད་པའི་
རང་བཞིན་མངོན་པར་རྫོགས་པར་སངས་རྒྱས་ཏེ་ཞེས་པ་ལ་སོགས་པ་དྲངས་པས་ཀྱང་
དེ་གཉིས་དགོངས་པ་གཅིག་པར་གསལ་ཞིང་། གཞན་ཡང་འཇམ་དཔལ་མཚན་
བརྗོད་ལས་ཀྱང་། དང་པོའི་སངས་རྒྱས་རིས་མེད་པ། །ཞེས་གསུངས་པ་དང་།
དུས་འཁོར་ལས་ཀྱང་། མཆོག་གི་དང་པོའི་སངས་རྒྱས་ཞེས་བཤད་པ་དང་།
རྒྱུད་གཞན་ལས་ཀྱང་། སངས་རྒྱས་སངས་རྒྱས་སྔར་སངས་རྒྱས། །ཞེས་བཤད་
པ་དང་། མདོ་པདྨ་དཀར་པོ་ལས་ཀྱང་། བསྐལ་པ་བྱེ་སྟོང་བསམ་གྱིས་མི་ཁྱབ་
པ། །དེ་ཡི་ཚད་ནི་ནམ་ཡང་མེད་པ་ནས། །བྱང་ཆུབ་མཆོག་བདེ་ནི་ངས་རྙེད་
དེ། །ང་ནི་རྟག་ཏུ་ཆོས་ཀྱང་རབ་འཆད་དོ། །ཞེས་པ་འདི་དག་ཀྱང་མི་མཐུན་པ་
མེད་པར་གནད་གཅིག་པ་ཡིན་པས་བདེ་བར་གཤེགས་པའི་གསུང་རབ་ལ་འགལ་འདུ་བོ་
ན་སེམས་པར་མི་བྱའོ། དེ་ལྟར་ནའང་འོག་མ་འོག་མས་ཕྱོགས་ཙམ་ལས་ཡོངས་སུ་
མ་རྫོགས་པས་གོང་མ་གོང་མ་དེ་ལས་ཞལ་གསལ་ཞིང་ཞིབ་པའི་ཁྱད་ཆོས་བཞག་ཏུ་
ཡོད་པའང་རྟོགས་དགོས་ཤིང་། དེར་མ་ཟད་སྔར་བཤད་པ་ལྟར་འཁོར་འདས་ཀྱི་
གཞི་དང་། བདེ་གཤེགས་སྙིང་པོའི་ཁམས་གཉིས་ཀྱང་ངོ་བོ་ཐད་དུ་ནམ་ཡང་བསམ་
པར་མི་བྱ་ཞིང་། ལྡོག་ཆའི་དབང་གིས་དབྱེ་བ། གཞི་སྣང་མཐར་ཐུག་དང་རིག་
པ་འོད་ཀྱི་ཁང་པར་གནས་པ་དང་མི་གནས་པ་ལ་སོགས་པ་ཕྲ་རག་གི་ཁྱད་ཆོས་རྣམས་
ཀྱང་ལེགས་པར་ཤེས་པར་བྱ་དགོས་པ་ཡིན་ནོ། གསུམ་པ་དེ་ལ། རྩོད་པ་སྤང་བ་
ནི། དེ་ཡང་ལྟ་བ་ཕྱོགས་རོལ་ཞེན་ཆ་ཞིང་བཟང་ངན་གཉིས་འཛིན་གྱི་སྒྲོག་གིས་
བཅིང་བདག་འདི་སྐད་ཅེས་དོན་དམ་པའི་ཆོས་ཉིད་བདེ་གཤེགས་སྙིང་པོ་ནི་སྐྱོན་ཀུན་ཟད་

ཡོན་ཏན་ཀུན་རྫོགས་སངས་རྒྱས་ཀྱི་རང་བཞིན་འབའ་ཞིག་པས་གྲོལ་གཞི་པོ་ན་ཡིན་གྱི་དེ་འཁོར་འདས་གཉིས་ཀའི་སྤྱི་གཞིར་བཤད་པ་ནི་ནམ་ཡང་མི་འཐད་དོ་ཞེ་ན། དེ་ལ་འདི་སྐད་ཅེས་བཤད་པ་བྱ་སྟེ། དབྱིངས་བདེ་གཤེགས་སྙིང་པོ་རང་ངོས་ནས་འཁོར་བའི་འཁྲུལ་སྣང་ཡེ་ནས་ལྷུན་གྲུབ་ཏུ་ཡོད་པ་མ་ཡིན་ཡང་། དེ་ལས་ཤར་བ་གཞི་སྣང་གི་དུས་རང་ངོ་ཤེས་མ་ཤེས་ལས་གྲོལ་འཁྲུལ་གཉིས་སུ་འབྱུང་བ་ཡིན་པས་བདེ་གཤེགས་སྙིང་པོ་སྤྱི་གཞིར་བཤད་པ་ལ་འགལ་བ་ཅུང་ཟད་ཀྱང་མེད་དེ། ཡིད་བཞིན་མཛོད་རྩ་འགྲེལ་ལས། གཞི་དེ་ཡང་འཁོར་བ་ལ་ལྟོས་པས་རྟེན་གཞི་ནམ་མཁའ་ལྟར་གདོད་མ་ནས་སྟོང་ཞིང་། ངོ་བོ་ཉིད་ཀྱིས་འདག་མེད་པ། ཉི་ཟླ་ལྟར་འོད་གསལ་ཞིང་ལྷུན་གྱིས་གྲུབ་པ་སྟེ། ཐོག་མ་མེད་པ་ནས་གནས་པས་འཕོ་འགྱུར་མེད་པ་སྤྲོས་པའི་མཐའ་ལས་འདས་པས་ངང་གིས་འོད་གསལ་བ་སྐུ་དང་ཡེ་ཤེས་འདུ་འབྲལ་མེད་པའི་དབྱིངས་སུ་གནས་པའི་བདེ་བར་གཤེགས་པའི་སྙིང་པོ་འཁོར་འདས་ཀྱི་ཆོས་རྣམས་བརྟེན་པའི་གནས་ལུགས་དོན་གྱི་ཀུན་གཞི་ཞེས་བྱ་སྟེ་འདུས་མ་བྱས་ཤིང་ཡེ་ནས་རྣམ་དག་ཆེན་པོར་གནས་པའོ། དེ་ཡང་འཁོར་བའི་ཆོས་ལས་དང་ཉོན་མོངས་པ་རྣམས་རྟེན་པ་མེད་པའི་ཚུལ་གྱིས་བརྟེན་པ་ནི། ཉི་མཁའི་ངོས་ན་སྤྲིན་ཕུང་བརྟེན་པ་ལྟར། གཞི་ལམ་རིག་མ་འབྱུར་ལ་དེའི་ངང་ན་གནས་པ་སྟེ། དོན་ལ་རང་བཞིན་མེད་པས་རྟེན་དང་བརྟེན་པར་མ་གྲུབ་བཞིན་དུ་བརྟེན་པར་སྣང་བས་བཏགས་པ་སྟེ། མྱ་ངན་ལས་འདས་པའི་ཆོས་རྣམས་ཉི་མ་དང་ཟེར་ལྟར་དབྱེར་མེད་དུ་བརྟེན་ཏེ་ཡེ་ནས་འདུ་འབྲལ་མེད་པར་གནས་པའི་ཕྱིར་རོ། །ཞེས་དང་། ཁྱད་པར་ཐེག་མཆོག་མཛོད་དུ། ཐོག་མའི་གཞི་ལ་འཁྲུལ་པ་མེད་ཀྱང་གཞི་སྣང་དུ་ཤར་དུས་རང་ངོ་མ་རིག་པའི་ཤེས་པ་ལྷུང་མ་བསྙན་མ་རིག་པའི་རྩ་བ་ཅན་དེས་གཞི་སྣང་རིས་སུ་བཅད་པས་སེམས་ཅན་དུ་འཁྲུལ་སྟེ། མུ་ཏིག་ཕྲེང་བ་ལས། ཁྱད་པར་ཆེན་པོའི་སྣང་བ་ལས། ཡོད་དང་མེད་པ་གཉིས་འབྱུང་སྟེ། །སྤྱི་ལ་འཁྲུལ་གཞི་ཞེས་བྱ་སྟེ། །མ་རིག་ཉིད་དང་སྦྲགས་པའི་ཕྱིར། །ཤེས་བྱ་ཉིད་ཀྱང་ཕྲི་པར་སྣང་། །ཞེས་པ་དང་། ཆོས་

སྐུ་ནམ་མཁའ་ལྟ་བུ་ལ། །གློ་བུར་སེམས་ཅན་སྤྲིན་གྱིས་བསྒྲིབ། །མ་འཁྲུལ་བ་ཡི་ཆོས་ཉིད་ཀྱང་། །བློ་ལ་འཁྲུལ་པའི་ཚུལ་དུ་སྣང་། །ཞེས་དང་། རྡོ་རྗེ་སེམས་དཔའ་སྙིང་གི་མེ་ལོང་ལས། །ཁམས་གསུམ་གྱི་སེམས་ཅན་འདི་དག་ཐམས་ཅད་ནི། །གཞི་ཅི་ཡང་མ་ཡིན་པ་ལས་འཁྲུལ་ལོ། །ཞེས་དང་། རྡོ་རྗེ་སེམས་དཔའ་འཁྲུལ་བ་མི་མངའ་ཡང་། །སེམས་ཅན་ལ་འཁྲུལ་པའི་ཚུལ་སྟོན་པའོ། ། ཞེས་སོགས་དྲངས་ནས་གསུངས་ཤིང་། ཁྱད་པར་རྐྱེན་གྱིས་སྐྱོན་ཡོན་ཆར་དབྱེ་བ་འདི་ལྟར་གསུངས་ཏེ། ག་བུར་དེ་ཚད་ནད་དུ་ཡོན་ཏན་སྣང་ལ། །གྲང་ནད་ལ་སྐྱོན་དུ་ཤར་ཡང་། ག་བུར་གྱི་ངོ་བོ་ལ་སྐྱོན་དང་ཡོན་ཏན་མ་གྲུབ་པ་བཞིན་དུ་གཞི་དང་གཞི་སྣང་གི་འཆར་ཚུལ་དེ་ཡང་རང་ངོ་ཤེས་པ་རྣམས་ལ་གྲོལ་རྐྱེན་ལྟར་དུ་སྣང་བས་ཡོན་ཏན་ལྟར་ཤར་ལ། མ་ཤེས་ན་ཆ་དེས་འཁྲུལ་བའི་གཞི་བྱེད་པའི་སྐྱོན་ལྟར་སྣང་ཡང་། གཞི་དེ་དང་དེས་སྣང་བ་སྐྱོན་ཡོན་ཏུ་གྲུབ་པ་མེད་དོ་ཞེས་སོགས་གསལ་བར་བཤད་པ་ལྟར་ཡིན་ཞིང་། དེར་མ་ཟད་འཁྲུལ་སྣང་འཁོར་བ་ལྟར་སྣང་བའི་དུས་ནའང་། །རང་ངོ་གདོད་མའི་གཞི་ལས་གཞན་དུ་གཡོ་བ་ཙམ་ཟད་ཀྱང་མེད་ལ་གཞི་སྣང་ཆོས་ཉིད་ཀྱི་རྩལ་ལས་ཤར་བའི་འཁོར་འདས་གཉིས་ཀྱང་བཟང་ངན་སྐྱོན་ཡོན་ཏུ་འབྱེད་པ་ཙམ་ཟད་མེད་དེ། དག་མཉམ་སྤྲོས་པ་དང་བྲལ་བར་གཏན་ལ་འབེབས་པ་ནི་ཐེག་ཆེན་ཐུན་མོང་མ་ཡིན་པ་ཡང་དག་གི་ལྟ་བ་ཡིན་ཏེ། ཆོས་ཐམས་ཅད་འབྱུང་བ་མེད་པར་བསྟན་པའི་མདོ་ལས། ལྟ་དང་ལྟ་མིན་གཉིས་ཀ་ཚུལ་གཅིག་སྟེ། ། མཉམ་དང་མི་མཉམ་དེ་བཞིན་མཉམ་པ་ཡིན། །སངས་རྒྱས་མེད་ཅིང་ཆོས་དང་དགེ་འདུན་མེད། །དེ་ལྟར་སུས་ཤེས་དེ་ནི་མཁས་པ་ཡིན། །ཞེས་དང་། ཀུན་བྱེད་ལས། སངས་རྒྱས་སེམས་ཅན་ལས་དང་བག་ཆགས་དང་། །བྱང་ཆུབ་སེམས་ལས་མ་གཏོགས་ཆོས་གཞན་མེད། །ཅེས་པ་ལ་སོགས་རྒྱ་ཆེར་བཤད་པ་ཡིན་ནོ། དེས་ན་གདོད་མའི་གཞི་བདེ་གཤེགས་སྙིང་པོ་གཅིག་གི་རྩལ་དང་རོལ་པ་ལས་ཤར་བའི་འཁོར་འདས་གཉིས་ལ་བཟང་ངན་སྤང་བླང་དུ་འབྱེད་པ་ནི་ཅི་ཡང་མེད་དོ། དེ་ལྟར་

མ་ཡིན་པར་ཆོས་ཉིད་བདེ་གཤེགས་སྙིང་པོ་མ་ཡིན་པའི་འཁོར་འདས་སྤྱི་མཚན་ལ་ལྟོས་བའི་ཡེ་གཞི་ཟུར་བ་ཞིག་འདོད་ན་དེ་ལ་འདི་སྐད་དྲི་སྟེ། དེ་ལྟ་བུའི་གཞི་དེས་སེམས་ཅན་ཐམས་ཅད་ལ་ཁྱབ་བམ་མ་ཁྱབ། ཁྱབ་ན་བདེ་གཤེགས་སྙིང་པོ་ལས་གཞན་པའི་སྤྱི་གཞི་ཞིག་ཁྱབ་བྱེད་དུ་ཡོད་ན་སེམས་ཅན་ཐམས་ཅད་ཀྱང་རྒྱུད་གཅིག་ཏུ་འགྱུར་བ་དང་། །ཡང་སེམས་ཅན་རེ་རེ་ལ་རྒྱུད་གཉིས་གཉིས་ཡོད་པར་འགྱུར་བ་དང་གཅིག་གྲོལ་དུ་ཐམས་ཅད་གྲོལ་བར་འགྱུར་བ་ལ་སོགས་པའི་སྐྱོན་འདུག་ཅིང་མུ་སྟེགས་གསང་བ་པ་རྣམས་འདོད་པའི་མཁའ་ལྟར་ཁྱད་པར་དགུ་ལྡན་དང་དབྱེ་བ་ཅུང་ཟད་མེད་པར་འགྱུར་ལ། མ་ཁྱབ་ན་ནམ་མཁས་གར་ཁྱབ་སེམས་ཅན་གྱིས་ཁྱབ་པར་གནས་པའི་གོ་སྐབས་ཀྱང་མི་རྙེད་ལ། འཁྲུལ་ཟིན་ནས་གྲོལ་བའང་མི་རིགས་ཤིག །ཁར་དོ་ལ་སོགས་པར་གཞི་སྣང་འཆར་བར་བཤད་པའང་མི་འཐད་ལ། དེ་ལྟ་བུའི་གཞི་བཤད་པ་ལ་དོན་མ་མཆིས་པར་འགྱུར་པ་ལ་སོགས་འགལ་འདུ་ཆར་ལྟར་འབབ་པར་འགྱུར་རོ། དེ་ལྟར་གཞིའི་འཆད་ཚུལ་ལ་གཞུང་གཞན་དང་རྫོགས་པ་ཆེན་པོ་གཉིས་ཁྱད་པར་ཅུང་ཟད་ཀྱང་མེད་དམ་ཞེ་ན། གདོད་མའི་ཡེ་གཞི་རང་གི་ངོ་བོ་འཆད་པ་ནི་ཁྱད་པར་ཅུང་ཟད་ཀྱང་མེད་ལ། དེ་ལས་འཁོར་འདས་སུ་སྣང་བའི་དུས་ན་གཞི་སྣང་ལྷུན་གྲུབ་རིན་པོ་ཆེ་སྒོ་བརྒྱད་ཀྱི་འཆར་ཚུལ་ཞིབ་པར་བཤད་པ་ནི་མདོ་རྒྱུད་གཞན་ན་ཤིན་ཏུ་གབ་པ་ཡོད་པ་ཉིད་རྫོགས་པ་ཆེན་པོར་རྒྱལ་དུ་བཏོན་ནས་བཤད་པའི་ཁྱད་ཡོད་པ་ཡིན་ལ། གནད་དེའི་དབང་ལས་ལམ་ཉམས་སུ་ལེན་པའི་གནས་སྐབས་ན་ཡང་རབ་ཚེ་འདིར་གྲོལ་བ་འོད་གསལ་ཐོད་རྒལ་གྱི་གདམས་པ། འབྲིང་བར་དོར་གྲོལ་བ་ཆོས་ཉིད་རང་སྣང་གི་བར་དོ་གཞི་སྣང་གི་འཆར་ཚུལ་དང་། ཐ་མ་སྲིད་པའི་བར་དོར་གཞི་སྣང་རང་བཞིན་སྤྲུལ་སྐུའི་ཞིང་དུ་གྲོལ་བ་ལ་སོགས་པའི་ཁྱད་ཆོས་གཞུང་འདིར་ཡོད་པ་གཞན་ལ་མེད་པ་ནི་ཤེས་པར་བྱ་བ་ཡིན་ནོ། །མཁས་པ་ཞྭ་རྒྱལ་པོས་གསུངས་སོ། །དགེའོ། །དགེའོ། །དགེའོ།།

Index

A Marvellous Garland of Rare Gems xvii
abandoning and accepting 24, 77
abiding mind 7
abode of all dharmas 33, 46
absence of clinging 76
absorption 6, 7, 25, 27, 74, 76, 94
actuality . . . iii, iv, xviii-xx, 1, 2, 9, 14, 24, 32, 44, 45, 47, 49, 50, 53, 58, 72, 73, 82, 85, 97, 109, 117
Actuality Treasury 47
actually experienced space . . . 59
adoption and rejection . . . 5, 30, 66, 72, 73, 79, 83
Advaita Vedanta . . . . . . xxiii, xxiv
adventitious . . . 34, 41, 51, 52, 85
adventitious discursive thoughts34
adventitious stains 41, 51, 52
Adzom Drukpa's edition of the Nyingthig Yazhi 55
affliction 85
afflictions 5,28,51,59,68,80,85,87
after-passing . . . . xxv, 71
after-passing teaching xxv
after-passing testament 71
alaya . . . . xi, 35, 44, 58, 86
All Creator 34, 39, 61
all phenomena . . . vii, 37, 42, 43, 47, 50, 61, 73, 78, 79, 90, 92, 94
All-Knowing Lord of Speech . xi
all-inclusive space vii
All-Knowing One 31, 86
alpha purity . . 23, 38, 45, 72, 80, 83, 86, 121
An Explanation of the Four Yogas Points out Superfact 7
antidote 5, 14, 23, 68, 76
appearance and becoming . . . 47, 73, 86
appearance factor of spontaneous existence 83
appearance factor of the bardo 55
appearance in the outer sky . . . 48
appearances of the sixfold group 24
approaches to the view 58
arhat 43, 96
assurance 23, 87
aural transmission . . . . xxviii, xxx
aural transmission for ordinary beings xxviii
awareness . . . 3, 4, 17, 22, 24, 59,

75, 76, 87, 89, 91, 93, 113, 122
bardo . . 19, 27, 48, 55, 62, 87, 92
becoming . . xxiii, xxv, 26, 30, 33, 34, 47, 49, 52, 62, 68, 69, 73, 79, 82, 86, 87, 92
Being Just So 28, 67, 74
best faculties 1, 5, 16
best, middling, and least 1, 5, 6, 16
beyond the reach of mind's thought 72
beyond-all fact 67
bindu with vajra chains 27
blemishes of latencies 4
bliss xi, 18, 21, 22, 27, 65, 74, 88
bliss, luminosity, and no-thought 74, 88
bliss-luminosity 27
Bodhgaya vi
bodhisatva xxviii, 88, 96, 102, 115
Bon . . . . xxiii, xxiv, 32
Bon teachings xxiii
Bon teachings and Buddhist teachings xxiii
Bon tradition's various mistaken claims 32
buddha, dharma, and sangha . . 54
buddhahood . . vii, 13, 14, 39, 41, 54-56, 96, 118, 120, 122
Buddhist Secret Mantra . . . xxiii
Buddhist teachings . . . . xxiii, 96
cage of hope and fear 75
cage of the afflictions 80
caged by their dualistic approach 57
caging the innate mind . . . 67, 75
camphor 60
causes and effects of samsara . . 14
chain of confusion 2
chakravartin emperor 53
channels and winds 18, 26
characteristiclessness 42
Chemchog Heruka 69
Chog Zhag 28, 67, 74, 88
Chogyam Trungpa . . . . xxiii, 52, 89, 114, 115, 123
clearness and stillness 3
clinging . . . 4, 20, 21, 28, 30, 57, 58, 67, 68, 73, 74, 76-78, 80, 81, 89
Collected Works . . . i, vi, xi, xvii, xviii, xx, xxvi, xxvii, 7
common awareness 3,17,75,76,89
compassionate activity . . . 36, 40-43, 45, 46, 49, 50, 62, 89
complete purity . . 21, 30, 45, 49, 51, 54, 58, 59, 67, 90
conceived effort . 3, 14, 28, 90, 95
conceived-of thing 90
concept labels 73, 90, 91
confused into a sentient being . 59
confusion . . 2, 25, 38, 45, 47-49, 57-60, 87, 91, 115
conquerors' mind process 2
conqueror's mind 4
Contained Understanding 34
containers and contents 23, 78, 91
contrivance . 3, 4, 15, 22, 67, 74-76, 78, 86, 92, 107
contrivance of rational mind . . . 3
contrived and contrived . . 68, 75
convention 47, 54, 96, 102
crow flies off from its perch . . 15
cyclic existence 89, 92,94,101,109
Dakini Quintessence ix
definitive meaning 54, 111
Derge Printery xviii
Descent into Langka 43
determined strivings of concept 75

Dharma King Trisong Deutsen xiii
dharmadhatu . vii, 34, 39, 40, 42, 45, 46, 71, 92
dharmakaya . . xiii, 2, 4, 5, 10, 23, 34, 36, 38, 42, 46, 62, 69, 73, 83, 92, 125
dharmata . . 19, 23, 24, 27-29, 38, 47, 51, 57, 61, 72-74, 78, 79, 82, 83, 92, 93
dharmata bardo 19, 27
dharmata sugatagarbha 47, 57, 61
dharmata's own entity 72
dharmin 73, 93
dhatu . . vii, xii, xiv, 9, 10, 27, 30, 33, 34, 39, 40, 42, 45-47, 49, 51, 52, 54, 55, 71-73, 92-94, 104, 123
dhyana 7, 25, 27, 94
dhyana day 27
Direct Crossing . . . . xvii, xxii, 18, 19, 26, 31, 49, 55, 62, 94, 121, 126
direct mind to mind transmission xxviii
direct perception . vii, 19, 24, 26, 41, 44, 51, 58, 90, 97, 98, 101
discursive thought . . 1, 2, 4-7, 9-11, 14-17, 23, 25-27, 73, 74, 76,94
discursive thought self-purifies 74
discursive thoughts of mind . . 82
distinguishing mind and wisdom 49
doha 9, 33, 38, 46, 95
door of shining forth 41
doors of spontaneous existence 48
doorway to actuality 9
dreams 26, 30
Drukchen Padma Karpo's Collected Works on Mahamudra 7
Drukpa Kagyu . . xx, 6, 8, 19, 124
dualistic clinging 80
dualistic grasping 29, 80
Dvagpo Kagyu 8
Dza Patrul . . . iii, vi, xvi-xviii, xx, xxi, xxiii-xxv, xxxv, 1, 31, 32, 57, 71, 125
Dzachuka . . . . . v, vi, xvi, xviii, xx
Dzogchen . . . . i, ii, v, vi, xv-xviii, xxi, xxiii-xxv, xxxiii, 65, 71, 104, 125
Dzogchen Monastery . . . . vi, xv-xviii, xxi, xxiv, xxxiii, 65, 71
Dzogchen Monastery lineage of Longchen Nyingthig xvi
Dzogchen Rinpoche xv,xvi,xxv,65
Dzogpa Chenpo vi
each side of dualistic grasping . 80
early lineage of the teaching . . ix
Eastern Tibet . . v, x, xv, xvii, xviii
effort 3, 14, 28, 90, 95, 116
eight analogies of illusion 48
eight doors' mode of shining forth 62
eight worldly dharmas 77
elaboration . . 7, 8, 25, 29, 61, 72, 83, 95
eleven topics of the *Word's Meaning* 31
eliminating opposing arguments 32, 57
empowerment . . xiv, xix, xxix, 18, 69, 125
emptiness . . . . viii, 2-4, 9, 15, 21, 25, 29, 37, 39, 42, 43, 49, 68, 72, 76-79, 94-96, 106, 110
empty entity 37, 50, 120
empty forms 19, 26, 82
empty-luminous dharmakaya

. . . . 69, 83
enlightenment mind . 35, 39, 40, 47, 49, 54, 61, 88, 96
entity . . . 2, 3, 15, 24, 25, 28, 36, 37, 40-43, 45, 46, 49, 50, 67, 72-75, 96, 110, 119, 120
entity, nature, and compassionate activity 36, 43, 49
equipoise . . . 3, 4, 10, 13-15, 23, 27, 28, 97, 111, 115
equipoise and post-attainment 4, 27, 97, 111
essence . . . ix, 39, 73, 89, 96, 109, 113, 117, 118
exaggeration 79, 97
excellence of objects 3
expanse . . . . xii, 51
experiences and realization . . . 21
expressions 72, 73, 97
expressions of words 72
external objects 4, 18, 82
extra-secret viii, ix, xxviii, 94, 121
extra-sensory perceptions . . 6, 28
extreme of becoming 82
extremes of elaborations 58
facsimile only of discursive thoughts 4
fact . . xviii, xix, xxviii, xxix, 1, 24, 30, 41, 51, 58, 59, 67, 68, 72, 75, 76, 79, 89, 91, 93, 95, 97-99, 101, 102, 105, 107, 110, 114, 117, 119
fact of the garbha is obscured 68, 75
factor of ground appearance . . 48
factual 44, 58, 73, 98, 99
factual alaya 58
familiarization 14, 26, 28, 98
father-son succession 31
Feature of the Expert Glorious King . . . . xix, xxi, 22
fetters of samsara 80
fictional 98, 99
field realm 99
finality obtained 99
first three empowerments 18
five eyes and the extra-sensory perceptions 6
five paths 19, 30, 100
five paths and ten levels 30
Flower Cave of the Great Secret . . . . xi, xiii
foremost instruction . . . viii, xxi-xxiii, 21, 23, 24, 100
foremost instructions . . . . iii, iv, xviii-xx, 1, 19, 100
Foremost Instructions Clearly Showing Actuality iii, iv, xviii-xx, 1
four appearances 27, 55
four appearances of luminosity 27
four turnings of the wheel of dharma xviii
fourth Dzogchen Rinpoche . . xv, xvi, xxv, 65
fourth empowerment 18
fourth-part-freed-of-the-three dharmakaya mind 23
free of ground and root . . . 69, 83
Freedom from Elaboration . 8, 95
freshness 16
fruition . . xxi, xxv, 14, 21, 22, 29, 37, 51, 66, 68, 72, 81, 83, 102, 103, 122
full definition of the ground in Great Completion 58
full-ripening 69, 81
furtherance and suppression . . 5, 85, 100

Gampopa 13, 107
Garab Dorje . . . . ix, xxi, 71, 125
garbha 32-36, 38, 39, 41-47, 49-58, 60, 61, 68, 72, 75, 101, 118-120
Garbha of the Secret 33, 38
general ground . . 47, 50, 57, 58, 61, 72
general ground of both samsara and nirvana 57
general ground of liberation and confusion 47
general ground of samsara and nirvana 72
generally characterized samsara and nirvana 44, 61
generic image 25, 101
good qualities . . 6, 19, 28, 38-40, 50, 51, 53, 54, 57, 105, 108
grasped-grasping . 30, 51, 80, 101
grasping at a self 25
grasping at a self in dharmas . . 25
grasping at I 80
grasping at the ground 80
great alpha purity 72
Great Bliss Chakra xi
Great Chariot xiii
Great Completion . . . . ii, iii, v-x, xiii, xvii-xxv, xxviii-xxxii, 1, 3-5, 16, 18, 20-24, 26, 31, 33-36, 38, 40-46, 48, 50, 51, 57-60, 62, 65, 67, 71, 73, 78, 83, 85-90, 92, 94-96, 103, 104, 106-111, 113, 117, 118, 121, 124, 125
Great Completion Hearing Lineage 16
Great Completion system of dharma vi
great groundless self-waking . 48
great juncture 67
Great Perfection . . . . vii, viii
great tantras of the quintessence level of the secret 31
Great Vehicle 32, 43, 61, 96, 100-102, 121
greater completion . . 67, 68, 73, 77, 78
ground and ground appearances . . . . xxiv, xxv, 48, 57, 58
ground and root free 102
ground and root-less dharmata 78
ground appearance 48, 49, 55, 62
ground appearances . . . . xxiv, xxv, 41, 47, 48, 50, 55, 57-62
ground of confusion 48, 60
ground of liberation 47, 48
ground of liberation and confusion 47
ground of samsara and nirvana 56, 72
ground, path, and fruition . . . xxi, 21, 37, 102
groundless phenomena of samsara and nirvana 78
ground's actuality . 32, 44, 45, 49
Guardian Nagarjuna 34, 80
Guru Rinpoche . xxv, 66, 69, 113
guru yoga of Longchen Rabjam x
Gyalwa Gotsangpa 8, 16
Gyalwang Yang Gonpa 6
Gyalway Nyugu . . . . . xv-xvii, xxv, xxviii, xxxiii, 31, 65, 71
hearing lineage 16
Hevajra 41
Highest Continuum . . . 36, 38, 40, 51, 53, 55
Highest Continuum Commentary 36, 38, 40, 51, 55

how sentient beings' confusion occurs 49
idea of perfection vii
identification . . . 4, 9, 11, 14, 22, 24, 26, 90, 103
identifying the ground 32
ignorance 45, 54, 59, 91, 98, 99, 103, 108, 110, 114, 117
illusion 26, 38, 48, 82
impurity's door 48
incorrect translation "Great Perfection" vii
indeterminate awareness not recognizing its own face 59
individually discriminating prajna 26
individually discriminating prajna's vipashyana 26
innate disposition 25, 68, 72,77,80
introduction . . . ii, iii, v, xvii, xxix-xxxii, 10, 18, 19, 24, 52, 67, 79, 88, 99, 104, 113, 125
introduction and to introduce 104
introduction to the nature of mind . . . . xxix, xxxii, 18
in-space . . 23, 24, 28-30, 67, 69, 72-74, 82, 83, 103
in-space of wisdom 74
Jamgon Kongtrul 53
Jigmey Gyalway Nyugu . xv-xvii, xxv, xxviii, xxxiii, 31, 65, 71
Jigmey Lingpa . . . x, xi, xv, xxxiii, 31, 67, 126
Jigmey Thrinley Ozer xv
joining of shamatha and vipashyana 6, 8
joining together shamatha and vipashyana 6, 7
Kagyu . . xvi, xviii, xx, xxi, 6, 8, 11, 19, 89, 104, 123, 124
Kagyu Mahamudra teachings . . . . xviii, xx
Kalachakra 26, 56
karma . 18, 33, 34, 52, 59, 61, 69, 79-81, 108, 123
karma and afflictions 59
karmamudra 18
kaya . . xii, xiii, 2, 4, 5, 10, 23, 34, 36, 38, 41, 42, 46, 50, 58, 62, 69, 71, 73, 74, 82, 83, 92, 104, 121, 125
kayas and wisdoms 58
key points . . . . iii, xii, xv, xix, xxii, xxv, 12, 15, 22, 23, 26, 31, 32, 42, 44, 48, 55, 65, 71, 75, 106, 126
Khadro Nyingthig ix
Khadro Yangthig 55
King of Samadhis Sutra 38
Lamp for a Dim Room . . . . . iv, 79
Lamp of the Three Key Points . . . 55
latencies . . . . xii, 4, 45, 52, 61, 79
latency 106
least faculties 10, 15, 16
levels and paths 7, 13
levels of Great Completion teaching viii
liberating afflictions 28
liberation and confusion . . 47, 58
liberation by sight 18
liberation by signs 18
liberation by taste 18
like a drawing on water 81
like a dream arising from sleep 47
like the front and back of the hand 48
like the swordsman in the midst of battle 13
liveliness . . 24, 26, 29, 61, 69, 74,

76, 82, 83, 106, 110
Longchen Nyingthig . . . v, vi, x, xv-xvii, xix, xx, 67, 71
Longchen Nyingthig transmission xvii
Longchen Quintessence . . vi, xv-xix, xxi, xxviii, xxix
Longchen Rabjam . . v, vii, x, xiii, 31, 86
Longchenpa . . x, xiii-xv, xxiv, xxv, 31, 32, 40, 42, 44-46, 55, 86
Longchenpa's seven treasuries . . . . xxiv, xxv, 44
Longchenpa's wisdom body . . . x
Longing Song of the Spring Queen xv
Lord Barawa 19
Lord Srongtsen 66
Lower Cave of Nyang . . . . xi, xiii
luminosity . . xi, 6, 19, 21, 24, 26, 27, 29, 30, 43-46, 50, 51, 55, 58, 62, 65, 71, 72, 74, 77, 88, 92, 103, 106, 110, 120
luminosity of the four appearances 55
luminosity or illumination . . 106
Luminosity's Appearance Aspect . . . . iv, viii, 52
luminous like the sun and moon58
Maha Ati 58, 107
Mahamati 43
Mahamudra . . . xviii, xx, xxii, 2-4, 6-8, 11, 18, 24, 75, 107, 117
Mahāsaṅdhi 67
Manjushrimitra . . . . xiii, xxv
manufacture and contrivance 75, 92, 107
meaning of common awareness 76
meeting and parting 50,58,59,108
mental examination and analysis 75
middling faculties 6, 16
migrator 86, 108
migrators . 20, 33, 46, 47, 52, 54, 62, 63, 66, 108
Milarepa 13
mind abiding 1
Mind and Space Sections xxii, 23
mind moving 1
mind of Great Completion . . 3, 5
Mind Section . . . . xx, xxii, 10, 18, 20, 23, 34, 35
Mind, Space, and Foremost Instruction sections viii
mindness . 21, 23, 27, 33, 38, 67, 72, 75-77, 109, 113
mindness king 67
mind-ness 73
mind's innate condition 73
mind's innate disposition 77
mind's nature of luminosity . . 72
Mitra Dzoki 4, 9
mode of confusion 60
most profound teaching of Great Completion viii
mother and son 27, 30
movement of thought 11, 12
movement seen self-purifies . . 76
naked rigpa 72, 76
naked rigpa-emptiness . . . 72, 76
nam mkha' klong chen 51
nam mkha' klong gsal 50
naturalness 68, 76
Nature Great Completion . . . 1, 31, 36, 45, 71, 87, 109
nature of all phenomena 42
Net of Illusion 38
Ngayab Glorious Mountain . . 69

nihilism 9, 50, 68, 78, 79
nine examples of the sugatagarbha 53
nirmanakaya . . . 41, 46, 62, 71, 83
nirvana . . . vi, 24, 30, 33, 37, 41-44, 46-48, 50, 52, 56-62, 69, 72, 73, 78, 79, 87, 92, 99, 105, 120, 123
nirvana's nature 43
no meditating 2
no trust in vipashyana 10
non-dual shining forth and liberation 73
non-dual wisdom 45, 116
non-stop 28, 42, 47, 109
not a state of perfection vii
not changed by abandonment 68, 77
not stopped 110
not-rigpa . . . 45, 51, 59, 103, 110
no-thought wisdom 26
Nyang Caves x
Nyang Tingdzin Zangpo . x, xiii
Nyoshul Khenpo xvii
object is visible in direct perception 26
one all-encompassing space . . vi
one-sided peace 82
output2, 21, 24, 29, 48, 69, 83,110
output of the emptiness 2, 21
outstanding faculties 3
own appearance 111
Pacifier 5
Padma Karpo . . . i, ii, vii, xiii, xx, xxi, xxix, xxxi, 7, 107, 118, 121, 123, 124
Padma Karpo Translation Committee . . . . i, ii, vii, xiv, xx, xxi, xxix, xxxi, 7, 107, 118, 121, 123, 124
Padma Laydray Tsal 55
Padma Rigdzin . . . . xv, 71
Padmasambhava . . . ix, x, 2, 114
path that proceeds in stages . . 80
Patience 19, 20
Pearl Strings 38, 59
perfection and imperfection . . vii
permanence 9, 50, 68, 78, 97
permanence and nihilism 9, 68, 78
person of great perseverance . . 48
phenomena of nirvana 59
phenomena of samsara . . 47, 58, 73, 78
phenomena of samsara and nirvana 47, 58, 73, 78
phenomena-ended dharmakaya mind 62
phenomena-ended rigpa 81
play of ground appearance . . . 49
post-attainment3, 4, 8, 27, 97, 111
Praise to the Dharmadhatu . 34, 39
prajna . . 2, 13, 19, 26, 40, 53, 111
Prajnaparamita . . 2, 13, 19, 40, 53
Precious Garland 36, 80
present appearance 48
present awareness 22
primal ground's actuality . . 44, 49
primal guardian 50, 111
primal guardian's good qualities54
primal situation 32, 44, 69, 72, 83
primal situation's general ground's element 49
primal situation's ground . 45, 61
primal situation's primordial ground 47, 49, 62
primal situation's sugatagarbha 55
primally empty of a supporting basis 58

primordial complete purity 45, 59
primordial emptiness 49
primordial ground . . . 43, 47, 49, 61, 62
primordial liberation . . 75, 79, 81
primordial meditation 6
prior time 47
profound emptiness 2
proliferation . 11, 12, 15, 27, 111
provisional and definitive meaning 111
pure vision xxv
quintessence . . . i, v, vi, ix, x, xii, xv-xix, xxi, xxii, xxiv, xxv, xxviii, xxix, xxxii, 16, 31, 36, 38, 41-43, 46, 50, 59, 125
Quintessence Great Completion . . . v, vi, ix, x, xvii, xxi, xxii, xxiv, xxv, xxviii, xxix, xxxii, 16, 36, 38, 41-43, 46, 50, 59, 125
Quintessence level of the secret 31
quintessential . . iii, xv, xxii, 31, 33
rational mind . . 2, 3, 5, 6, 18, 22, 23, 25, 29, 35, 37, 58, 68, 74, 75, 78, 79, 91, 112, 121
rational-minded approaches to the view 58
rational-mind-made meditation 8
rdzogs pa chen po 109
realization . . . vii, xii, xiv, 21, 30, 31, 49, 88, 95, 103, 104, 112, 113
reference . . . xiv, 2, 3, 12, 42, 90, 91, 100, 108, 111, 113, 116, 124, 127
reference and referencing . . . 113
requirements for transmission xxviii
rigpa . . . . xi, 9, 10, 21, 22, 24-28, 30, 40, 45, 47-51, 54, 57, 59, 67, 69, 72-74, 76, 77, 81-83, 87, 88, 101, 103, 110, 113, 114, 125
rigpa enlightenment mind 47, 49
rigpa king 69, 82
rigpa self-arising wisdom 47
rigpa's liveliness 69, 74, 82
rigpa-wisdom 40
root guru 66, 71
sambhogakaya's appearance . . 83
samsara . vi, 7, 14, 24, 30, 33-35, 37, 39-44, 46-48, 50, 52, 56-62, 68, 69, 72, 73, 78-80, 82, 83, 87, 90, 92, 94, 98, 99, 105, 114, 116, 119, 121
samsara and nirvana . 24, 30, 37, 41-44, 46-48, 50, 56-62, 72, 73, 78, 92, 99, 105
samsara's confused appearances 58
samsara's nature 43
samsara's unsatisfactoriness 68, 80
Samye Chimpu x
Saraha 20
satva and sattva 88, 114
seal with the deity and mantra 24
Secret Mantra . . xix, xxiii, 32, 33, 61, 115
seeing the view's own face 74
seeking mind 1
self-appearances of the bardo . 62
self-arising wisdom . . . 2, 19, 22-24, 39, 45, 47, 56, 115
self-liberating appearances . . . 24
self-liberation . . . viii, 21, 23, 24, 28, 29, 67, 69, 74, 82, 83
self-liberation nakedly seen . . 67
self-output 21, 24, 29, 48
self-output of deity and its mantra 24
self-output of no-thought 29

self-purification 15
self-recognition . 8, 9, 48, 76, 113
self-recognizing and not self-recognizing 58
Self-Shining Forth 46
sentient beings . . . 34, 35, 40-42, 45, 48, 49, 60-62, 66, 77, 96, 99, 102, 105, 108, 114, 118, 122
Seven Dharmas of Vairochana 10, 115
shackled by clinging and dualistically grasping 57
shamatha 6-10,12-14, 26,116,122
shamatha and vipashyana . . . 6-9
shamatha practice 8, 13
shang shang 66
shifting events 116
shiftless 62, 116
shine forth, shining forth . . . 116
shines forth as ground appearances 59
shining forth and liberating continuously 82
shining forth and liberating without trace 76
shining forth as meditation . . . 28
Shri Singha xxv
simile wisdom 25
similes of the thoughts 81
simultaneous shining-forth-liberation 81
single cause in rigpa 48
six migrators 47, 54, 66
sixfold group 24
small piece of wood 12
snying thig ix
solidification . . . . . xiii, 117, 121
Sound Breakthrough 36, 41
space having nine features 61
Space Section 23, 51
spoilage of contrivance . . 22, 67, 74, 78
spontaneous existence . 4, 27, 39, 47, 48, 50-53, 58, 62, 69, 83, 117
spontaneous existence mandala 53
spontaneous zone of rigpa . 67, 74
spontaneously existing three kayas 74
stains 41, 51, 52, 72
state . . . . v, vii, viii, xi, xv, xxix, 9, 10, 14, 16, 17, 20-23, 25-30, 47, 59, 69, 72, 74, 76, 77, 80, 82, 83, 87, 90, 92, 95, 101, 111, 116, 118
state of space-like dharmata . . 82
stillness 3, 21
striving 14, 40, 75, 80, 96
stronghold 83
subject-object becoming . . 69, 82
suchness 36, 43, 98
sugata . 32-36, 38, 39, 41, 42, 44-47, 49-51, 53-58, 61, 72, 101, 118-120
sugatagarbha . 32, 34-36, 38, 39, 41, 42, 44-47, 49-51, 53-58, 61, 72, 101, 118-120
sugatagarbha element 56
sugata's garbha 33
Summation of the Vidyadharas . 70
*Sun, Moon, Planets, and Stars*49, 55
superfactual . . 44, 45, 53, 57, 73, 79, 98, 99, 119
superfactual dharmata sugatagarbha 57
superfactual truth 53, 119
superfice, superficies 119
superficies of illusion 82
suppression and furtherance . 28,

30, 77
Supreme Vehicle Treasury 47, 55, 59, 60
sutra section of the Great Vehicle 32
Sutra Showing All Phenomena to be Without Origination 61
sutras of the middle turning of the wheel 42
system of instruction vii
tantras ... iii, xix, xxii, xxv, xxviii-xxx, 14, 26, 31, 38, 40, 41, 43, 46, 50, 51, 59, 62, 87, 94, 95, 97, 103, 104, 109, 111, 117, 118, 125
tantras of Nature Great Completion 31
tathagatagarbha 43, 120
tathagatagarbha teaching 43
tenth level bodhisatvas xxviii
terminology and style of expression xxx
testament 71
the aggregates 80
the authentic 37, 43, 61, 120
the beginning .. xxiii, xxv, 17, 38, 44, 55, 59, 60, 68
the birthless state 74
The Condensed 40
the element 32, 36, 120
the innate ... 6, 22, 67, 68, 72-77, 80, 82, 83, 113
the innate disposition . 68, 77, 80
the innate's liveliness 24
the light channels 48
the light output 83
the name Great Completion .. vii
the nature .. xxix, xxxii, 8, 18, 27, 29, 42, 43, 45, 49, 50, 52, 57, 67, 74, 76, 77, 79, 104, 107, 109, 120, 122
the nature left untouched . 67, 74
the nature luminosity 50
the nature's luminosity 43
the primal situation .. 32, 44, 69, 72, 83
the space of objects 69, 82
The Sutra Petitioned by Brahma Special Mind 42
the vajra seat vi
The Vajrasatva Garbha's Mirror 60
the way to practise the path .. 76
The Words of Manjushri ... 38, 40
The Words of my Most Excellent Guru xx
theistic habits vii
third order thousandfold world system 120, 121
Thorough Cut ... ii, vii, xvii, xxi, xxii, xxix, xxxi, xxxiii, 18, 24, 31, 73, 88, 92, 94, 99, 101, 113, 121, 125
three body postures 26
Three Chariots and Seven Treasuries xv
three gazes 26
three kayas xii, 46, 50, 74, 82, 121
three kayas as path 82
three lines of transmission . xxviii
Three Lines teaching of Garab Dorje xxi
three realms .. 34, 35, 40, 47, 60, 66, 113
threefold entity, nature, and compassionate activity 36, 43, 49
Tibet ... 1, ii, iv-vi, ix, x, xv, xvii, xviii, xxiii, xxvi, xxvii, xxx, xxxii, xxxiii, 17, 35, 36, 39, 44, 46, 50, 52, 56, 66, 67, 75, 79, 86,

88, 91-93, 95-97, 99, 103, 104, 106, 107, 109, 113-115, 117, 118, 121-127, 129
time of practise in this life 48
Tirthika 7, 43, 61, 121
Tirthikas 7, 43
total purity kaya 38
transmission via symbolic means xxviii
Treasury of Abhidharma ... 33, 46
Treasury of the Birthless 37
truly complete buddhahood .. vii
truly complete buddhas 43
Tshogdrug Rangdrol 65
Uddiyana .... vi, vii, 2
uncompounded 23,38,39,44,53,59
unconfused dharmata 72
uncontrived innate 83
uncontrived self-knowing rigpa 73
undistracted mindfulness .. 9, 10
unification 9, 24
uninterrupted flow of the innate 82
unique style of expression ... xxx
Unravelling the Symbols of the Great Secret Treasury xiv
unsurpassed . ix, xxviii, 24, 39, 94
un-grasped liveliness 82
un-stopped 109, 120
Upper Cave of Nyang .... xi, xiii
vajra chains 27
Vajra Guru mantra 70
Vajra Vehicle .. 33, 96, 102, 104, 115, 121
Vajradhara 38, 111
Vajrasatva 60, 115
Vasubhandu 33
verbal expressions 72, 73, 97
very special path of unification 24
vidyadhara ... xxiii, xxviii, 52, 65, 67, 69, 70, 123
vidyadhara Gyalway Nyugu .. 65
view of alpha-purity's Thorough Cut 73
view that does not accumulate karma 81
view, meditation, and conduct .... xxv, 121
Vimalamitra .... ix, x
vipashyana 6-10,13,14,26,74,121
vipashyana of unmistaken actuality 14
wanting 27, 79-81
wanting a fruition 81
warehouse of the oceanic good qualities 53
warnings xxix
way of preserving 1
White Lotus Sutra 56
winds not moving 26
wisdom ... vii, viii, x, xi, xiv, xv, 1, 2, 5, 19, 22-26, 29, 30, 39-42, 44-47, 49, 51, 52, 56-58, 72-74, 77, 79, 87, 89-93, 97, 104, 108, 112, 113, 115, 116, 118-120, 122
wisdom freed of all elaborations 72
wisdom's spontaneous existence 27
wishlessness 42, 43
wish-fulfilling jewel 33, 38
woodblocks ..... xviii, xxvi, xxvii
Words of Manjushri 38, 40
Word's Meaning Treasury .. 49, 55
works of the Tirthikas 43
Yang Gonpa 6, 9
Yeshe Tshogyal ix
yogin .. xii, 4, 69, 77, 81-83, 103
"after-passing" teaching xxv

www.ingramcontent.com/pod-product-compliance
Lightning Source LLC
Chambersburg PA
CBHW021841220426
43663CB00005B/347
* 9 7 8 9 9 3 7 5 7 2 6 4 4 *